Tourism, Culture and Development

TOURISM AND CULTURAL CHANGE
Series Editors: Professor Mike Robinson, *Centre for Tourism and Cultural Change, Leeds Metropolitan University Leeds, UK* and Dr Alison Phipps, *University of Glasgow, Scotland, UK*

Understanding tourism's relationships with culture(s) and vice versa, is of ever-increasing significance in a globalising world. This series will critically examine the dynamic inter-relationships between tourism and culture(s). Theoretical explorations, research-informed analyses, and detailed historical reviews from a variety of disciplinary perspectives are invited to consider such relationships.

Other Books in the Series
Irish Tourism: Image, Culture and Identity
Michael Cronin and Barbara O'Connor (eds)
Tourism, Globalization and Cultural Change: An Island Community Perspective
Donald V.L. Macleod
The Global Nomad: Backpacker Travel in Theory and Practice
Greg Richards and Julie Wilson (eds)
Tourism and Intercultural Exchange: Why Tourism Matters
Gavin Jack and Alison Phipps
Discourse, Communication and Tourism
Adam Jaworski and Annette Pritchard (eds)
Histories of Tourism: Representation, Identity and Conflict
John K. Walton (ed.)
Cultural Tourism in a Changing World: Politics, Participation and (Re)presentation
Melanie K. Smith and Mike Robinson (eds)
Festivals, Tourism and Social Change: Remaking Worlds
David Picard and Mike Robinson (eds)
Tourism in the Middle East: Continuity, Change and Transformation
Rami Farouk Daher (ed.)
Learning the Arts of Linguistic Survival: Languaging, Tourism, Life
Alison Phipps
Tea and Tourism: Tourists, Traditions and Transformations
Lee Jolliffe (ed.)

Other Books of Interest
Recreational Tourism: Demand and Impacts
Chris Ryan
Shopping Tourism: Retailing and Leisure
Dallen Timothy
Sport Tourism Development
Thomas Hinch and James Higham
Sport Tourism: Interrelationships, Impact and Issues
Brent Ritchie and Daryl Adair (eds)
Tourism Collaboration and Partnerships
Bill Bramwell and Bernard Lane (eds)
Tourism and Development: Concepts and Issues
Richard Sharpley and David Telfer (eds)

For more details of these or any other of our publications, please contact:
Channel View Publications, Frankfurt Lodge, Clevedon Hall,
Victoria Road, Clevedon, BS21 7HH, England
http://www.channelviewpublications.com

TOURISM AND CULTURAL CHANGE 12
Series Editors: Mike Robinson and Alison Phipps

Tourism, Culture and Development

Hopes, Dreams and Realities in East Indonesia

Stroma Cole

CHANNEL VIEW PUBLICATIONS
Clevedon • Buffalo • Toronto

Library of Congress Cataloging in Publication Data
Cole, Stroma
Tourism, Culture and Development: Hopes, Dreams and Realities in East Indonesia/Stroma Cole.
Tourism and Cultural Change: 12
Includes bibliographical references and index.
1. Tourism–Social aspects–Indonesia–Ngada. 2. Economic development–Indonesia–Ngada. 3. Ngada (Indonesia)–Economic conditions. I. Title. II. Series.
G155.I5C65 2007
338.4' 7915986–dc22   2007020003

British Library Cataloguing in Publication Data
A catalogue entry for this book is available from the British Library.

ISBN-13: 978-1-84541-070-4 (hbk)
ISBN-13: 978-1-84541-069-8 (pbk)

Channel View Publications
An imprint of Multilingual Matters Ltd

UK: Frankfurt Lodge, Clevedon Hall, Victoria Road, Clevedon BS21 7HH.
USA: 2250 Military Road, Tonawanda, NY 14150, USA.
Canada: 5201 Dufferin Street, North York, Ontario, Canada M3H 5T8.

The policy of Multilingual Matters/Channel View Publications is to use papers that are natural, renewable and recyclable products, made from wood grown in sustainable forests. In the manufacturing process of our books, and to further support our policy, preference is given to printers that have FSC and PEFC Chain of Custody certification. The FSC and/or PEFC logos will appear on those books where full certification has been granted to the printer concerned.

Typeset by Saxon Graphics Ltd.
Printed and bound in Great Britain by the Cromwell Press.

Contents

Part 2: Perceptions, Priorities and Attitudes

Part 3: The Influence of Tourism

Plates

Preface

How much does tourism change a village? What effects does tourism have on a culture? Can tourism help a poor remote community to develop? How can a village have the benefits tourism offers without the problems it can cause? These are the questions that have grown in me over the past 20 years, fed by questions from the villagers to whom I introduced tourism.

Only a handful of backpackers had ever passed through Wogo in 1989 when I began taking small groups of tourists to stay with the villagers. Village stays were not only a resounding success for the tourists but also for the villagers. They became the unique selling point of our tours and our business success was laid on the foundations of our visits to Wogo. But in the long term, what would be the impact of introducing tourism to this village? And how could the villagers benefit from the growing numbers of tourists that came to their village?

After six years of taking tours (1989–1994) and frequent short visits, I spent eight months (1998–1999) seeking to understand tourism from the perspective of the different stakeholders. I felt indebted to the villagers and answering their questions became central to my research. I wanted to understand the conflicts of tourism development and offer the villagers potential solutions. The long-term research continued with visits in 2001 and 2003; in 2005, with the assistance of a British Academy grant, I was able to evaluate the success of one of my suggestions.

This book provides the story of the lives of real people in real villages. I have not changed their names. Following discussion with the villagers, we were sure that anybody reading the text, familiar with the area, would be able to work out which villages I was writing about and therefore there was no point in keeping them anonymous. In nearly all cases, the villagers are proud to be part of the study and wanted their real names to be used. I have respected their wishes.

My fieldwork was conducted in Indonesian and Ngadha languages, mainly the former – especially in the earlier phases of my work. I have translated both into English. For ease of reading I have limited the amount of foreign words in the text. However, at times the translation is provided in italics. The translations may be from either language but most of the time I have used Indonesian. Where the Ngadha term is used I have either stated so or used Ng to indicate Ngadha language. There are, however, a few terms that I feel are best left untranslated, as there is no equivalent term in English.

Ngadha words: *Nua* = a collection of Houses found in two parallel lines with the associated *bhaga, ngadhu* and megaliths. *Bhaga* = a miniature house representing the first female ancestor of a clan. *Ngadhu* = carved tree trunks, with conical thatched roofs representing the first male ancestor of a clan.

Indonesian words: *Adat* = Indonesian word of Arabic origin meaning custom, customary law and customary behaviour. In Ngadha, it is used to mean the complex of beliefs and rituals associated with the ancestors. *Malu* = Indonesian expression meaning modest and bashful, used to express feelings that lie between the English for shy, ashamed and embarrassed but also respectful and humble.

In order to differentiate between traditional named 'houses' locally referred to as *sa'o* and other homes I use House (with a capital H) for the former and house (with a lower-case h) for the latter.

Using an anthropologist's eye and a high degree of trust, this book uncovers the story of tourism development in two small villages on one remote island. However, the study has ramifications beyond the locality. Many other villages in Indonesia are experiencing similar issues. Many of the challenges are of relevance to peripheral communities across the globe. Themes in this book will resonate with studies of tourism, tourists, development, globalisation and cultural change from around the world.

Acknowledgements

The research for this book would not have been possible without the kind help and support of many villagers in Ngadha – my sincerest appreciation goes to them all – *Tima ti'i woso*. It is not possible to mention everyone individually but I would like to express special thanks to Siprianus Batesoro for his insightful comments, frequent readings and corrections of my work, emails of support and his brotherly love. Also to Pak Yohannes Wawo for his generous hours of teaching, explaining and advice; to Nene Yuli for her lessons and love; and to all those who are named in the book who gave up their time and shared their thoughts and lives with me.

I would like to thank Michael Hitchcock for suggesting I develop my initial research more fully. and for his supervision. Thanks also to David Harrison for his constructive comments as the work unfolded. I am indebted to a number of other people who have supported me through the writing of this book. My thanks to Lisa Goodson for her support and understanding; to Ruth Fryer for her tremendous moral support and her comments, suggestions and help; to Kathleen Adams for her supportive comments; to Mike Robinson for his editorial support; and to the production team at Channel View.

Some of the research for this book was carried out under the auspices of the Lembaga Ilmu Pengetahuan Indonesia (LIPI) with sponsorship from the Universitas Nusa Cendana in Kupang. I am grateful for their permission and assistance. I would also like to express my gratitude to Buckinghamshire Chiltern University College for its financial support and sympathetic time-tabling that has made the research possible and for the Fellowship that allowed the writing of this book to become a reality. I am also grateful for the grant from the South-East Asia Committee of the British Academy that enabled the most recent phase of the research.

During the journey to produce this book I have published widely about tourism in Ngadha (Cole, 1997a, 1997b, 1998, 1999, 2003, 2004a, 2004b, 2005, 2006, 2007) and I have presented material at numerous conferences worldwide. My thanks to all those who have commented on my work, pointed out its flaws and contributed to its progress.

I would like to express my thanks to Brian for the continual support and belief that I would eventually finish. Last but not least, I would like to express a very special thank you to Mira, my daughter, who has supported me with her love, humour and patience both in the field and back home.

Chapter 1
Introduction

Arriving

After eight hours of hairpin bends, knife-edge ridges, spectacular views, dry riverbeds, dust and bumps we branched off the Trans-Flores highway. After a mile or so down a seemingly unpassable track my co-tour leader, Hilman, asked the driver of the local bus we had chartered to halt. Immediately we were surrounded, half-dressed children appeared, pushing their faces against the windows while others began climbing on the bus. Drums and gongs could be heard. Hilman and Pak Ben (a representative from the Department of Education and Culture) alighted through the back door, informing me simply '*Sudah tiba*' we had arrived.

The 13 tourists were clearly nervous as I translated our arrival and told them to follow me off the bus. Getting down from the bus past masses of children, I could see through the village entrance. Men were waving swords as they stamped the ground. With anxiety and trepidation I persuaded the tourists not to worry about their belongings on the roof and join me at the entrance. Behind the sword waving men, women, also in full ceremonial costume, danced.

The 'welcome dance' appeared more like a threatening war dance. The villagers didn't seem to be smiling. The swords looked menacing and the repetitive rhythms on the drums and gongs compounded our sense of fear. Although I was leading my first tour, I knew that containing my own fear was necessary for the well being of my clients. My outward expression of excitement masked my inner turmoil of combined surprise and apprehension.

Following instructions from Pak Ben we followed the villagers around the village of Wogo passing in front of the 32 majestic wooden houses with high thatched roofs, to a house where we crowded on the terrace. In the centre of the village we could see stone structures or megaliths, clan posts (*ngadhu*) and miniature clan houses (*bhaga*) (see Plates 1 and 2). We were presented with drinks: very sweet coffee and sugared water (as tea). The children began by keeping a safe distance and staring. As they gradually inched forward, an adult would chastise them and they would retreat a few metres.

1

Plate 1 The *lenggi* and some *ngadhu* in Wogo

Plate 2 Re-thatching a *bhaga* in Bena

The 13 tourists were split between four houses to get to know their host families. Hilman and I shared our time between houses to help translate and settling. We ate our main meals in a fifth house but host families kept up a constant supply of snacks: roast sweet potatoes, boiled bananas and baked cassava.

The next 42 hours were partly negotiated on our reconnaissance trip[1] but the villagers had put the main activities together. Briefly it involved: a cultural description of the village centre; a walk to observe local agriculture and palm toddy tapping; visiting villagers' garden homes; walking to the local volcano to observe volcanic activity; bathing in a pool that had hot and cold water sources; a walk to the old village site and megaliths, where we had a picnic lunch of rice, pork and vegetables cooked in bamboo tubes over a fire, washed down with palm toddy; and a cultural show of songs and dances by adults and children.

As I had refused to allow individual tourists to tip individual villagers or households, the tourists had made a collection for the village. This raised a significant amount of cash which, following a discussion the villagers, was put towards a project to bring water to the village. After we had visited the village with three groups, the water project was up and running, and some of the villagers had had the opportunity to take part in a festival of international bamboo music in Bali. When we met again they asked me 'How can we have tourism and not end up like Bali?' The disturbing aspects of Bali that they described were the volumes of scantily clad tourists; the traffic jams; the wealth disparities, mansions and beggars; shops, hotels, and restaurants everywhere; and no peace at all.

On our fourth visit the villagers were faced with decisions of what to do with future finance raised from tourism. No consensus was reached during our visit. Unlike in any previous visit we felt unhappy about leaving money in the village. There were disagreements about who should look after it.

It was also on the fourth visit that our tourists encountered other tourists in 'their' village. In the afternoon a few independent tourists, arrived, looked around and departed. Later that evening, a guide arrived with a group of tourists just as our cultural show was about to start. I approached the guide and told him that we had sponsored the show and therefore found it unacceptable for his tourists to 'watch for free'. The presence of other tourists detracted from my clients' special event. The guide claimed to have permission from a villager, whom he had paid. I was powerless.

Visiting remote, untouched villages with anthropologists had become the unique selling point of our tours. When I heard my clients' comments that the village was 'obviously getting touristy', I knew the competitive advantage of my company relied on finding a remoter village. However I have continued personal visits to Wogo for shorter (days) and longer (months) periods ever since.

On my visits we would always discuss tourism, its development and how things were changing, or not. As my visits continued and my role changed from tour operator to academic researcher it became clear that tourism was developing, but that the process was outside and beyond the villagers' control. Their village was visited, and they became passive recipients of visitors without any signs of development. The village was not becoming 'like Bali', but the villagers were deriving no benefits from tourism, yet at the same time I felt sure that tourism was changing the village. Was the passivity confined to this village and if so why? From the early days of excitement and enthusiasm for tourism, why had their attitudes changed? With my changed role I ventured further afield to other villages in the Ngadha area to learn from them of their experiences and see for myself how they coped with tourism.

The Ngadha villagers have been incorporated into the cash economy requiring cash for taxes, schooling, health care and basic commodities. The opportunities for economic development in the area are minimal. Steep slopes and a harsh climate limit agricultural development. The area has no known mineral resources but does have thermal power. Industrial development is unlikely due to the region's peripheral position, far from markets and lacking entry ports either by sea or air. Cultural tourism development could potentially provide the villagers with opportunities to obtain cash. The villages have the raw cultural resources to provide the context for tourism although development requires their refinement for tourism consumption. Too little refinement and there is minimal economic benefit from tourism, too much and the resource is spoilt. Understanding the intricacies of the culture and the value systems of the actors is crucial to ensuring the sustainability of their tourism. This book details the first 20 years of tourism development, examines the values of key actors to identify real and potential conflicts, and discusses the ways tourism is incorporated into two of the villages: Wogo and Bena.

Themes: What This Book Is About

This book provides a holistic picture of the first 20 years of tourism development in two remote marginal villages. It provides the tourism story from multiple perspectives. It contrasts the values, attitudes and priorities of the different actors in tourism. It discusses how tradition, ethnicity and culture are strategically articulated, moulded, manipulated and used, to serve the different actors' purposes. In doing so, the book reveals the 'conflicts of tourism' both between actors and because of tourism processes.

Based on 16 years of visits from 1989–2005 this book provides a rare longitudinal study revealing not only socio-cultural change and development but also changes in tourists', villagers' and the mediators' attitudes and priorities. The book focuses on two villages and makes comparisons between them; this micro-level analysis shows the importance of very local detail and thus challenges some of the assumptions in the tourism development literature.

While this book is about tourism and socio-cultural change, it also highlights how globalisation can be about powerlessness and a lack of change. The ethnography provides a rich description of life in a non-western marginal community in a contemporary global context and how they face the challenge of balancing socio-economic integration and cultural distinction. It tells the story of how tourism has entered social processes in the villages, has brought dreams and hopes, and has affected the balance of power but has done little to change the economic situation of the villagers.

This book is not an exhaustive ethnographic study. It is a partial ethnographic study that deliberately focuses on some areas of the respondents' lives. While the narrative concentrates on tourism and the changes it has brought about, it should be remembered that it is not possible to disaggregate socio-cultural change brought about as a result of tourism from other influences. Using a series of stories, vignettes and quotations from all the stakeholders I will attempt to evoke what life is like for the villagers in Ngadha. Their experience is only one part of the complex story; by examining the views of the other actors I hope to present a holistic picture, to reveal the connections and contrasts, and how these change.

Location

The Ngadha live in the rugged mountainous region between two active volcanoes: Inerie and Ebolobo[2] in the south-east quarter of the Ngada regency. The regency (*Kabupaten Ngada*) is located in central Flores in Eastern Indonesia (see Figures 1.1, 1.2 and 1.3). Formerly part of the Dutch East Indies, the regency is known after its colonial name, Ngada, which is a misrepresentation of local pronunciation of the name. (The Dutch appear to have difficulty rendering the local 'dh' sound and wrote it as 'd'.) The people in this study, however, call themselves – and are referred to by neighbouring groups when speaking Indonesian – as *orang Ngadha*.

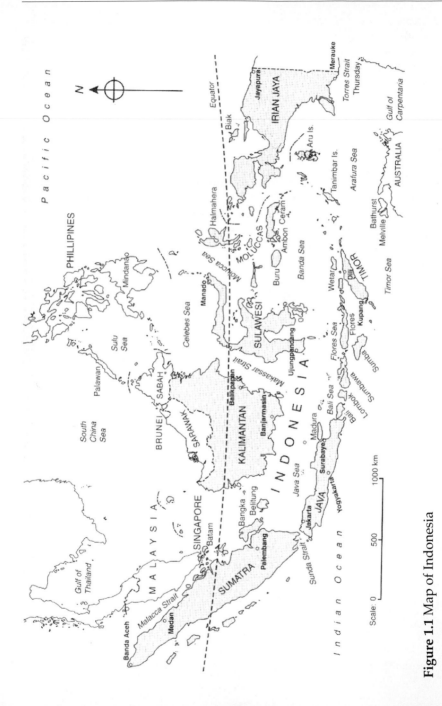

Figure 1.1 Map of Indonesia

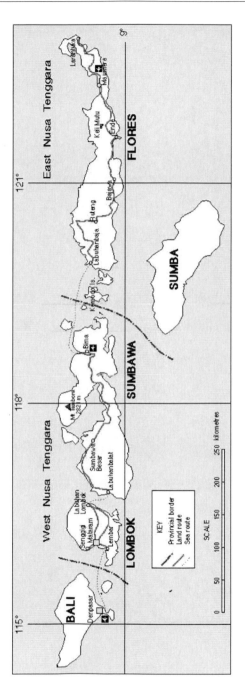

Figure 1.2 Map of the Eastern Isles

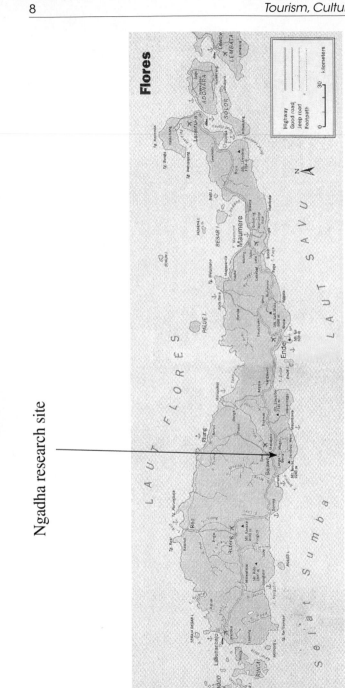

Figure 1.3 Map of Flores showing the location of the study

Outsiders continue to be confused by this, since the regency, a geographical designation, is spelt one way, Ngada, but a group of people living in the south-east corner use Ngadha.

The Ngada regency lies between 8 and 9 degrees south and 120 and 121 degrees east (Kabupaten Ngada, 1998). As with so many areas of Flores, the area is subject to frequent seismic activity. The young volcanic soils are littered with volcanic boulders. Gradients vary across the region but over 40% of the land is very steep (Kabupaten Ngada, 1998). The area receives 1750mm of rain in the rainy season (October to April) and 157mm in the dry season, far more than the rest of the Kabupaten (Kabupaten Ngada, 1998). Temperatures range from between 20°C and 33°C in the day but can get down to less than 10°C at night in the mountains. However, significant variation exists between villages in terms of temperature and rainfall due to altitude and aspect.

The population of the regency in 1997 was recorded at 212,271, giving a population density of 70/ sq. km. However the Ngadha part of the regency is by far the most populated, supporting an average of 184/sq. km (*ibid*). The area is economically poor with one of the lowest per capita incomes in Indonesia (Rp900,000/yr approximately US$180) (Kabupaten Ngada, 1998). Communications in Ngada are also among the poorest on Flores. The area has one major tarmacked road, the Trans-Flores Highway, which runs east–west across Flores. Small single-tracked, partially tarred roads run off this main artery. A small airport north of the capital exists but has not been in regular use.

The Ngadha language is currently classified as belonging to the Central Malayo-Polynesian (CMP) language group, a branch of the Austronesian family (Blust, 1984) and is part of what Fox (1998) calls the central Flores linkage[3]. The exceptionally rugged terrain of Flores helps to explain its extraordinary ethnic fragmentation. The Ngadha are separated to the west from the Manggarai and Mbae peoples by the river Moke (Hicks, 1990). Three other groups occupy the Ngada regency: the Nage and Keo to the east, and the Riung, who occupy the north of the regency. The work on linguistic (Fox, 1998) and cultural (Molnar, 2000) linkages suggests a continuum of languages/cultures exists with neighbouring groups in areas of Flores[4].

The capital of the regency, Bajawa, is included in the study. It is the least developed regency town on Flores. Lying in a 'bowl' surrounded by steep mountains, the possibility for this town to expand is limited. Despite serving a population of over 200,000 in 1998, the town did not even have a chemist. It is the only regency town on Flores not to have an agent's office for the East Indonesia newspaper (*Pos Kupang*). It is in this town that tourists inevitably stay before and after their visits to the villages. It has 12 guesthouses, 5 of which are regularly used by tourists and 3 'tourist- style' restaurants.

How: My Encounters and Representations

The research upon which this book is based began in 1989 when I started taking tourists to stay in Wogo, one of the villages central to this study. The first six years of research were for personal and business interests. As I had studied anthropology,[5] I had a personal interest in discovering the cultural background of the village. As a tour leader, leading a cultural tour marketed as 'led by anthropologists', my business depended on providing detailed cultural information for my clients. During these visits, I established an excellent rapport with the villagers. Hilman and I were officially 'adopted' by the villagers and I was accepted as 'family' when I returned to stay for eight months to carry out further research.

During the main period of fieldwork (1998–1999) my daughter (aged seven) and I lived in three homes in two villages. By moving around, I got to experience the differences of living in traditional houses and in the 'modern healthy' homes. I experienced living in the centre of a 'touristy' village with onlookers on my terrace on a daily basis and I experienced living just outside a traditional village and seeing how little tourism is part of their lives. As a successful tour operator I had credibility with the villagers, which, combined with my long-established relationships, meant that a strong bond of trust developed. This enabled the deep understanding necessary to interpret values, views and actions in the villages.

Research involved participant observation and interviews in villages that received tourists. Interviews were carried out in Indonesian, the villagers' second language. I also held focus groups with different sections of the communities: men, women and young people in both villages, Bena and Wogo. I interviewed tour operators, staff in relevant government departments and hotels. My research into guides and guiding involved a focus group, interviews, and covert and participant observation.

I have been exposed to cultural tourists in the villages of Ngadha over a period of 16 years. In the years that I had my company, I did not think of my clients as informants but many of their impressions have, without doubt, influenced my research and interpretation. During fieldwork I did not have any difficulties interacting with western tourists that visited Ngadha[6] I observed, interviewed and surveyed them at different points and under three different circumstances: in the villages; in Bajawa, the local town; and in the gateway towns. In Bajawa, there was precious little night-life and tourists readily gave their time. At the gateway towns, it was similar. In the villages, my dress, frequently in my local *kain*[7], and conversation with villagers aroused suspicion among tourists that I was not a tourist. I found that tourists were attracted to me for conversation and to gather knowledge. Unable to converse with villagers, talking to me either filled the awkward vacuum of time or allowed them to feel they were blending in. Sometimes I had to adopt strategies to avoid them such as entering the house (going back-stage) until they had passed.

I have returned to Ngadha for frequent visits, lasting from days to weeks ever since my early days in Flores, sometimes to attend family events, for holidays, and to conduct formal research[8]. Elsewhere I (Cole, 2004b) have discussed at length the advantages and challenges associated with long-term research, how relationships with key people in this story have changed over time and how these relationships have affected the nature of the data collected and how their story is told. I do not believe in an ethnographer's neutrality. I am implicated in the material presented here, I have affected the self-image of the communities,[9] and my presence and actions have impacted on the tourism development process.

The Structure of the Book

This book is divided into three parts: Part 1 offers the background, Part 2 contrasts the views of the different actors in tourism and Part 3 draws these perspectives together to highlight the conflicts of tourism, how tourism affects the balance of power of the competing forces in the villagers lives, and examines the changes that have taken place.

Following this introduction, Chapter 2 looks at some of the theoretical themes in the anthropology of tourism: globalisation and social change, authenticity and commodification. It also provides the background literature about stakeholders and the conflicts of tourism.

In Chapter 3 tourism and development in less economically developed countries is examined from a general perspective and also from a national and regional view. It examines some of the previous ethnographies from the region highlighting how tradition has been conceptualised. The chapter also details how wider global and national agendas have impacted on tourism development in Ngadha.

Chapter 4 gives a background on the villages. Rather than a complete ethnography, it examines the livelihood, social organisation and the belief system as a necessary background to understanding tourism and socio-cultural change.

Chapters 5, 6 and 7 present the perceptions of tourism from the perspectives of the villagers, tourists, mediators, government and guides, and how these have changed over the past 20 years.

Chapter 8 compares and contrasts these perceptions to show how the different groups of actors hold different views and where their underlying values conflict with one another. It also examines the conflicts of acculturation that result from the tourism development process.

Chapter 9 examines the different discourses in the villagers' lives and how tourism is incorporated into the nexus of forces that shape Ngadha society. It looks at how tradition, culture and identity have new meanings and how they are strategically manipulated in the competition for power and survival. Further, it examines how tourism is a globalising and localising force in Ngadha.

Chapter 10 presents the conclusions and looks at the first 20 years of tourism, the changes that have occurred and how the villagers have incorporated tourism into their lives.

Notes

1. I was taken ill and did not make it to Wogo on our reccy. This partly explains my anxiety during our 'welcome'.
2. Ine means mother and her partner, Ebolobo, also known as Suru Laki, facing her is considered father of the region.
3. Up until Fox's reclassification, the language was often described as belonging to the Ambon-Timor group (Barnes, 1972). Through an examination of the languages spoken on Flores, Fox (1998) argues that the linkage has more in common with Sumba than eastern parts of Flores. This link to Sumba gives credence to the local story of origin, which claims that the Ngadha arrived in the area from Sumba.
4. Molnar's (2000) work on the Hogo Sara, a village on the border between Ngadha and Nage, shows many characteristics in common with both groups.
5. Both as an undergraduate in Indonesia and for an MA at the School of Oriental and African Studies, London.
6. Andrew Causey (2003) found it difficult to interact with western tourists on Samosir and used a questionnaire to gather data about their perceptions.
7. A full length tubular ikat cloth, worn over clothing from the shoulders to the toes when cold; or as a wrap after bathing. Sometimes turned over at the waist for freedom of arm movement and, in my case, sometimes removed in the heat of the day, at which point my dress was probably akin to a conservative tourist.
8. In 2005 the British Academy funded research into the effectiveness of the code of conduct drafted with the villagers, guides and government in 2003 as a result of my research findings.

9. As Foster *et al.* (1979) discuss, carrying out long-term research differs from once-in-the-field studies. Firstly, because of the enduring ties, long-term research is more likely to be action or advocacy orientated, and secondly, 'the research can make an important contribution to the communities' "self-image" giving the villages a sense of *esprit* that would otherwise be lacking' (1979: 346).

Part 1

Theoretical and Contextual Issues

Chapter 2
Theoretical Issues in the Anthropology of Tourism

Social anthropology is the study of human social life. Its subject matter is culture, and anthropologists examine the similarities and differences between societies. Tourism, and in particular cultural tourism to less economically developed countries, involves people from very different societies meeting in different circumstances. Social anthropologists, using their distinct methodology, ethnographic fieldwork, are in a particularly strong position to examine this phenomenon. It may be surprising then, that so few ethnographies of tourism exist. Many authors have commented that the anthropology of tourism has been slow to emerge considering the synergies between anthropology and tourism, and given that 'tourism bears directly on a number of time-honoured themes in anthropology' (Crick, 1994: 1). Although anthropological interest in tourism can be traced back to the 1960s, it did not gather momentum until the publication of the first edited collection of papers on the anthropology of tourism: *Hosts and Guests* (Smith, 1978), and it was nearly two decades later before full ethnographic monographs began to appear. Crick's work on Sri Lanka was published in 1994, followed by Waldren's (1996) work on Mallorca; Kottak's examination of social change in a Brazilian village appeared in 1999; followed by Ness' (2002) ethnography of tourism in the Philippines, Causey's (2003) examination of the interactions between travellers and woodcarvers in North Sumatra, and McLeod's (2004) study of tourism and globalisation in the Canaries. This book adds to these contributions by giving the 'native-voice' or hosts'[1] perspective[2] of international tourism but from a different cultural region.

Despite the slow start, the anthropology of tourism is now firmly established as a sub discipline with a number of interconnected themes. In this chapter I will briefly examine each of these themes in turn to provide the theoretical background for the ethnography of Ngadha tourism.

Tourism, Globalisation and Socio-cultural Change

The social and cultural impacts of tourism has been a significant area of interest for anthropologists, with special attention being given to the changes bought about due to the contact between different peoples. Like other strangers, tourists are 'agents of contact between cultures and directly or indirectly the cause of change particularly in less developed regions of the world' (Nash, 1989: 37). Anthropological studies of people in tourist destinations and cultural change have had two inter-related foci: the political economy of tourism and development; and cultural commodification, homogenisation/hetetogeneity and the associated processes of globalisation. These strands will be examined in turn.

Political economy

Anthropological studies of tourism challenged the idea that tourism was a panacea for economic development[3] by focusing on the position of the hosts, or tourates[4] – the people in tourist destinations. Numerous studies have sprung from the anthropological concern with cultural contact and cultural change, in particular, contact between the more powerful tourists and the less powerful tourates in less economically developed countries.

Many of the early studies in the anthropology of tourism were 'embedded in concerns of development and dependency' (Selwyn, 1994: 34). Using the dependency paradigm (also known as underdevelopment theory), studies showed how tourism has evolved in a way that matches historic patterns of colonialism and economic dependency[5]. Thus, tourism has been viewed by some as a form of imperialism (Britton, 1982; Nash, 1978) or neo-colonialism (Crick, 1994; Hunter, 2001). International tourism dominated by foreign, frequently trans-national, ownership has resulted in the perpetuation of existing inequalities[6] as local people find themselves in a globally integrated system over which they have no control (Brohman, 1996: 55).

The political economy of tourism has built on a debate, analysing how islands, in particular, on the periphery, have become economically, politically and culturally dependent on tourist generating countries, in the centre. A useful analytical tool is to view tourism as being organised within a framework of politically dominant centres and marginalized peripheries (Parnwell, 1993; Selwyn, 1996). This framework for analysis focuses on the economic and political domains. In the case of Ngadha it is instructive to remember that the region is part of what we might term the super-periphery. This conceptualisation of super-periphery is not used in a static deterministic sense but in order to portray the relative situation of the area as a result of geography, past processes and economics. The region is hundreds of miles from the provincial capital, Kupang, which itself is a remote outpost of a nation, itself peripheral to the world system. Combined with its remote geographical position, the region has minimal industry, and as a result is super-peripheral in both geographic and economic terms. Further, the Ngadha are Catholic and the majority of Indonesians are Muslims. The Ngadha are not part of the Indonesian mainstream in terms of cultural history, having never been part of one of the major Javanese or Malay kingdoms. Moreover, nothing yet has put the Ngadha on the 'cultural map' of Indonesia, unlike some other minority groups (e.g. the Toraja, Batak or Dani).[7]

It is the very nature of their peripheral position that has meant many communities that are weakly integrated into the world system are the sites of today's cultural tourism. For many western tourists marginal communities represent a backward stage of human development, remnants of a disappearing world, dwindling refuges of difference (Azarya, 2004). This type of tourism, discussed in more depth in Chapter 3, is frequently referred to as ethnic tourism, MacCannell suggests that 'touristsified ethnic groups are often weakened by a history of exploitation, limited in resources and power, and they have no big buildings, machines, monuments or natural wonders to deflect the tourists' attention away from the intimate details of their daily lives' (1984: 386). Furthermore, as most of the money involved does not change hands at the site, there is little economic advantage for such groups. It is the underdevelopment of these groups that is their resource, it is their marginality that is their major source of attractiveness, and preservation of their distinctiveness is a crucial pre-condition for the sustainability of their tourism. Furthermore, their representation tends towards essentialisation: they become known by distinct, easily recognisable, traits (Cohen, 2001). In many cases the most immediately apparent symbols, that carry the most exotic connotations, are selected and emphasised[8].

Acculturation

Ethnographic studies that have paid attention to the diachronic, dynamic dimensions of culture have examined how tourism has contributed to change in societies over time (for example, Kottak, 1999; McLeod, 2004; Waldren, 1996). Working on the assumption that the elements of a sociocultural system are interconnected, change in one element will necessarily lead to changes in other aspects of the system. If this change is induced through contact with another culture, as is the case in tourism, the process is known as acculturation.[9] According to Matheson and Wall, the underlying assumptions of the acculturation framework are that cultural changes occur primarily on the indigenous traditions, customs and values rather than to the visiting group. Furthermore, these cultural changes are leading to a global homogenisation of cultures in which local identity is being assimilated into stronger visiting culture (1982: 160). This idea that tourism leads to global homogenisation is however contested and, as we shall see in relation to tourism in Ngadha, this oversimplification is not borne out; reality is a far more complex picture.

The 'demonstration effect' is a concept commonly used in tourism to describe a process whereby local people copy visitors' behaviour and aspire to own their material possessions. A large number of tourism texts[10] suggest that: changes in behaviour patterns may be brought about simply by observing tourists; the young people are considered particularly susceptible and attempt to imitate dress, language and habits since they are thought to be exciting alternatives. Most consider the process to be inevitable or unavoidable. Although some writers (e.g. Murphy, 1985; Williams, 1998) note that the demonstration effect may be beneficial if it encourages local people to adapt to work for things they lack, most consider it negatively. I consider the notion that purely by observing foreign tourists, local people will want whatever they see with some scepticism. It masks the locals ability to chose which, if any, elements they may wish to copy, and why. What the villagers have copied and why is discussed in Chapter 9.

This book will examine the processes leading to the essentialisation of elements of Ngadha culture and examine how far tourism brings about acculturation (including the demonstration effect). These are two aspects of socio-cultural change that anthropologists have observed that result from tourism. The book also explores the inter-related process of modernisation, globalisation and localisation that are also frequently associated with tourism in remote less economically developed regions.

Globalisation

Globalisation is often described as the 'intensification of world-wide relations which link distant localities in such a way that local happenings are shaped by the events occurring many miles away and vice versa' (Giddens, 1991: 64). It is a concept that describes the tightening network of ties that connects people around the world. It is a useful concept in this case because it goes some way to explain how the lives lived in Flores are becoming increasingly governed by forces and affairs many miles away. Although globalisation and westernisation are not coterminous (Scholte, 2002) the two processes are intimately connected (Schuerkens, 2003). Globalisation has resulted mainly from the forces of modernity such as rationalist knowledge, capitalism, automation, and has spread western patterns of behaviour, values, commodities and priorities (i.e. westernisation) across the globe (McLeod, 1999; Scholte, 2002).

Globalisation can be seen to have its historic roots in the European trading of the 16th century or even earlier. For example, Walters (1995) considers the spread of the great universalising religions that offered a generalised set of values and allegiances standing above and beyond the state, as evidence of early cultural globalisation. Scholte (1997) considers the process of globalisation to have begun from the later colonial period when the world began to be interconnected through expanded transport and communication technologies. Over the course of the 20th century, the pace and extent of globalisation have increased. As tourism involves the massive movement of people and cultural capital, uses high technology, and is supported by a huge media, it is considered to be both a cause and consequence of globalisation (Azarya, 2004; Salazar, 2005) helping to both reinforce and accelerate it.

While intimately connected, there is a danger in assuming globalisation equals Westernisation (e.g. Howell, 1995a; Scholte, 2002), since the flow of commodities and values is not unidirectional. Things and ideas also flow from the east to the west. Even when western goods are transferred to remote parts of Asia, the meanings associated with them may not be (Hannerz, 1990). Western cultural meanings do not enter a void; they are made meaningful by reference to existing experiences and cultural understandings. A cultural inflow is filtered by local experience, which allows acceptance, refusal, interpretation and transformation (Schuerkens, 2003). This ethnography adds to a growing literature about the active and creative roles of people in remote locales and how they experience, relate to and negotiate global influences.

Further globalisation does not necessarily imply homogenisation, merely greater connectedness and de-territorialisation (Scholte, 2002; Walters, 1995). It is a differentiating and diversifying process rather than the encroachment of western values and commodities. As Howell (1995b) argues, and the evidence in this ethnography supports, it is a mistake to overestimate the extent of westernisation and correlatively underestimate the degree to which societies are only superficially affected by it.

Tourism transforms difference into the global discourse of consumerism, a process by which 'otherness' becomes a commodity to be consumed. 'Othering' is thus a prerequisite, an aspect and a consequence of tourism. '[T]he nostalgic longing for untouched primitive peoples' (Mowforth & Munt 1998: 69) in the minds of the tourists is part of the process of 'othering'. Mowforth and Munt suggest this is 'a kind of institutional racism that celebrates primitiveness' (1998: 270) as suffering and poverty have become aestheticised by tourists' accumulation of images of the poor. Human practices are redefined as commodities as tourists are exposed to cultural differences and local cultural variation is confirmed. Much contemporary tourism to remote less economically developed locations, such as Ngadha, is founded on the 'Quest for the Other', who belong to a premodern, pre-commoditized, imagined world and is authentically social (Selwyn 1996: 21). The framing of 'Others' as primitive and traditional represents cultural ignorance and leads to conflicts in tourism, which are highlighted in this ethnography. The framing of tourates as primitive through tourism, not only colours, but also reflects the way the west looks at other cultures, and this has consequences beyond the tourate–tourist encounter. The quest for the traditional 'Other' leads to differentiation, a revival of culture and ethnicity, essentialisation and a paradox that is central to cultural tourism in peripheral regions.

This paradox is at the heart of cultural tourism development in less economically developed countries. To develop is to modernise: if a remote cultural tourist destination modernises, it is no longer 'primitive' and it loses its appeal. The challenge of balancing socio-economic integration with cultural distinction (Li & Butler, 1997) is a challenge fraught with conflict. As cultural assets are refined as consumables for tourists, culture becomes commoditised. As the destination modernises, a process, many suspect, of becoming more like the western tourist's society, it becomes less different and distinct. The destination appears less authentic and so the value of the tourism product is reduced.[11] Azarya's analysis of globalisation and tourism in developing countries details the link between marginality (or peripherality) and globalisation. He concludes that in tourism 'marginality is related to a perception of primitivism in western eyes towards places and people that become objects of their curiosity'. And that for the tourates the economic incorporation opportunities depend on a continued representation of marginality – 'an ultimate paradox of globalisation' (Azarya, 2004: 965).

In order to grasp how culture is changed as a result of globalising forces including tourism, it is helpful to recognise that traditions are not bounded, fixed or unchanging, they are creations in the present, socially constructed in an ongoing process (Wood, 1993). As Causey (2003) discusses, in the context of cultural tourism, in relation to carving traditions in Northern Sumatra, and we will see in relation to weaving in Ngadha, traditions are modified not only by internal innovations but also outside influences. The questions that need to be asked are not about how tourism impacts on a culture but how tourism is used and how the facets of culture are articulated in the face of increased tourism. As Wood discusses, 'the central questions to be asked are about process, and about the complex ways tourism enters and becomes part of an already on-going process of symbolic meaning and appropriation' (Wood, 1993: 66).

For many commentators, globalisation generates ambivalence and uncertainty and leads individuals to emphasise their identity and security of their location (e.g. O'Riordan & Church 2001; Schuerkens, 2003). This emphasis on the local or localisation is considered 'inextricably bound together' (Featherstone, 1990: 47) with globalisation. They are two sides of the same coin. The search for identity is pursued in terms of ideas about tradition, history, locality and community (Robertson, 1992). The search leads to 'an intensification of local particularism and differentiation and a proliferation of asserted differences'(Schuerkens, 2003: 217). In Ngadha, tourism has become a vehicle through which localness is asserted, traditions are attested and communities are affirmed.

Tourism has important consequences for identity and ethnicity. As this book will describe, one of the changes resulting from tourism has been the affirmation of local identity. The creation of an 'Ngadha' ethnicity is a response to and consequence of difference and 'otherness' becoming consumable tourist commodities. By understanding ethnicity as a set of social relationships and processes by which cultural differences are communicated,[12] ethnicity can be understood as a resource to be mobilised. A distinct cultural identity is a marketable resource for a tourism destination. Elements of culture may be commodified through tourism, but a self-conscious awareness of traditional culture as something local people possess, which attracts tourists, can bring political legitimacy (where traditional culture and the identity associated with it have hither to been debased). Tourism has provided this marginalised community with an awareness of the political capital that tradition can provide. Furthermore, a specific identity and associated culture can also bring pride and confidence. Pride, confidence and increased community cohesion combined with access to external contacts, new language skills and better access to information can all be very positive benefits brought by tourism. As this ethnography of tourism in Ngadha will portray, together these factors are important in the empowerment process for remote communities in less developed regions.

Authenticity and Commodification

Authenticity and commodification are closely related concepts frequently used in academic debates about social and cultural issues in tourism. As we have seen the commodification of certain aspects of tourates' culture is considered as a consequence of tourism. We will also see how visiting authentic cultures is part of the experience tourists to peripheral communities in the third world seek.

The 'commodification of culture' is considered as a negative impact of tourism when the inherent meanings of cultural artefacts and perform-ances are lost, as they are modified to suit tourist markets.[13] Debates about the commodification of culture are inter-linked with debates about authen-ticity and identity. Authenticity is a western cultural notion that implies 'genuine, of undisputed origin, or established authorship' (*Oxford English Dictionary*). Since MacCannell's (1976) provocative work, *The Tourist*, there has been a debate on authenticity among social scientists in tourism. Authenticity is associated with the past, with the 'primitive other', and in opposition to modernity. The view of a dichotomy between a pre-modern (authentic) and modern (inauthentic) has been criticized (Meethan, 2001; Olsen, 2002). Further analyses have attempted to deconstruct the notion.[14] While accepting the notion is problematic I use it because so many of the tourists that visit Ngadha do. However, the meanings and values they attach to the notion vary.

Authenticity does not have an objective quality, it is socially constructed and therefore negotiable, it varies according to the tourist and their point of view (Cohen, 1988). Authenticity is a value placed on a setting by the observer and is a notion embedded with power implications (Appadurai, 1986). Authenticity is not fixed but, as Barker *et al.*'s (2006) analysis of Balinese dance demonstrates, it changes over time. Further, as we will see, differences of perspective between tourists, the local community, and the local government have important consequences for development in Ngadha villages. It is the different meanings of authenticity, the compet-ing voices, and the inter-play with power relations that give meaning to our understanding of how the villagers relate to, and experience, tourists and tourism.

A common view in the anthropology of tourism literature is that tourism turns culture into a commodity, packaged and sold to tourists, resulting in a loss of authenticity. Taylor has suggested that the moment a culture is defined as an object of tourism, its authenticity is reduced (Taylor, 2001). Researchers have examined how crafts, performance, photography, hospi-tality and identity have been transformed by the presence of tourists. There is a rich literature in relation to the commodification of crafts and performance in Indonesia, which I examine below before turning my examination to the actors in tourism.

Crafts and souvenirs

The authenticity of souvenirs has been linked to the process of 'other-ing'. Souvenirs are tangible representations, expressions of cultural differ-ence between tourist and tourate (Graburn, 1987). The quest for ethnic art objects links the tourist with the traditional primitive life (Dougoud, 2000). Souvenirs are material proof of a tourist's intimate contact with the 'other' (Graburn, 1984). It has been suggested that the more educated and status-conscious the traveller, the more concerned they are that their souvenirs are authentic (Graburn, 2000: xiii). Purchasing souvenirs at the point of manufacture is one way to obtain authenticity; another way is to choose objects that seem to preserve ancestral traditions. Causey (2003) found that tourists tended to look for 'authentic', 'traditional' and 'primitive' carvings on their travels to Samosir Island, Sumatra.

Crafts are modified, with or without tourism, by the presence of new tools, materials and even images. Many crafts sold as souvenirs do not differ from local products for local consumption. However, tourism may be an important force for change in craft production. Graburn outlines a non-unilinear evolution of traditional art to souvenirs i.e. from 'authenticity to memento' (1984: 415). This process included miniaturisation and changes in production methods, to the importation of products made more cheaply by outsiders. If the changes that take place lead to them being alienated and losing their original meaning, the crafts are commoditised.

As part of the process of nation building, the visual and decorative arts of Indonesia have benefited from an unprecedented degree of official promotion (Picard, 1996). This is particularly true for textiles, one of the three crafts produced in Ngadha. Craft production in Ngadha villages, like other areas in Eastern Indonesia, is subject to prohibition and specialisation.[15] As Barnes (1989) found, in the islands off the eastern end of Flores, the specialisation is not only based on differentiation between villages but also by gender. Females produce ikat[16] cloth in one of the villages in this study, Bena, and males in the other, Wogo, do blacksmithing.

Crafts produced for the tourist trade are modified to make statements about ethnic identity (Van der Berghe & Keyes, 1984). Part of their appeal depends on a definable ethnicity and thus the souvenirs become ethnic markers. Frequently, in Indonesian societies, cloth is bought by tourists and becomes an ethnic marker,[17] including the cloth produced in Ngadha villages. As Smedjebacka (2000) discusses, all the ingredients of the burials tourists see on Sumba, are featured on the textiles to be sold as souvenirs. This incorporation of the tourists' gaze helps to sell the cloth, as it serves better as memorabilia.[18]

Performing arts and rituals

Performing arts have also become commoditised as a result of tourism (Daniel, 1996). Just as art objects are miniaturised, performances are shortened and made more varied to appeal to tourists (Sanger, 1988; Soejono, 1997). Performances can also act as ethnic markers.

Living arts have their own special meaning in the development of a national culture and can be a great asset in national tourism. As Picard (1990, 1997) discusses at length with reference to Bali, culture is simultaneously perceived as cultural heritage that should be looked after and as tourist capital to be exploited. Cultural shows are listed in the Indonesian government's definition of an *obyek parawisata* (tourist object or tourist attraction) (Article 4 Statute No. 9 1990) 'to be taken care of, developed, safe-guarded and preserved' (Sufwandi Mankudilaga, 1996: 332). The state has sponsored 'cultural studios' (*Sanggar Budaya*). As a result, groups of local people who practise local 'traditional' music and dance have proliferated in the provinces (Erb, 2000).

Staged cultural events are criticised on the one hand as 'reducing the religious element' (Hutajulu, 1997) and 'losing customary importance and resulting in cultural poverty' (Lathief, 1997). On the other hand, they are celebrated for the opportunities they offer: revitalising traditional culture,[19] reinforcing social solidarity and social cohesion, and providing the opportunity for travel (Sanger, 1988). Furthermore, they provide the setting, time and opportunity for innovation, diversification and creativity, (Hughes-Freeland, 1993).

I consider it necessary to make an analytical division between ritual and performance, that is, between performances put on specifically for tourists, and rituals, essentially performances for the ancestors, that tourists happen to observe. Performances are essentially profane or already secularised. They are not sacred events in the same way as rituals.[20] As discussed in Chapter 7, the separation between performance and ritual in Flores is at an early stage. In line with Indonesian policy to develop and preserve traditional practices, ritual dances are removed from context to be displayed at competitions and festivals. According to Rahyu Supanggah (1994), the Indonesian performing arts festival[21] in Maumere in 1994 was an attempt 'to get society to value its culture and to put Eastern Indonesia on the arts map of Indonesia'. Staged attractions or pseudo-events as Boorstin (1964) called them, have the potential to reduce community disturbance and can provide a forum for local people to take pride in their culture (Murphy, 1985).

The attendance of tourists at rituals rather than events staged for them has received less discussion. One of the exceptions is the significant research and analysis of tourists' attendance at funerals in Tanah Toraja, Sulawesi, Indonesia, by a number of anthropologists,[22] Tanah Toraja is a remote, Christianised, mountainous community that shares much in common with the Ngadha. However, tourism began in Toraja much earlier and the preservation of the ritual system became the goal of the villagers and the urban modernisers. Initially, positive consequences were reported: the former negative embarrassment of local culture was transformed into a positive encouragement of ritual practices with a dramatic alteration in self-image (Crystal, 1978). However, when he returned in 1976, Crystal discovered a tenfold increase in tourists, bewildered locals and rituals that had been commercialised as spectacles for foreigners. With increasing tourist interest, competitive funeral feasts increased at an extraordinary rate (Volkman, 1985). This played a role in the movement to revitalise ... *aluk* (the traditional religion of Toraja). Tourism has changed the death rituals of Toraja, which are now staged for tourists and the media (Adams, 1993; Yamashita, 1994). The rituals of Ngadha however have not been re-orientated towards the tourists; they remain ceremonies for the ancestors and local communities. This book explores why tourists are important guests at Ngadha competitive feasts but how, so far, they have not been important agents of change.

The debates about authenticity and cultural commodification go beyond the literature concerning crafts and performance. Cohen *et al.* (1992) have examined the photographer–photographee interaction. In the tourists' (photographers') attempts to capture authentic images of tourates (photographees), they do not reciprocate in the social exchange. This may lead to the tourates asking for immediate rewards. The photographer–photographee interaction is then commoditized. In Ngadha, payment for photographs was important in narratives from tourists, guides and villagers. It was an issue around which opinions about the limits of acceptable commodification appeared to crystallise. Furthermore, as suggested above, and will be discussed in relation to Ngadha ethnicity, identity can also become commoditisied.

While cultural commodification is frequently regarded as a negative aspect of tourism, this ethnography will present an alternative view. People can use cultural commodification as a way of affirming their identity, of telling their own story and establishing the significance of local experiences (MacDonald, 1997). Far from rendering culture superficial and meaningless, commodification can be seen as 'part of a very positive process by which people are beginning to re-evaluate their history and shake off the shame of peasantry' (Abram, 1996: 198). Tourates are active strategists and they manipulate their 'otherness' to their own ends. Tourism is used to support a variety of versions of culture, tradition, identity and authenticity. And, as this case describes, commodification may be a pragmatic response for the poor and can also be a step on the ladder to empowerment (Cole, 2004a).

The Stakeholders and Conflicts

In order to provide a holistic view, this book presents tourism development in Ngadha from the perspectives of the different stakeholders. A stakeholder is defined as 'any person, group or organization that is affected by the causes or consequences of an issue' (Bryson & Crosby, 1992). Tourism involves many stakeholders from the tourists to the tourates and all those that mediate their relationship: governments, media, international organisations, non-governmental organisations (NGOs) and a wide variety of industries. This section examines the pertinent background literature of the key stakeholders: tourists, guides, government and guidebooks. It then provides a brief theoretical orientation to stakeholder conflicts. The background literature that deals specifically with the tourates can be found in Chapters 3 and 4.

Tourists

Anthropological studies of tourists have focused on two themes: tourism as a form of pilgrimage and how far tourists are in search of authenticity. Graburn (1978) traced the structural similarities between tourism and sacred experiences. Following Van Gennep's *Rites of Passage*, originally formulated in 1908, Graburn analysed tourism as an annual sacred journey that separates us from our ordinary profane lives: 'During vacations, tourists are in a liminal (betwixt and between) status and may experience a heightened sense of life or reality which results in a sense of communitas or togetherness' (Graburn & Moore, 1994: 235). The liminal state of tourists whilst on holiday is used to explain their 'inverted' (and sometimes irresponsible) behaviour.[23]

According to MacCannell (1976) the tourist searches for authenticity in order to recover the senses of wholeness and structure absent in everyday life. This argument has been challenged on two counts. Firstly, Cohen (1974) has argued that there is no such person as *the tourist* but a variety of different tourist types. Indeed I found it essential to segment the tourists that visit Ngadha in order to develop a deeper understanding of their behaviour, values and priorities. I built on the work of Cohen (1974) and Smith (1978), and their typologies are discussed in Chapter 6. Secondly, Urry (1990) has argued that tourists do not always seek authenticity and are happy to accept inauthentic experiences. As discussed above authenticity was an important factor for the majority of the tourists that visit

Ngadha. This contested notion lies at the centre of many of the conflicts of tourism that are central to this book.

Prepared to stay in relatively low standard accommodation, backpackers are the most numerous type of tourists to visit Ngadha like many remote marginal communities. Research has shown that backpackers are a very heterogeneous (Hampton, 1997; Spreitzhofer, 1998) and increasing diverse demographic group (Scheyvens, 2002). Many backpackers themselves believe that they are more discerning and responsible travellers than mere tourists, and several researchers suggest that backpackers provide more net benefits to local communities than do mass tourists (Hampton, 1998; Scheyvens, 2002).

Despite their heterogeneous character and the debates about better or worse (cf. Goodwin, 1999), exploring other cultures is an important motivation and, for those that travel to less economically developed countries, this includes sharing the local lifestyle and meeting people in out of the way locations (cf. Cohen, 1989). They often express a desire to see different cultures and generally experience how other people live and are keen to gain an understanding of different cultures (Huxley, 2004).

As explored in Chapter 6, the types of tourists that have visited Ngadha over the past 20 years have changed quite dramatically and as I have argued the term backpacker is becoming increasingly blurred. More importantly, they differ in terms of the experience they seek in cultural tourism situations. Zeppel (1993) who studied tourist experiences among the Iban in Sarawak sub-divides cultural tourists into 'cultural sightseeing' and 'meet the people' (1993: 62) The former spent less time in the villages than the latter and concentrated on taking photographs that matched pre-conceived images. For the latter, personal encounters and opportunities to socialise such as sharing drinks and meals were important. Goffman (1961) divides interaction between that which is 'unfocused' i.e. those interpersonal communications that result solely by virtue of persons being in one another's presence, and that which is 'focused', when people effectively agree to sustain a flow of cognitive and visual attention and an encounter results. Cultural tourists can then be divided between those who seek unfocused interaction, i.e. sightseeing, and those who want focused interaction and want to 'meet the people'. The tourists' desire for social interaction, their ability to adapt to local cultural norms, their sources of information and the occasional lasting relationships that they developed with tourates, are the most important aspects of this stakeholders relationship to this story of tourism development in Ngadha.

The mediators

Anthropological studies of the mediators of tourism are less common than work on tourists and tourates. Although under the broad heading of the seminology of tourism, work has been undertaken on images produced by the industry to market tourism,[24] there has been limited analysis of the significance of the mediators of tourism by anthropologists (Smith, 2001). Tourism is a thoroughly mediated activity, dependent on mediation by others who are neither tourists nor tourates (Chambers, 1997). The mediators in tourism are those who act as go-betweens or culture brokers: they are the agents who interpret and negotiate between the tourists and tourates. Mediators in tourism include guides, governments, tour operators, travel agents and international organisations such as the World Tourism Organization (WTO) (Smith, 2001).

Guides

Tour agents, guides and leaders who act as culture brokers between tourists and tourates are crucial elements in tourism (Hitchcock *et al.*, 1993). Guides are important front-line employees in tourism, they are often the first (and only) local people that tourists can converse with, and tourists frequently view guides as representative of a place. Cohen (1985) is one of the few social scientists to have studied the importance of guides as mediators of the tourist experience. In his paper *'The tourist guide, the origins, structure and dynamics of a role'*, he discusses how the modern tour guide's role has developed from the 'pathfinder' and the 'mentor'. Cohen divides the guide's work into leader and mediatory spheres and into interactional and communicative components. While Cohen distinguishes between 'original guides' and 'professional guides', Bras (2000) recognised a number of other divisions. Guides may be licensed or unlicensed, formal or informal. On Lombok, Bras (2000) distinguished between professional, site-related, odd-jobbers and network specialists.

Crick (1992) describes the tour guides in Kandy as rough and poorly educated. Frequently, they were in the role for short periods of time and were highly individualistic. The guides in Ngadha come from a mixture of educational backgrounds but some are highly educated and they tend to be in their role for years, decades in some cases. Dahles and Bras' (1999) work on guides in Indonesia examines the work of guides as entrepreneurs or brokers who manipulate strategic contact with other people for their own profit. Bras (2000) claims that social relations and narratives are sold in pursuit of profit. However, tourism on Flores is less well developed than on Java or Lombok and differs in several fundamental ways. The Ngadha guides have not become *Balinized* (cf. Causey, 2003) or entered the 'gigolo scene', for example they would not fondle a western girlfriend in public, as guides reportedly do elsewhere in the archipelago.

Not only have there been very few anthropological studies of guides, the role of a tour guide has also received little attention in the tourism development literature (Gurung *et al.*, 1996). Probably due to guides' lack of profile and status and therefore visibility to researchers, the impact of guides has largely been glossed over (Weiler & Ham, 2001). In the vocational literature, guides are seen as ambassadors (e.g. Mancini, 1990); the same stance as is taken by many governments and used in guide training programmes.

Guides regard the dissemination of information as a key feature of their work. Although Cohen (1985) separates information provision from interpretation, in the case of cultural tourism the information to be provided requires interpretation, therefore rendering such a division unnecessary. There is an evolving body of literature on nature tourism guides that examines the vital role the guide can play in the management of tourist behaviour.[25] Weiler and Ham maintain: 'There is increasing evidence that what a guide says to her or his clients can influence how they think and behave with respect to the places they visit.' (2001: 261). Through their ability to understand the culture of both tourist and tourate, the guide has a role to prevent misunderstandings caused by cultural differences (de Kadt, 1979). Furthermore, as the narratives here reveal, guides are, as Salazar (2005) suggests, key actors in the folklorising, ethnising and exoticising of the local culture.

The guides in Ngadha, like the guides studied by Bras and Dahles (1999) in Lombok and Yogyakarta, work in the informal tourism sector, are inclined toward risk-avoidance strategies and imitate the product and services of others. They have both co-operative and competitive relations with each other and share profits with family and friends instead of reinvesting them. They do not feel that they have a voice in tourism development but many have been key agents of change. Several young men who have worked as guides have developed long-term relations with tourists, who have sponsored their education, have provided them with the opportunities to leave Flores and, in two cases, travel abroad. The expanded social networks of these men have influenced lives beyond these individuals; the benefits have fed back into their families and their villages. These issues are explored in Chapter 5.

The government
The state plays a crucial role in structuring the tourist encounter (Wood, 1997). While state involvement is necessary, as is often the case in less

economically developed countries, the state is riddled with inefficiency, inexperience, corruption, poor policy formulation and implementation. This is often accompanied by low skills levels and 'a dire need for trained and educated personnel in tourism' (Harrison, 2001: 253). Richter's (1993) analysis of tourism policies in South East Asian countries suggests tourism policies are elite-driven, centralised and the regulatory frameworks are weak. The governments aspire to hosting luxury international and business travellers and have neglected issues of sustainability.

Tourism is not only seen as a generator of foreign exchange but also a means to promote pride in a country's heritage. In the case of ethnically plural nations, such as Indonesia, the government has to strike a balance between forging national consciousness and promoting regional and local identities (King, 1993). The Indonesian state has fostered the recognition of regional identities over smaller ethnic group identities (Picard, 1993; Wood, 1997). The Indonesian government has used tourism to present cultural differences in a benign and non-threatening way (Sofield, 2000). The state mediates cultural change through sponsoring tourism and affirms authenticity through the state licensing of guides and the marketing of ethnic markers (Wood, 1984). The state shares with tourism the presentation of destinations as unique and distinctive.

The underlying theme of Taman Mini Indonesia Indah, Indonesia's ethnographic theme park, is that the nation's foundations are its people, its different customs and cultures held together by common traditions (Hitchcock *et al.*, 1997: 228). The park acts as an official repository for culture (Stanley, 1998: 55). However, 'decisions have been made as to which cultures to privilege and which to ignore' (Stanley, 1998: 59). Some ethnic groups, for example Toraja, get official recognition while others, for example Ngadha, do not.

Picard's (1996) work traces the development of tourism on Bali from colonial times to the 1990s. His analysis demonstrates how Balinese cultural tourism is an outcome of history and a complex series of policy decisions made by the Dutch, the Indonesian state and more recently the Balinese intelligentsia. His work underlies the importance of the state's role, which has systematically disembodied Bali's culture into component parts, so that custom, politics, religion and art have been separated in the process of touristification. The definition of culture has shifted from one expressed in terms of values, concerned with appropriate social relations, moral behaviour and so on to one that is focused on artistic expression or cultural arts. Culture is then objectified, reified, externalised and detached from the Balinese, in order to be displayed and marketed to tourists (Picard, 1996). This is part of the essentialisation discussed above.

This book examines this process in relation to Ngadha and examines how the government objectifies components of a lived culture, removing them from context and obscuring their meaning. The story unveils how tourism becomes a force in the interpretation of culture and tradition and how some stakeholders want to preserve culture and while others fragment it.

The importance of supra-national organisations as mediators in tourism should not be omitted. Foreign governments, global financial institutions and development agencies exert a high degree of influence on tourism policies. However, there has been no significant impact of international organisations in Ngadha's tourism to date beyond their impact on tourism to Indonesia generally, which is discussed in the next chapter.

Guidebooks

Guidebooks also act as mediators although they and their authors are not direct stakeholders. They form a common, little analysed, crucial part of the touristic process, mediating relationships between tourists and their destination as well as between host and guest (Bhattacharyya, 1997). They are both useful and powerful. They help to navigate tourists around an unfamiliar area. Guidebooks not only exert an inordinate amount of power over the tourist experience (McGregor, 2000), they can also make or break local businesses, depending on how they are written up (Wheat, 1999). For many tourists, guidebooks are the chief means of making sense of a country (Abram, 2000).

McGregor (2000) discusses how guidebooks affect tourists' pre-arrival images, how they experience Tanah Toraja, and what they gaze upon. He concludes that travellers in Tanah Toraja were tutored by the texts to gaze and experience destinations in a particular way. Guidebooks create a particular type of interest and participation, and constitute a form of social control. In reference to tourism on Samosir Island, Sumatra, Causey concluded that the 'guidebooks historicizing portrayals were attempting to repair the disjuncture between what the visitors desire to see and what they actually see' (2003: 85).

Bhattacharyya's (1997) semiotic analysis of Lonely Planet's *India: A Travel Survival Kit* discusses how the language used by Lonely Planet was authoritative, leaving many tourists unquestioning about what they read. As the texts and photographs concentrate on the natural world, historic monuments and the social life of the exotic, to the exclusion of contemporary ordinary life, the book 'perpetuates the view of the Orient as spectacle' (1997: 587). Furthermore, the Lonely Planet guidebook gives visitors virtually no guidelines on culturally appropriate behaviour and there is no presumption that tourists are expected to behave in culturally appropriate ways.

The analysis, in Chapter 5, of the guidebooks used by tourists visiting Ngadha, also suggests that they do little to educate tourists. They have an important impact on which villages the tourists choose to visit and on the success and failure of local businesses. Furthermore, guidebooks are read by locals and work as a feedback mechanism. They have directly or indirectly influenced local actors to preserve tradition but in doing so they may be one of the forces preventing important aspects of village development.

Stakeholder conflicts

Tourists and tourates

As mentioned, the tourists that visit Ngadha are a heterogeneous group who will be further sub-divided in order to develop a better understanding of them. However, nearly all of them are westerners and thus their visits result in encounters between different value systems. The differences result in misunderstandings and friction, and a tension at the heart of Ngadha's cultural tourism development.[26] Values are culturally constructed and tourism involves the meeting of different cultures. Values are a dominant cultural variable in differentiating cultures. They specify which behaviours in a culture are important and which should be avoided. Values determine attitudes, behaviour and perceptions (Reisinger & Turner, 2003), and barriers arise from the substantial differences in cultural patterns and expectations between tourists and tourates (Blanton, 1992). What is normal in one culture, another may find insulting or irritating. The greater the differences in the cultural background, the more likely it is that behaviour will be misunderstood and lead to friction.

The familiar assumptions, values, behaviour and ideas of residents are constantly challenged while they cope with 'tourists behaviour which is often a product of heightened expectations, deflated hopes, exaggerated fears or frustrated plans' (Blanton, 1992: 6). Unskilled in the rules of the tourates' culture, tourists often feel inadequate or embarrassed. They often suffer from anxiety and culture shock (Pearce, *et al.*, 1998). The differences in cultural values can result in miscommunications, suspicions, shortcomings, misunderstandings and conflict. Misunderstandings frequently occur due to ignorance and arrogance (Kripendorf, 1987; Pearce, 1995) or a combination of the two. Misunderstandings frequently underpin resentment and conflict. The transitory, superficial nature of the tourist–tourate encounter is a primary breeding ground for deceit, mistrust, dishonesty and a lack of responsibility.[27]

Making generalisations about Asians and their values is problematic, however there are some common themes in 'Asian values discourse in Asia' (Bhopal & Hitchcock, 2001: 7). Among others, Asian values include respect for authority, saving face and the avoidance of embarrassment; the desire for harmony and avoidance of clashes; and precedence of the group over the individual. Even generalising about Indonesian values is difficult. However, an important aspect Indonesian culture is that it is a collectivist culture that stresses deference and harmony, which means individual behaviour is regulated to ensure peace and order in the social domain; the unity of the community is guarded by restrictions to individual freedom (Zanial Kling, 1997). Indonesians avoid unpleasantness and public affection, and touching between people of different gender brings shame. A number of further value clashes specific to tourism settings have been identified. Firstly, in relation to time: Indonesians see time as stretchable, and being in a hurry is an indication of impatience. By contrast, western cultures focus on efficiency and punctuality. Secondly, in relation to dress: in Indonesia dress expresses respect of other people and must conform to the occasion to a greater degree than in western societies. Thirdly, solitude is perceived negatively by Indonesians, leading to misunderstandings about privacy. Fourthly, in Indonesian society, conflict and disagreement are avoided to assure a conflict-free and psychologically comfortable life. Fifthly, in relation to greetings: in Indonesian culture, on meeting, one must acknowledge the other's presence with a smile and it is advisable to talk for several minutes by enquiring politely about the other person's family and affairs. Finally, with reference to the expressions of emotions: in Indonesia negative or positive expressions of emotions are avoided and expressions of love are not acceptable in public. Westerners tend to be more direct, individualistic and self-assertive (Reisinger & Turner, 1997).

Other stakeholder conflicts

Conflicts in tourism do not only arise from differing cultural values between tourists and tourates. As Saremba and Gill (1991) discuss, values may conflict between different user groups. Disharmony and conflict may be 'the creation of outcomes of decisions, objectives and activities selected by initiators [e.g. governments and operators] away from the scene of the encounter '[between tourists and tourates]' (Boniface, 1999: 2).

Greenwood (1989) discusses the 'conflictual arenas' that result from claims over rights, ownership and consent. Robinson's (1999b) review of the cultural conflicts of tourism stresses how conflict can be between tourists and tourates, the industry and tourates and among the tourates themselves. Conflicts can also arise between neighbouring groups[28] and even villages. Communities cannot be seen as a single homogeneous group of hosts, but in fact are made up of 'an agglomeration of factions and interest groups often locked in competitive relationships' (Joppe, 1996: 475). There are major differences that exist between men and women, generations, the dominant and the disadvantaged, decision-makers and workers, and those with money and those without. Where boundaries are drawn, who is included in a community and who is not, who is local and who is not, are vital considerations as conflict over limited resources can result in tourism being a divisive force. Chapter 8 examines how, in Ngadha, tourism has become the focus for tensions both between and within villages.

As Robinson (1999b) discusses, cultural conflicts can to some extent be compensated for in economic terms and that the extent of the dependency has bearings on that compensation. Robinson's broad-ranging discussion indicates the links between cultural commodification and conflict. We know commodification of culture takes place, 'we need to analyse the political basis upon which it occurs, the degree of selectivity involved, whether cultural rights are transgressed and whether owners of culture receive the revenues generated through gazing tourists' (1999b: 13).

The different actors – tourists, villagers and mediators –hold different perspectives on tourism, which relate to their cultural norms, values and positions, on a number of different levels. As Cohen, in one of his earliest papers, suggested, an analysis of the different values, priorities and attitudes of the various parties in tourism 'will enable one to pinpoint the source of the 'conflicts of tourism' (Cohen, 1979: 30). If such conflicts are to be resolved, a rich understanding of each party's position is a prerequisite (Pearce, 1995). This book unpicks the nuances of the different stakeholders, views, attitudes and priorities to examine the sources of the conflicts of tourism in a marginal community in Eastern Indonesia.

Conflicts of acculturation

The villagers not only experience value clashes and conflicts with other stakeholders but also as a result of the processes of tourism development. As we have seen cultural tourism involves fulfilling the desires of tourists 'to access primitive societies ... to taste traditional ways of life ... to see ...exotic practices' (Sofield & Birtles, 1996). Tourism, as an important form of globalisation, results in greater socio-economic integration with the wider world. The processes of socio-economic integration result in modernisation, a loss of the 'primitive' and results in the tourist product being, from the tourists' viewpoint, 'spoilt'. On the one hand, tourism brings (or has the potential to bring) wealth and modernisation, while, on the other hand, for the product to remain attractive, the villages must remain 'primitive, traditional and exotic'. These conflicts between modernising and remaining traditional I refer to as 'conflicts of acculturation'.

As King suggests, 'the interrelationships between tourism and culture are complex; they are not generalisable and they have to be demonstrated in given cases' (1993: 100). Anthropologists working in tourism have thus called for more ethnographies and more long-term studies. This book provides one such study. This chapter has outlined some of the theoretical building blocks used to frame the research and the ethnography that follows. A number of important inter-linked themes recur in the literature that relate to the cultural processes of tourism development in remote marginal communities. As tourists seek to quench their thirst for a pre-modern exotic other, tourates' arts, crafts, ceremonies and relationships change. While many analysts have examined this commodification process resulting in the loss of authenticity and cultural distinction as a threat to cultural tourism development, few have examined how tourism can be used, as a force to be mobilised and the resultant affirmation of identity, increased pride and empowerment that can follow.

In order to provide a holistic view, and identify 'the conflicts of tourism' this book will examine tourism from the perspectives of the different stakeholders. In tourism substantial cultural barriers exist between tourists and tourates, the literature that identifies the cultural differences between Indonesians and westerners has been explored to provide a backdrop to the narratives that follow. The next chapter explains the context surrounding tourism development in a remote village of Eastern Indonesia – a little understanding of tourism as a tool for development and the history and politics of Indonesia is necessary to understand tourism development from the perspectives of the mediators and the circumstances of the villagers' lives.

Notes

1. The term host, coined for people in tourist receiving communities following Smith's (1978) book is controversial. See Selwyn (1996).
2. Cf. Crick (1994) and Nash (1996).
3. For example Greenwood (1972), Crystal (1978), Urbanowicz (1978).
4. Andrew Causey (2003) coined this term. As he suggests it is better than touree coined by Van den Berghe to mean those gazed upon in tourist destinations, and which I have previously used. Tourates denotes action (tourism) but also

indicates that its members simultaneously have some degree of agency in that action and are changed by it.

5. See for example Lea (1988), Oppermann (1993), Oppermann and Chon (1997).

6. As discussed by Harrison (1992), Nash (1978), Madeley (1999), Broham (1996), Britton (1982) and Murphy (1985).

7. See Stanley (1998) and Volkman (1990) on the official designation of some ethnic groups in Indonesia.

8. Adams (1997) examined the role of travel agents in South Sulawesi and how they acted as brokers in ethnicity selecting and emphasising symbols from neighbouring Torajan culture.

9. Acculturation theory has been long established in anthropology (mentioned in *American Anthropologist* as early as 1936 with social science research council attempting an exploratory formulation of the subject in 1954).

10. For example Cooper *et al.* (1993: 101), Burns and Holden (1995: 84), Burns (1999: 101), Hashimoto (2002: 213), Bleasdale and Tapsell (1999: 190), Murphy (1985: 119), Williams (1998: 152), Pearce (1989: 221). Van Harssel (1994: 189) refers to it as 'the imitation effect'.

11. Cf. Swain (1989), Dearden and Harron (1992), and Go (1997).

12. Cf. Hitchcock (2000).

13. This view developed from Greenwood's (1978) initial analysis of the Alarde festival of Fuenterrabia in Spain, which led him to conclude that a performance for participants was turned into a show for outsiders and that tourism turns culture into a commodity, packaged and sold to tourists. Although Greenwood's assumptions were later criticised (Wilson, 1993) and even reversed (Greenwood, 1989), his work has been influential.

14. Selwyn (1996), for example, differentiates between cool and hot authenticity while Wang (1999) differentiates between objective authenticity; constructive authenticity, and existential authenticity.

15. The production of pottery industry was exclusive to a few villages at the foot of Mount Inerie (Slamet-Vilsink 1995). This has now been replaced by brickmaking as aluminium has replaced earthen cooking pots.

16. Ikat is originally an Indonesian term that has entered the international textile vocabulary (Hitchcock, 1991). It should be noted that the Indonesian verb '*ikat*' literally means 'to tie'. In reference to weaving, it has come to refer both to the verb i.e. the process to tie a bundle of treads so that they resist the dye, and the finished product of cloth produced using this technique. This common use of ikat as the product as well as the process is probably a direct result of tourism. For example, Sumba style textiles are mass-produced in factories in Java (Hitchcock, 2000). These cloths are sold to tourists on the beaches of Lombok as ikats. The tourists have accepted this (incorrect) terminology and it is common to hear ikat used for a variety of woven cloth in Indonesia.

17. For example, the *ulos* in Toba Batak culture (Causey, 1998), the *hinggi* in Eastern Sumba (Forshee, 1998) and Jambi Batik from Jambi (Hitchcock & Kerlogue, 2000).

18. Smedjebacka (2000) also discusses how men have started weaving and how young women have started to practice ikat and dyeing, where previously this was the preserve of the privileged few. In some cases, women have lost artistic

control as men have taken over the creation of the designs and women are left to take care of the less creative stages.

19. See for example Daniel (1996), Sanger (1988), Hughes-Freeland (1993) and Soejono (1997).
20. It would appear from Sanger's (1988) work that the villagers in Singapadu make this distinction by keeping the most sacred Barong for rituals and not using it for tourist performances. Picard (1997) asserts that the distinction is made by outsiders and not by the Balinese themselves, and that there is a complex interaction between the two. In other societies, varying strategies are developed to preserve the sacred from tourist consumption.
21. Masyrakat Pertunjuk Seni Indonesia.
22. Crystal (1978), Volkman (1985, 1987 and 1990), Adams (1984, 1990, 1993, 1995 and 1997), Yamashita (1994).
23. See for example Lett (1983), Wickens (2000), and Erb (2000).
24. See for example Dann (1996a, 1996b), Selwyn (1996) and Rojek (1997).
25. See for example Gurung *et al.* (1996), Pond (1993) and Weiller and Davis (1993).
26. The villagers asked me: 'How can we have tourism and not end up like Bali?' 'Is it possible to have tourists but only those that keep their clothes on?' 'How can we have tourism and still show respect for the ancestors?'
27. As discussed by MacCannell (1984), Dahles and van Meijl (2000), and Hunter (2001).
28. Adams (1990, 1997) examines the consequences of tourism on Toraja ethnic relations and the conflicts that have emerged as the Toraja jostle to control their tourism planning. Toraja is situated in the province of South Sulawesi. At the provincial level, political power is in the hands of Islamic Buginese, age-old ethnic rivals of the Toraja. The provincial officials refused to allow unlicensed Toraja guides to operate. Access to licences (from the provincial capital, Ujung Pandang) was easier to obtain for their ethnic rivals, who would deny the Toraja the opportunity to represent themselves to outsiders. Further, their Muslim rivals would be likely to misrepresent the Toraja as pagan and backward.

Chapter 3
Placing Ngadha's Tourism Development in Context

In order to comprehend the effects of tourism on Ngadha villages it is necessary to understand development and tourism in Indonesia, both at the national level and more specifically in Eastern Indonesia. It is equally important to appreciate how wider global and national events have affected the development of tourism in Ngadha. The latter half of this chapter links this case with the theoretical arguments about tourism as part of the development process in less economically developed countries. The brief background here concentrates on the most recent development discourse: poverty reduction (cf. Mowforth & Munt, 1998). This is because the people of Ngadha are poor[1] and tourism in Ngadha is small scale and, in the near future, unlikely to become 'mass'. Tourists visit Ngadha for its culture and for this reason I have unpicked some of the academic debates about this phenomenon, and explain why I reject the often-used concept of 'ethnic tourism' and the complications of the term 'indigenous tourism' particularly in the Indonesian setting.

Development in Indonesia

Three forces have shaped life in Ngadha villages: the state, the Church and the ancestors. The history of Indonesia and its present governance shapes the way tourism is mobilised and how the villagers experience it. A little history and politics of the nation is thus essential to understand the way the village works and way the villagers interact with tourists and tourism.

Indonesian nationalists declared independence on 17 August 1945. Most of the vast archipelago of the former Dutch East Indies finally became an independent state in 1949. Although Flores was first colonised by the Portuguese, who brought Catholicism[2] to the island, the colonial legacies are largely Dutch. Dutch legal and political institutions and bureaucratic systems still affect the workings of the state across the archipelago, as do the extremely uneven patterns of development that the Dutch began.

Under the leadership of the first president of Indonesia, Sukarno, the tenets of *Pancasila* (the five principles to safeguard national unity) were formulated. *Pancasila* remained the national ideology under the New Order government of the second president, Suharto, who treated the principles as religious in nature (Erb, 2001b) and used them as an ideological justification for authoritarian rule (Schwarz, 1999). In order to maintain unity, stability and economic growth, the New Order maintained order and control through authoritarianism, patronage and bureaucracy. Development planning is embedded in the national ideology, which means that Indonesians 'should submit to the collectivity and put the needs and demands of the nation before individual, local, regional, ethnic and class interests' (King, 1999: 61). Furthermore, as discussed in Chapter 2, 'the Indonesian culture is highly collectivistic and group orientated. The focus is on group rights and needs …. In all social relations the importance of group harmony and living together in harmony is emphasised' (Reisinger & Turner, 1997: 142). The government has been heavily committed to a centralised, bureaucratic process of decision-making. Each of these factors has permeated to the lowest levels in the Indonesian state structure, and has consequences for tourism development.

Across the archipelago, we can also see Javanese concepts of power and authority,[3] whereby reverence towards people in power or otherwise high social standing prevails. Accordingly, from high-level political jurisdictions, down to the village level, the top-heavy traditional perspectives of power remain strong (Timothy, 1999). The authorities make decisions and they cannot be questioned. Individuals place themselves at the disposal of the nation to support efforts of national development (*pembangunan*) with guidance, support and direction from the government (King, 1999). Villagers accept and expect political and social control to be in the hands of the government. They are taught blind obedience to central government (Erb, 2000), and there is a belief that the government knows best (Gede Raka, 2000). The villagers' and local government's attitudes to tourism development need to be understood against this backdrop.

Unity and nationalism have been the most important aspects of *Pancasila* in the building of the Indonesian state. However, other aspects of *pancasila* have had important bearings on the lives of the Ngadha villagers including how tourism is articulated and how individuals negotiate their position in their daily lives. Belief in one God, the first of the five principles, has resulted in state support for missionaries and Catholic conversion. Catholicism is one of the villagers' realms of social organisation, a discourse of modernisation, which competes for authority in the lives of the villagers.

Social justice for all, or '*pancasila* equity', has undermined the power of local ethnic groups and affected gender relations '[b]y claiming all its citizens are equal the state undercut local claims to political power based on principles of kinship' (Blackwood, 2000: 4). In doing so, it has undermined the power of the ancestors, another force shaping the lives of the villagers.

The focus of the New Order government was on economic development, upon which its legitimacy and that of the state bureaucracy was based (Schmidt *et al.*, 1998). The unity and political stability attracted foreign investors. Development was a national ideology and there is no doubt that national wealth increased. The New Order's record on economic development must not go unquestioned, for a number of reasons. Firstly, the success grew from a very low starting point because under Indonesia's first president, Sukarno, economics had taken a back seat to political struggle. Secondly, poverty indicators are notoriously unreliable, Schmidt *et al.* (1998) consider the artificially low poverty line means that statistics given for the numbers of the poor are unrealistic. Thirdly, government policy has exacerbated the very uneven development across the archipelago.[4] Fourthly, growth has in many cases been at the expense of the environment, for example the loss of forests. Finally, growth has been at the expense of free expression and years of *'pancasila* democracy', infused with fears of national disunity (Schwarz, 1999), have resulted in a society politically ill-prepared for involvement in the decision-making process and frightened of change.

Economic development in Indonesia has followed the top-down authoritarian model, based on Javanese and colonial structures, for the purposes of order and control. 'The bureaucracy has positioned itself as the "prima donna" of economic development at the expense of political development' (Gede Raka, 2000: 29). The tendency for decisions to be made by bureaucrats, who then inform the people, is due to a perception among government planners that the population is uneducated (Timothy, 1999). Encouraging local involvement in decision-making has then to overcome official reluctance to listen and consult (King, 1999).

Tourism in Indonesia

Tourism to Bali pre-dates the Indonesian state: an association for tourist traffic and an official tourist bureau were opened in 1908 (Picard, 1996). An Indonesian term for tourism (*parawisata – para* = many, *wisata* = visitor)) was first coined in 1958 by the first president, Sukarno, and since then has been part of the nation's development plans (Gunawan, 1997). Considered as a smokeless industry of the future, based on the country's natural assets of a diversity of culture and environment, tourism is seen as a leading sector for promoting economic growth (Wiendu Nuryanti, 1998). Growth in arrivals from half a million in 1980 (Booth, 1990) to over five million in 1997 (Hall, 2000) has meant that tourism is the country's fourth most important generator of foreign exchange after oil/gas, timber and textiles (Wall, 1997).

Generalising about tourism in Indonesia is dangerous and does not reflect the situation on the ground in Ngadha. For example, Wall (1997) suggests that as Indonesia straddles the equator and gets tourists from both hemispheres, it suffers less from seasonality than other destinations. Further, in general, Asians, with Singapore, Japan, Malaysia and Taiwan contributing more than half the country's arrivals, dominate visitation to Indonesia (Hall, 1997; Go, 1997). However, these patterns are not reflected in the tourism in Ngadha.

Indonesia has five-yearly development plans (REPELITA), which establish the country's regulations, policies and programmes for its development. The 1994/1995–1998/1999 plan had ambitious targets to maintain tourism growth at 11–13% per annum in line with the previous decade (Kuntjoro–Jakti, 1997). In the same plan, emphasis was placed on regionalisation and the reduction of social inequalities. Tourism was to be used to meet government's goals of economic development throughout the regions.[5] Areas of high poverty in Eastern Indonesia were targeted because tourism was seen as an engine to drive overall economic development.[6]

The national tourism strategy utilised Butler's (1980) tourist destination life cycle as a major tool for analysis.[7] It recommended that Bali be used as a 'hub' to encourage 'spoke' developments in regional locations (Wall, 1997). The strategy recommends concentration on the 'beach plus' concept. The plan supports coastal tourism development and concentrates on high-quality, high-spend, beach tourism. This is not surprising considering that official figures show that the large-scale luxury end of the industry accounted for 60% of the gross income and over half the value-added generated in the tourism sector (Booth, 1990). *Indonesia's Tourism Vision* suggests that local communities should be given the maximum opportunity to participate in tourism development and that there is a commitment to empowering communities (Gunawan, 1999). Furthermore 'the community is at the heart of the development plan; local norms and values must be appreciated and respected' (Gunawan, 1999: 159). At least the rhetoric of community participation existed.

Ngadha falls into the Lesser Sunda region of the national tourism development plan with Bali's airport (Nguruh Rai) as the gateway. Although Wiendu Nuryanti (1998) shows that Nusa Tenggara has the highest growth rate in hotels, this is starting from a very low base level. Ngadha is positioned between two of the region's primary attractions: Komodo to the west (home of the world's largest monitor lizards *varanus komodoensis*) is the main pull factor for visitors to Eastern Indonesia (Erb 2000); Keli Mutu, a volcano with three different coloured lakes, draws the tourists further east. As I have outlined elsewhere (Cole, 1997a), a cultural attraction between two major natural attractions serves tourists' needs for a varied itinerary.

Komodo National Park attracted nearly 31,000 tourists in 1997/1998 (Warpole & Goodwin, 2000: 561). Nearly half of these came on cruise ships (Goodwin *et al.*, 1997). When P&O ceased operating in the late 1990s due to the political and economic turmoil in Indonesia, arrivals were nearly halved. According to park records, the number dropped to 15,000 in the period from 1998 to 2000, by 2002/2003 the number climbed to about 17-18,000 (RARE 2003). Although local charters continue to take tourists to the island, P&O had not resumed operations in 2007. The Ata Modo people, who have a distinct language and social organisation, sparsely populate the park (Hitchcock, 1993). They come into contact with 5000 tourists a year but tourism employment is limited to 6 boat crew and 17 wooden dragon carvers and only 1% of tourist expenditure accrued to people living in the park (Warpole & Goodwin, 2000). These data suggest that tourism is doing very little to alleviate poverty in this locale.

Indonesia's official tourism policy has either tacitly ignored or actively discouraged backpackers[8] although the government agreed to encourage small-scale projects, especially in the outer islands (Dahles, 1999). The government's lack of support for backpackers is surprising since they are considered the pioneers in tourism development and it is imprudent to ignore trend-setters. Furthermore, backpacker tourism creates a demand for cheap accommodation and a parallel structure of transport, restaurant and support services. Due to lower capital requirements, facilities for backpackers are more likely to be locally owned, resulting in a greater economic benefit to the local economy, as suggested earlier. Furthermore, the evidence from Komodo suggests that, following external crisis, back-packers return more quickly than mass tourists.

Backpackers are defined as surviving on less than £10 per day, use local transport, and carry all their belongings on their back. They bargain for goods and services and guard against 'rip-offs'. They attempt to get away from crowds and discover new places (Bradt, 1995). However, this is an increasingly diverse demographic group (Scheyvens, 2002), which, some researchers suggest, requires further segmentation (e.g. Hampton, 1997). This ethnography highlights some of the differences in Chapter 6. Not only have the tourists changed over time, but also significant variation exists depending on their direction of travel, and their use of guides.

The clearest and most recent indicator that the Indonesian government ignores the importance of backpackers comes from the visa policy changes. In the 16 years I have been studying tourism development on Flores this change has had the greatest impact. In 2003 and 2004 there were several changes (with the changing government and ministers) which resulted in considerable confusion. The policy is intended to be good for tourism generally, but is very detrimental to Flores and other remote marginal destinations that are dependent on backpackers.

Prior to the changes tourists were entitled to a 60-day visa issued on arrival. This Visa on Arrival (VoA) is now limited to 30 days and costs $US25. It is free for ASEAN (Association of South East Asian Nations) countries, and also Peru, Chile and Morocco under reciprocal arrangements. The number of countries issued with VoA has changed constantly since 2003. This visa policy change is considered 'the most dramatic U-turn in the country's history of tourism' (Travel Impact Newswire, 2003). The policy was initially justified to fight terrorism and prevent terrorists entering the country, however, all the terrorists that have operated in Indonesia have been home-grown.

The visa fee triggered massive protests. In Bali local tourism players staged a street rally, not only fearing that the fees would put tourists off and thus the move would further dent the country's beleaguered tourism industry, but also that the fees were collected by the central government and were not being given to Bali. In 2004 US$29 million was collected (Hudiyanto, 2005). Furthermore VoA are only issued at certain entry points. Lombok, for example, has not been included 'even before the new measures 62% of hotels in Lombok could not cover their costs' (Osbourne, 2004).

For Flores the problem is the limited time the tourists are allowed to stay in Indonesia. During my research in 1998/1999 many tourists claimed to be running out of visa time, being in a hurry, or not spending as much time on Flores as they had wished. At the time tourist visas were issued for 60 days. The majority of tourists were Europeans, and Australian, many on travels through South East Asia, on their way to or from Australia. In 2005 very few long-term travellers were in Flores. Backpackers that 'did' Indonesia only had time for Bali, the Gili Islands and the iconic sites of Java; visa time did not allow them to travel further afield. While tourists numbers in August 2005 were at record levels, the season in Flores was the shortest they had known and the type of tourists had changed (see Chapter 6).

East Nusa Tenggara: Culture and Society in Eastern Indonesia

An in-depth discussion of the culture and society of the villages in this study can be found in Chapter 4, however, here I would like to provide a broad outline of the cultural similarities between Ngadha and other people in Eastern Indonesia. The section provides details not only of shared roots and traditions with other neighbouring people but also of *adat* – the force of the ancestors – a contested notion that lies at the heart of this ethnography.

Flores is one of the major islands of the Nusa Tenggara Timor (NTT) province of Indonesia. East Nusa Tenggara or NTT is the driest and poorest province in the Indonesian archipelago, with a per capita income of less than a tenth of that in the capital, Jakarta. The World Bank estimates 17% of Indonesia's population lives below the poverty line, but this figure rises to 30% of the nearly four million people who live in NTT (Michaud, 2002). Other estimates suggest the figure is closer to 50% e.g. Human Development Report (2001). Average annual per capita incomes are much less than US$100 (Russell-Smith, 2005). Infant mortality in the province is 57 per 1000 (BPS, 2005) and while estimates suggest 76% of Indonesians have access of clean water, the figure is less than 50% for NTT (UNESCAP, 2004).

There is a large variety of ethnographies about various communities on Flores and the other islands in NTT.[9] The Ngadha share general features in common with their neighbours which are useful to examine to provide the ethnographic context to cultural tourism in Ngadha. Like the Tana' Ai, the Ngadha have houses of consanguinally related women and their brothers, and inheritance that passes through the female line, presenting another case of 'house-based matriliny'. However, as they remember ancestors on both sides of the family, and are often involved in rituals on their father's as well as mother's side, they should be considered bilineal or cognatic (Rodgers, 1985). However, local guides use the labels 'matrilineal' and even the more evocative 'matriarchal' to describe the Ngadha. As Waterson (1990) suggests, the social organisation based around matriliny, combined with matrilocal residence and the association of women with houses provides a social structural dominance of women to complement the official ideology of male dominance. In Ngadha society[10] root/tip (or trunk/ shoot) symbolism is fundamental to their notions of order. The root or base is female, and the tip is male. This botanical idiom of life is common in Eastern Indonesian societies (Fox, 1980).

The ranking of people is also a common feature in East Indonesian societies.[11] Waterson (1995) contrasts ranking of people in some societies (e.g.

Toraja) with the ranking of houses in others, but in Ngadha both are ranked. A number of scholars have noted the importance of the house as an indigenous category and principle of social organisation in the societies of Eastern Indonesia (and elsewhere). The house is a central organising principle in Ngadha society. All members of Ngadha society belong to a named house. As in the Levi-Straussian concept of '*societas a maison*' (1983), Ngadha houses endure through time, through the holding of property and the transmission of names. As Carsten and Hugh-Jones remind us, the house is not only a ritual construct related to ancestors, embodied in heirlooms and titles, it is also 'a group of people, concerned with day to day affairs, sharing consumption and living in shared space' (1995: 45). In Ngadha, as elsewhere (cf. Waterston, 1990), through symbolism, ritual and indigenous cosmologies, houses are considered living. As the stories illustrate, house-based rituals play an important part in the tourists' experiences and the villagers' narratives about tourism to the area.

Houses belonging to a number of clans are found in collections of two parallel lines (Barnes, 1974), referred to as *nua*.[12] *Nua* is usually translated as village but confusion then occurs with the Indonesian *desa*, which is also usually translated as village. The administrative villages (*desa*) subsume a number of *nua*. Various authors have used other terms: original, ancestral, ancient and traditional [13] but as none of them apply to both the villages central to this study I have chosen to retain the local term in this case, and use *nua* to refer to the nuclear settlement of traditional houses and associated structures: *ngadhu, bhaga* (see Chapter 4), *lenggi* and other megaliths.

Megaliths are another common feature of Eastern Indonesian, indeed South East Asian, villages. These 'structures made of large stones, usually rough and unhewn, which conform to certain well marked types' (Perry, 1918: 10) are connected with religious life; they serve as a medium to connect the living with the dead. In Ngadha, megaliths reveal a great diversity of forms and purposes.[14] Waterson warns against the temptation to label any use of stones as megalithic as the word has 'a romantic appeal to Europeans' (1990: 23). As some stones are several metres across, the use of the word seems appropriate in this case. The male-female complementary dualism, found throughout the symbolism of this society, is reinforced in the stones: upright males stones are found in pairs with flat female stones[15] (see Plates 1, 3 and 9).

According to Fox (1980), Eastern Indonesia societies are preoccupied with control over the flow of life. Certainly, in Ngadha society the unity between past and present members of a clan and house is constantly maintained. Ancestors are constantly remembered, fed and referred to, and

Plate 3 Megaliths in 'Old Wogo'

Plate 4 Reading messages from the ancestors in the lines of a pig's liver

their approval is sought. In return they protect, bless and provide food, health and harmony for the living. As in Sumba, 'the dead continue to be enmeshed in on-going social relations, becoming more powerful after death as they have the ability to enforce supernatural sanctions and demands on their descendants' (Hoskins, 1987: 146). The unity between past and present generations is maintained through rituals and particularly through sacrifice. Howell (1996) argues that during sacrifice in Eastern Indonesia direct communication takes place between human sacrificers and non-humans (ancestral spirits) in two ways. Firstly, the utterance of an invocation that precedes a sacrifice and the offering of blood and cooked food are the way in which the living 'speak' to the ancestors. Secondly, an augury after the event is how the living read messages from the ancestors. In Ngadha, this involves reading the lines in the liver of sacrificed animals (see Plate 4).

The importance of sacrifice goes beyond communication with the ancestors. The size and amount of livestock sacrificed is important for the social standing of the living. A Toraja's worth is validated through sacrifice and every gift of meat contains a message about status (Volkman, 1985). Daeng (1988), in his claims of the ecological function of competitive feasting among the Ngadha, noted that the ancestors always favour the host whose feast lasted the longest and was attended by the most people. Furthermore, as this book discusses, the further guests travel the greater the status bestowed on the host. Tourists can then, under the right circumstances, help further the social standing of those hosting rituals.

Traditional religion has been devalued for political reasons and missionaries were actively supported in the conversion of those supporting minority religions (Dove, 1988). As Hoskins points out, 'true conversion is not really possible until the nature of indigenous conceptual systems have undergone a substantial transformation' (1987: 137). Missionaries believing that local religious practices were satanic and anti-Christian found it easier to proscribe specific actions than to prohibit ideas and thus many local beliefs have remained unchanged (cf. Forth, 1998).[16] Several scholars report how villagers have been subjected to significant pressure to cut down the number of animals slaughtered at major ceremonies (Daeng, 1988; Forth, 1998; Molnar, 1998). Indeed the slaughtering of fewer animals is one of the greatest changes that have taken place in Ngadha over the past 30 years.

Adat

Adat is a concept that lies at the heart of this ethnography; it is one of the forces that shapes the villagers lives and how many conceptualise tradition.

The local people refer to the villages as *kampung adat* (customary villages). Tourists visit Ngadha villages to gaze upon the symbols of *adat*: Houses, *ngadhu, bhaga*, megaliths, rituals etc. Originally from Arabic meaning law or custom, *adat* is accepted across the Indonesian archipelago to mean custom or tradition but it is far more all-encompassing.[17] As Picard discusses, 'it is essentially a religious concept, in the sense that it refers to a social order founded by the ancestors to an unchangeable cosmic order' (1996: 12). It has become institutionalised and needs to be understood as the 'internal methodology for members of a society to understand and perceive the patterns of social relations' (Zainal Kling, 1997: 49). It exists to ensure harmony in the universe. The villagers in this study perceive *adat* as the way of the ancestors. It governs relationships between the individual and community and gives guidance for relationships.

Adat means consensus, a state of equilibrium, and it means order (Zainal Kling, 1997). Any offence against *adat* disturbs the universal order and produces undesirable results, from minor sickness to major epidemics and crop failure (Caslake, 1993). As Picard suggests, *adat* 'is specific to a particular ethnic group' (1996: 153) and refers to 'ways' bequeathed by the ancestors. The contemporary meaning has evolved with different emphasis in different parts of the archipelago. The Ngadha terms are *ebu po, nusi pera*[18] (the advice of grandparents, the teachings of great-grandparents) or *uku adha*[19] (rules of respect). Ngadha *adat* has not been subject to desacralisation to the same extent that it has in Bali but has been separated from religion.

In Toraja, the mission made the decisive strategy of formally separating religion from *adat* (Volkman, 1987). *Adat* was what was secular and social and was deemed acceptable. In a similar vein, the Church accepted ritual as culture (*adat*) but not ritual as religion (ancestor worship) in Manggarai, Flores (Erb, 2001a). *Adat* has been appropriated by the state so that it is used not only in opposition to religion but also to administration (Soemardjan & Breazeale, 1993). In sponsoring material culture, especially houses and textiles, the state has objectified tradition. The social institutions of *adat* and its religious aspects are downplayed in favour of cultural objects that legitimate ethnic groups (cf. Allerton, 2001; Hutajulu, 1997).

Although the majority of studies on East Nusa Tenggara societies have stressed the normative and traditional parts of culture (Vel, 1994), there has been a number of recent studies that has examined the ordinary everyday life of women and men. Vel (1994) focuses on the changing economy of the Uma in Sumba, with special mention to the poorer segments of the local population. Her study concludes that the Church will have the largest influence on Uma economic life. The villagers in her study (like those in this study) made increasing exchanges with strangers in order to raise money required for church taxes, health and schools. Forshee's (2001) study focuses on how the villagers in Sumba have responded to the international market for their textiles.

While this book is about the everyday lives of the villagers (and some very special days in the tourists' lives) as they adapt to tourism processes, *adat* takes centre stage in much of the ethnography. What constitutes *adat*, the way it is contested, and how tourism affects that contestation, is at the core of the villagers' experience of tourism development.

Wider Global and National Political Agendas and their Impact on Ngadha's Tourism Development

In Chapter 2 the globalisation discussion focused on the process of westernisation and cultural change. In this section I would like to discuss how global (and national) events, many miles from Flores, shape the tourism development that has taken place. In many cases the villagers are unaware or do not understand why the number of tourists that visit fluctuates or why their tourism dries up without explanation. Forest fires, the Asian financial crisis, political turmoil, media reports, bombs in Bali, foreign travel advisories, SARS (Severe Acute Respiratory Syndrome) and the Indian Ocean tsunami have all impacted on Flores' tourism development.

When in 1991 I stopped taking tourists to Wogo and moved to a more remote village, the villagers (and I) were sure that they were at 'take-off'. The village had entered the Lonely Planet guidebook and independent travellers visited the village on a daily basis. Despite the first Iraq war (which severely affected world tourism) and events in East Timor that continuously dented Indonesia's image, the numbers of tourists to Indonesia generally and Flores in particular increased through the 1990s. Erb (2000) reports an 18% annual increase between 1990 and 1995 in Manggarai (the regency of Flores to the west of Ngada).

Between 1987 and 1997 Indonesian inbound tourism grew from just one million to over five million. By 1997 tourism accounted for 10.2% of Indonesia's exports (WTO, 1999). In that year, Bena's best, 9000 tourists visited the village. As discussed in Chapter 4 statistics for tourism to Flores are extremely hard to come by and are extremely unreliable. Here I will discuss what has happened to Indonesia's tourism and in particular Indonesia's most popular island Bali. The vast majority of tourists that visit Flores also visit Bali and we can therefore extrapolate from the data that are available for that island.

Indonesia's tourism fortunes started to take a dive in 1997 when forest fires caused a smoke haze to spread across the northern part of the archipelago (and Singapore and Malaysia). Television news screened pictures of sickness and impaired visibility. The smoke did not reach Bali and Flores but tourism there was affected when prospective tourists in Europe and America 'assumed all of Asia was in a dense brown cloud' (Leiper & Hing, 1998).

In 1977 the Asian financial crisis unfolded. In June, Indonesia seemed far from crisis. Unlike Thailand, Indonesia had low inflation, a trade surplus of more than US$900 million, huge foreign exchange reserves of more than US$20 billion, and a good banking sector (World Bank, 2002). In July, Thailand floated the baht, and by August the rupiah came under severe attack. In September the rupiah and Jakarta Stock Exchange touched a new historic low. The rupiah lost 45% of its value between January and September (Henderson, 1999) and the country experienced *krismon* (monetary crisis). By Novemeber the crisis had intensified, businesses failed, there was large-scale unemployment and prices increased. The inflation of the rupiah resulted in steep hikes in the prices of food staples – the price of rice trippled - so many people could not afford to eat more than once a day (Hall, 2000). An estimated 50 million people were forced into poverty (Henderson, 1999).

Dissatisfaction with the government's handling of the crisis led to riots that began in Jakarta, where more than 500 people died, and quickly spread to other cities. This was locally refered to as *krispol* (political crisis). The political unrest reached its peak in May 1998 when President Suharto was forced to stand down. 'Graphic images of rioting, killings, destruction of commercial districts in Java and images of mass air evacuations of expatriates from Jakarta in May 1998, made the selling of pleasure travel to indonesia a difficult task for marketers' (Prideaux *et al.*, 2003: 481). Flores experienced the price rises and those living in urban areas needed the income from tourism more than ever. Despite relative calm on the island, tourism virtually dried up.

Beginning in the capital, ethnic tensions flared, and the Chinese community in particular became scapegoats and were targeted. Attacks against ethnic Chinese were extensively covered in the media. This had a severe impact on bookings and led to cancellations from important markets to Indonesia: Tawain, Hong Kong and Singapore (Prideaux *et al.*, 2003). However, as I have suggested these are not important markets for Flores. The ethnic and religious unrest spread across the archipelago. While relatively minor in Flores (some Chinese shops were burned), in some provinces the violence escalated and the negative image of Indonesia was reinforced. In Ambon, for example, militant Muslim fundamentalist groups declared jihad on the island's Christian population. In 2007 tourists were still advised to avoid the area due to recurrent clashes.

The crisis did not affect tourism equally across the country (WTO, 1998). As Hitchcock (2001) discusses, Bali weathered the storm better than some other regions. The devaluation of the rupiah made visiting Indonesia very cheap but hotel occupancy fell from 48% in 1997 to 35% in 1998 (Henderson, 1999) – the limit at which a hotel can break even.

In 1999 East Timor voted for independence and violent clashes erupted between residents, local militia and the Indonesian army. The Indonesian troops and anti-independence militia followed a scorched earth policy when they pulled out. They destroyed public buildings, looted banks, bombed bridges and devastated the infrastructure. Not only did the outbreak of violence devastate the East Timor economy, but also the brutality of the Indonesian army dealt another massive blow to Indonesia's tourism industry.

For the first time, the travel writing community[20] in Britain put out a press release suggesting tourists and tour operators should boycott Indonesia. In New Zealand a 'Boycott Bali' campaign emerged (Hitchcock, 2001). The Australians also took a strong stance, cancelling tours to Indonesia. As Burns (1999), Wheat (1999) and Holden (2005) discuss, such a boycott raises many ethical questions. Local people, dependent on tourism in Bali and beyond, may have been very unhappy about the actions of the Indonesia military but were incapable of influencing them. Boycotting tourism to Indonesia may have sent an important message to the Indonesian government but it further impoverished the lives of many who had become dependant on tourism.

While the events in East Timor had comparatively little overall impact on tourism to Indonesia, Flores' tourism was disproportionately affected for several reasons. Firstly due to Flores' proximity to East Timor, military personnel were based on Flores and returned there. Secondly, Flores took in thousands of refugees from the conflict. Thirdly, markets that are particularly susceptible to human rights news e.g. Australia and the UK were important markets for Flores.

In 2000 tourism to Indonesia began to pick up with foreign arrivals rising to over five million but the 11 September 2001 terrorist attacks in New York halted the positive trend (Wiradji, 2005). The World Travel and Tourism Council (WTTC) estimates that worldwide international travel declined by 5.1% and that 85% of this was attributable to 9/11. Belau (2003) suggests that counties highly dependent on US markets, long-haul destinations and those in the Muslim world were most affected. Indonesia, despite being a long-haul destination from Europe and the US and having a largely Muslim population was less severely affected than predicted. The adverse affects of 9/11 were essentially a downturn in outbound travel from the US and to some extent Europe. As intra-Asian travel is so important to Indonesia, there was a slight increase in visitor arrivals in 2001.

Spring and summer 2002 saw a return of the tourists, then, on 12 October the two car bombs exploded in Kuta, Bali, killing 202 people and injuring 300 others. The tragedy shocked not only Bali but also the world as a terror attack specifically targeted at tourists. Immediately after the attack Bali's tourism virtually collapsed, airlines re-routed and hotel occupancy tumbled from a comfortable 70% to less than 10% (World Bank, 2002).

Indonesia made special efforts to prevent total breakdown by heavily marketing to neighbouring ASEAN countries, East Asia, China and domestic markets. These cost-effective packages kept Bali's tourism afloat – necessary as 70% of Bali's economy depends on tourism – however, despite some Asian and domestic tourists spending small amounts in Bali, these tourist types do not travel to destinations further afield such as Flores.

The impact of the terror attack was made worse by the travel advisories. Criticised as politically motivated (see Tourism Concern's campaign), and unfair, Australia, the US and the UK all advised its citizens against non-essential travel to Indonesia. While tourists were encouraged to visit New York after 9/11 and were not advised against travel to Madrid following the terrorist attack there, the travel warnings worked to keep tourists out of Indonesia. Sales revenues dropped by 71%, and 30% of schools reported children dropping out because their parents could not afford school fees. Australia's ban was still in place some three years later – but was being ignored by many. The UK, under pressure from Tourism Concern, changed its advice in June 2004.

Despite the devastating impact of the October Bali bombing and the subsequent travel advice, SARS had an even greater impact on tourism. SARS spread by travellers infected more than 4000 and killed 230 in 25 countries. However, this is far fewer than die from seasonal influenza, and SARS is five times less infectious than measles (APEC, 2003). It was the SARS-induced panic that led to the mass cancellations and devastation to tourism across Asia. Indonesia saw a 60% drop in arrivals despite no reported cases in the country. Europeans feared transit in Singapore, Hong Kong and Bangkok, all countries that had SARS. Asians feared flying as the media reports emphasised that the virus travels with ease in confined aircraft cabins (LaMoshi, 2003).

Terrorists targeted tourism in Indonesia again in August 2003 bombing the Marriott Hotel in Jakarta. The bomb killed 12 people and injured scores of others. Indonesia's image and tourist arrivals had begun to recover when terrorists struck again bombing the Australian Embassy in September 2004 killing another 11 people.

The Indian Ocean tsunami in December 2004 caused death and destruction across Asia (and east Africa). Although the affected area was 3000 kilometres away from Bali, visitors, particularly from Asia, were still deterred. However, visitor arrivals picked up and 2005 promised to be a golden year for Indonesia's tourism (except in Sumatra which was still severely affected by the tsunami). Occupancy levels in Bali reached 95% in August (Hudiyanto, 2005). In Labuhan Bajo, Flores, record numbers of tourists arrived and exceeded the town's carrying capacity. All the hotels were full to bursting and tourists had to sleep on boats.

Then, in October 2005, tourists in Bali were targeted for the second time. Three bombs in Kuta and Jimbaran killed 22 people. However, this second bombing of Bali did not result in the same mass exodus and many analysts are suggesting that tourists are factoring in the risk of terrorism to travel plans (e.g. Economic Intelligence Unit Limited, 2005). Australian travel advice, warning tourists to avoid all but essential travel to Indonesia was still in place when the 2005 bombs went off. Personal observation and booking levels in Bali, in August, suggest that many Australians were choosing to ignore their government's advice. Following the second bomb neither the Japan nor Malaysia strengthened their advice. However, newspapers reported occupancy levels falling to 20% and less in November (Flores Paradise, 2005).

For nine years global and national, natural and political disasters have besieged Indonesia's tourism. The country's destination image has been constantly damaged by one event after another. As soon as recovery looks possible another calamity dashes hopes. It should be noted that the greatest single cause of damage was SARS-induced panic; a media-induced fear of a disease that never reached Bali. Meanwhile a rabies outbreak on Flores posed a far greater threat to tourists but was never reported despite the deaths of 113 people (Windiyaningsih, 2004). The media's impact on tourism should never be underestimated.

The events damaged Indonesia's hope that tourism would continue to increase in the same way as it did in the 1980s and early 1990s – a 475% increase between 1987 and 1997 (WTO, 1999). However, a look at the statistics shows relatively minor decline for the nation as a whole when compared with specific areas. For example, while Indonesia saw declining figures from 1997–1998 and 2001–2002 (both amounting to approximately

11%) overall the figures have remained stable between 4.7–5 million visitors. Compare this with Komodo National Park, which saw a 50% decline (from 30,000 to 15,000) and has never fully recovered (RARE, 2003). The later figures are a much more useful indicator of tourism arrivals in Flores and how seriously its tourism has been damaged.

Tourism and Development in Less Economically Developed Countries

Tourism's potential contribution to development is the fundamental justification for establishing tourism. Defining development is problematic. In early post-second World War conceptualisations development was narrowly conceived as western-style modernisation and virtually synonymous with economic growth. During the 1970s the acceptance of social indicators such as health care and education and broader aims including poverty reduction were included as aspects of development (Sharpley, 2002). To this, notions of human rights, political freedom, gender rights and sustainability were added (Telfer, 2002). Scheyvens (2003) sums up present-day conceptions of development as a multidimensional process leading to 'good change' and seen to embrace self-sufficiency, self-determination and empowerment as well as improved standards of living.

Tourism is seen as a vehicle for development and has been promoted as a strategy for economic growth in Ngadha as it has in many developing countries.[21] Tourism is a growth industry, and it contributes to foreign exchange earnings, creates employment and leads to economic diversification. Tourism makes use of the natural 'free' infrastructure such as beaches and mountain views and as such has relatively low 'start-up' costs. Furthermore, tourism has the ability to attract inward investment for capital projects (Williams, 1998) and infrastructure improvements needed for tourists will also help local communities. Unlike nearly all other industries, it is not subject to trade barriers such as tariffs and quotas (Lickorish, 1991). Tourism is labour intensive industry and many less developed countries have severe unemployment problems (Tribe, 2005). As tourism delivers consumers to the product, locals have a new market for their products and services. Thus tourism has the potential for linkages particularly to traditional livelihood occupations such as agriculture, fishing and handicraft production. This means that tourism expenditure has the potential to generate a large multiplier effect, which can stimulate the local economy. Furthermore, tourism is considered a smokeless industry that has less negative environmental impact than other industries and can provide the economic incentive to protect habitats, which might otherwise be destroyed. Seen from this perspective, it is not surprising that so many less developed countries promote tourism as an important economic development strategy. This is especially the case in areas that have few primary resources and a small industrial base, such as Ngadha, where tourism often constitutes the only viable economic opportunity (Oppermann & Chon, 1997).

While the above is an impressive list of reasons to develop tourism for economic growth, it does not address the other aspects of development. As many analysts (Britton, 1982; Crick, 1989; McKean, 1978) have bemoaned, the rapid development of tourism in less developed countries has not been without problems: excess foreign dependency, the reinforcement of socio-economic and spatial inequalities, environmental destruction and rising cultural alienation (Brohman, 1996). As a result of studies that have highlighted the negative consequences of tourism, representing Jafari's (1989) cautionary platform, combined with a changed era in development thinking, there has been a growing concern for environmental protection, sustainability and community participation in tourism.

As many less developed countries struggle to develop their tourism due to inadequate infrastructure, lack of trained personnel and corrupt, inefficient and inexperienced government bodies (Harrison, 2001), attention has turned to initiatives that develop tourism from the bottom up such as 'community based tourism', 'pro-poor tourism', or 'alternative tourism'. A number of reasons for this new focus exist: if tourism is to be a tool for development it must focus attention on poverty alleviation. Evidence from the literature suggests small-scale enterprises present greater opportunities for control and profit by local people (Rodenburg, 1980) and that guesthouses import less than hotels and as a result the multiplier is greater. Furthermore Britton (1982) argued that small-scale tourism enterprises have a greater impact on improving rural living standards, reducing rural–urban migration and countering structural inequalities of income distribution. Small-scale tourism places value on natural and cultural resources and can be developed without great capital investment in remote and marginal regions that have disproportionate numbers of the poor. Much of the labour requirements are for unskilled workers, improving the opportunities for women and disadvantaged groups to earn money.

As I suggested in the previous chapter, developing tourism in poor remote areas has benefits that go beyond the economic. Tourism can be a powerful tool to empower marginal communities. Many researchers have discussed how tourism brings about pride.[22] Tourism can also enhance community cohesion. Tourism increases access to information and external contacts,[23] as well as new language skills and globalised media (Williams, 1998). Through tourism, communities come to value their cultural assets;

it increases their confidence and can strengthen their political identity (Johnston, 1992; Swain, 1990). These are all signs of empowerment.

From the bottom up?

A consensus of opinion in the tourism and development literature suggests that to bring about tourism that will be effective as a tool for development in its widest sense, community participation is essential. This ethnography raises fundamental questions about this received wisdom, raising questions not only about 'who makes up the community?' and about how they can participate in something about which they understand so little, but also because so many factors, so far from local community control, make tourism an unreliable prospect on which to base economic hopes.

The reasons for community participation in tourism development are well rehearsed in the tourism literature. As a service industry tourism is highly dependent on the goodwill and co-operation of host communities. Service is the key to the hospitality atmosphere (Murphy, 1985) and community participation can result in an increased social carrying capacity (D'amore, 1983). Virtually all tourism surveys show that the friendliness of the local people rates high on the list of positive features about a destination (Sweeny & Wanhill, 1996). Support and pride in tourism development is especially important in the case of cultural tourism where the community is part of the product. Furthermore, involvement in planning is likely to result in more appropriate decisions and greater motivation on the part of the local people and protection of the environment is more likely to be supported (Tourism Concern, 1992). Not only does local community participation look good on paper, but also it is often essential in securing funding. Community participation is considered necessary to get community support and acceptance of tourism development projects and to ensure that benefits relate to the local community needs. Tosun and Timothy (2003) further argue that the local community is more likely to know what will work and what will not in local conditions, and that community participation can add to the democratisation process and has the potential to increase awareness and interest in local and regional issues. Furthermore, they suggest that democracy incorporates the rights of the individual that often encourages various forms of equity and empowerment.

While the reasons for community participation in tourism are many, the paradigm is subject to great debate. Some debates surround how to define 'the community' and 'participation' while many researchers question how community participation can work in practice due to the heterogeneous nature of communities.[24]

The approach to defining the community that should participate or have control is subject to a number of interpretations. As we shall see in Ngadha, arguments over who is included in 'the community' has been at the centre of conflict over tourism revenue. Murphy's (1985) important early work focused on the host community, identifying their goals and desires for, and capacity to absorb, tourism. Using an ecosystem approach or ecological community model and the notion of social carrying capacity, he emphasised that the planning system must extend down to the micro-level, to the community. By identifying the community as synonymous with place, this approach fails to focus on decision-making and control. It assumes that all parties have equal opportunities to participate in the political process. Determining who in the community should participate involves ruling some people in and some people out, who is local and who is included are vital considerations as conflict over limited resources can result in tourism being a divisive force. Tourists are seen as a resource and conflict can arise over who has a right to access them.[25]

Notions of community, defined by territory, are fixed, discrete and relatively stable. However, communities need to be seen as more complex and fluid. Consideration needs to be given to power and decision-making between and within community groups. While the heterogeneous nature of communities is frequently referred to, few analysts unpick how communities are fractured along lines of kinship, gender, age, ethnicity and existing levels of wealth (Crehan, 1997). Forshee's (2001) ethnography details the impact of caste, gender and ethnicity and how these factors inter-play with power and local textile production for sale to tourists. In this ethnography we will see how tradition is articulated by some community members to underscore a return to traditional hierarchies, and how tourism impinges on gender hierarchies.

Identity, space and place are interconnected and notions of community need to be dynamic and fluid.[26] A community is far more than an environmental or geographical territory and our understanding of community needs to extend to psychological and intangible aspects as well as the political. Notions of 'community spirit', for example, may be grounded originally in 'place' but values are shared and negotiated between evolving groups of people. As members of communities travel, new networks are created, new social relationships become possible and notions of community become multi-layered and blurred. The late 20th century offered the people of Flores opportunities to travel, study and work on other islands of Indonesia (and abroad). Members of houses, clans and villages are increasingly spread geographically while still remaining part of the community.

Participation is also open to a variety of interpretations.[27] A ladder of participation exists, ranging from passive participation, 'being consulted' (often only being told of a fait accompli) to self-mobilisation – being able to determine every aspect of the development process. While all communities in tourism destinations are at least passive participants i.e. sharing a despoiled environment, receiving menial jobs or getting a percentage of gate fees to a national park (Scheyvens, 2003), community participation that will result in tourism being a successful tool to alleviate poverty needs to concentrate at the top end of the ladder.

Even if definitions were easier, and communities less complex, there is a number of reasons why active community participation is hard to achieve in practice: lack of ownership, capital, skills, knowledge and resources all constrain the ability of communities to fully control their participation in tourism development (Scheyvens, 2003). In many communities, such as the ones documented here, where monetary exchange is a relatively recent phenomenon, villagers fail to accumulate capital. There is often pressure from relatives to redistribute gains from tourism, and/or a desire to gain prestige from the conspicuous public display of wealth, such as donating livestock for rituals, and so consequently gains from tourism are short lived for many marginalised people.

A lack of knowledge about legal and financial processes makes the poor vulnerable to exploitation by local elites and outside business interests. Both Sofield (2003) and I (Cole, 2006) have discussed how a lack of knowledge is the constraining factor in marginalised communities in the world. Differential access to knowledge affects participation, those with better access have more opportunities. As I have discussed, participation beyond lip-service and rhetoric cannot be achieved without elucidation (Cole, 1999). Knowledge of tourism must be a precursor for those who want to participate in decisions about tourism planning and management. Many communities lack any real understanding of what it is they are supposed to be making decisions about (Sofield, 2003). The villagers in Ngadha bemoan their lack of understanding of tourism and this is one the reasons the reality of bottom-up development remains so elusive.

While many researchers have recognised the need for and value of considerable public education,[28] I have questioned the ethics behind public education programmes to date (Cole, 2005). As discussed in Chapter 5 the public tourism education to date has been an attempt by the government to gain villagers' support for tourism development. The essence of the programme was that tourists are the nation's guests, so the villagers should be good hosts to them. Kadir Din considers ignorance as the greatest barrier to participation but that the ignorance is not restricted to residents but 'also affects the planning machinery and bureaucracy vested with implementation' (1997: 79).

Evidence suggests community responses to tourism are partly determined by their prior access to local resources, the level of consensus and cohesion in the community and the degree to which they are able to work with outside institutions. Communities have adopted and adapted to tourism when in productive and sympathetic partnerships with external agencies such as NGOs and private-sector players (Harrison & Price, 1996). The ideal of many 'community based initiatives' is for the local community to have a high degree of control over the activities taking place and that a significant proportion of the benefits accrue to them (Scheyvens, 2003: 10) but as we have seen locals are not likely to ever have a high degree of control over tourist arrivals due to global and national events out of their control. It is for this reason that any tourism development strategy must be part of an integrated development strategy; tourism should only ever be one string on a community's bow.

Cultural, ethnic or indigenous?

The fascinating traditions and expression of Ngadha material culture are the *raison d'être* of tourists' visits to the villages. Their visits therefore fall into a category of tourism referred to as cultural tourism, ethnic tourism or indigenous tourism depending on the author, their standpoint and the flexibility with which the English language is used. In this section I will briefly explore these concepts. The later two have nuances that carry negative connotations, which I explore before I reject them.

Cultural tourism can be broadly defined as travel motivated by the desire to experience a destination's culture. Although clearly demarcated as an elite niche market, variation exists in the understanding of what it involves. The term *'cultural tourism'* is subject to many definitions (Sofield & Birtles, 1996) and much confusion (Hughes, 1996) and is symptomatic of Tribe's (1997) 'indiscipline' of tourism. Like other forms of special interest tourism it appeals to tourists from higher socio-economic groups, who are well educated and travel frequently.

Cultural tourism is distinguished from ethnic tourism by some authors. In her seminal book, *Hosts and Guests*, Valene Smith makes the distinction: 'ethnic tourism is marketed to the public in terms of quaint customs of indigenous often exotic peoples' (1978: 4). Wood further defined ethnic tourism by its focus on people living out a cultural identity, whose uniqueness is being marketed to tourists (1984: 361). The focus of tourists' visits is on cultural practices according to Wood, and on 'native homes and villages, observations of dances and ceremonies and shopping for curios' (Smith,

1978: 4).All these observations are appropriate to tourism in Ngadha, though the distinction is problematic for two reasons. Firstly, both Wood (1984) and Smith (1978) differentiate between ethnic and cultural tourism whereas in fact a continuum exists (Cole, 1997b). Secondly, the use of the term ethnic is problematic. The popular use of the term ethnic implies a minority, a framing of the 'other'. As discussed in Chapter 2 'the nostalgic longing for untouched primitive peoples' (Mowforth & Munt, 1998: 69) in the minds of the tourists is part of the process of 'othering'.

Creating a conceptual dichotomy between ethnic and cultural tourism, where the former is used for the 'primitive other' and the latter for the high arts in developed nations (as Richards (1996), for example, uses it), serves to entrench inequalities between the rich and poor. MacIntosh and Goeldner (1990) use the concept of 'cultural distance' to refer to the extent a tourist's home culture differs from that of the area being visited. At present, western academics use the term 'ethnic tourism' when the cultural differences are great and 'cultural tourism' when they are less so. All communities have culture, the further removed that culture is from the tourist's, the more exotic it will appear.

Further, the term ethnic group is usually used to define a specified racial or linguistic group.[29] If ethnicity and identity are seen as processional, contested and changing, it is inappropriate for the groups and their ethnonyms to be reified by tourism. Such reification draws boundaries with potential for conflict.

The terminology is further confused by the term 'indigenous tourism'. Hinch and Butler refer to indigenous people as those who 'are endemic or native to a destination region' (1996: 9). This shows little understanding of the movement of people and their settlement of areas. Kadir Din, a Malaysian scholar is much clearer: 'They can be native groups or descendants of pioneer settlers' – but more importantly: 'the dividing line is that the indigenous group was already on the scene before the onset of development' (1997: 76). The indigenous label is further complicated in the Indonesian setting. In a country with 240 million people from over 500 ethnic groups speaking more than 600 languages (LOC 2005)[30], who would be considered the indigenous peoples? The official line under the New Order government was that all Indonesians are equally indigenous (Li, 2000). Ethnic identity was considered a danger to state unity and the government put policies in place to eliminate ethnic identities (ADB, 2002).[31] The government saw isolated people (*masyrakat terasing*) as a social problem, still '*primitif*' and in need of development. To be classified as indigenous, isolated or native was negative and brought shame. In 1999 the isolated people label was changed to *adat* community, which refers to 'groups of people who have origins inter-generationally in a certain geographic territory and also have their own value system, ideology, economy, politics, culture, society and territory' (ADB, 2002: 5). It is estimated that 50–70 million people live in such communities, 9000 of them in NTT (ADB, 2002). As discussed by the Asian Development Bank (ADB, 2002) report and Li (2000) the new label has benefits and local groups are starting to articulate their ethnic identities for their own ends. In the case of Ngadha, tourism is one of the forces behind the strategic articulation of an ethnic identity.

Cultural tourists are interested in seeing these communities. They want to experience ways of living and being in the world that are unlike their own. As Causey (2003) discusses, the two cultures of tourists and tourates are assumed to have boundaries that separate them. The process of distinguishing boundaries is easier where cultures can be defined as discrete entities. Cultures and traditions come to belong to particular groups and, as discussed in Chapter 2, identities become commoditised.

In considering the evolution of ethnic tourism referred to from here on as cultural tourism for the reasons discussed above, Cohen (2001) suggests that the tourates become active agents, achieving a degree of empowerment while gaining little financial reward, mainly through the sale of crafts. He goes on to suggest that, as tourism matures, some inhabitants accumulate some capital and gain familiarity with the tourists' tastes and increasingly gain a share of tourists' expenditure. Hospitality, performance and the arts then become commoditised or at least re-orientated towards outsiders. MacCannell suggests that, when a group sees itself as an ethnic attraction, the group members begin to think of themselves as representatives of an ethnic way of life, and any change has economic and political implications for the whole group. The 'group is frozen in an image of itself or *museumized*'(1984: 388). As Butcher (2001) discusses, cultural tourism can create a straightjacket for communities. Their culture becomes cast in stone. Furthermore, levels of economic development are seen as part of culture and inequality becomes reinterpreted as 'cultural diversity', tourism can then preserve poverty. I will trace Cohen's generalised evolution in this particular case and examine '*museumization*' from the insiders' perspective. We will see how the villagers resist the straightjackets and examine the more mouldable plastic nature of their culture. The villagers are still in poverty but this cannot be put down to preservation through tourism alone.

This chapter has placed Ngadha's tourism development in the context of development and tourism in Indonesia and the culture and society of Eastern Indonesia. The examination of the tourism development literature suggests that tourism can be a positive tool for pro-poor development. However, this chapter has highlighted some of the challenges associated with the 'bottom-up' and 'community-based' ideals of tourism development. I have disentangled some of the tourism vocabulary around tourism based on a community's cultural resources, and examined how global and national events beyond the villagers' control have limited the efficacy of their economic development through tourism.

Notes

1. Poverty on Flores is such that 100% of villages receive Indonesian IDT (*Inpres Desa Tertingal*) grants paid to villages 'left behind' by development. Poverty indicators vary substantially depending on the source but most are based on Indonesia's National Household Survey (SUSENAS), which includes both consumption indicators and access to services indicators. See for example UNESCAP (2004), Indonesia's Human Development Report (UNDP, 2004) or Indonesian government statistics (BPS, 2005).
2. Dominican missionaries were sent to the island for the first time in the 1550s (Prior, 1988). In 1667 the Dutch East Indies Company took control of Flores and the Dutch continued to send Catholic missionaries (Ricklefs, 1993).
3. Cf. Anderson (1972).
4. See for example the discussion in Parnwell and Arghiros (1996) or Hall and Page (2000).
5. See Wiendu Nuryanti (1998), Sofield (1995), Gunawan (1999).
6. As discussed by Gunawan (1997) and Simpson and Wall (1999).
7. According to Gunawan (1997) Flores falls into the region of Lesser Sunda and is in the development stage. The region includes Bali and South Sulawesi. According to Soffield (1995), Nusa Tenggara, the province, falls into the exploration stage, although it receives more visitors than South Sulawesi, which is placed in the development stage.
8. See Richter (1993), Hampton (1998), Erb (2000).
9   For example, Hicks (1976, 1990) studied the Tetum of Timor, Forth (1981) the Rindi of Sumba and more recently (1998) the Nage of central Flores. James Fox (1977) chose the islands of Roti and Savu, and Traube (1986) studied ritual exchange in Timor. Lewis (1988) studied the social life and ritual among the Tana'Ai, central Eastern Flores. Smedal (1993) and Molnar (2000) studied communities in Ngada.
10. As among the Rindi (Forth, 1981) and Mambai (Traube, 1986).
11. Cf. Howell (1995b) on the Lio, Gibson (1995) on the Makassaresse, Forshee (2001) in reference to the Subanese, Hitchcock (1996) on the Bimanese and also among the Savunese, S'adan Toraja and the Tetum of Timor according to Waterson (1990).
12. *Nua* is almost certainly a cognate of the word *banua*, which has a wide distribution throughout Austonesian languages (Waterson, 1990).
13. Barnes (1974) uses 'old village', Traube (1986) 'origin villages', Hoskins (1986) 'ancestral villages', while Forth (1998) uses both 'traditional villages' and 'ancient villages'. All of these terms could be applied to one of the villages in

this study, Bena, which is an old original ancestral village. The other village, Wogo, however, is not the original site, being only about 60 years old, but is traditional or at least has all the elements that custom demands.

14. Cf. Van der Hoop (n.d.).
15. This is similar among the Tana'Ai (Lewis, 1988) and the Lio (Howell, 1995b).
16. For example, tooth filing, a common initiation rite for women, was prohibited (cf. Forth, 1998; Suzuki, 1959).
17. For further discussion see Soemardjan and Breazeale (1993).
18. *Ebu* means grandparent, *po* means advice, *nusi* means great-grandparents and *pera* means teachings.
19. *Uku* means rules or restrictions and *Adha* means showing respect.
20. The British Guild of Travel Writers.
21. Cf. de Kadt (1979), Pearce (1989), Matheson and Wall (1982) and Richter (1993).
22. For example see Adams (1997), Boissevain (1996), Cole (1997b), Crystal (1978), Erb (1998), Mansperger (1992), and Van den Berghe (1992).
23. Cf. Ashley *et al.* (2001) and Forshee (2001).
24. For example Joppe (1996), Warburton (1998), Braden and Mayo (1999), and Harrison (1996).
25. Forshee (2001) describes a fight resulted from conflict over who had rights to sell cloth to a Dutchman in a Sumba village.
26. Cf. van de-Dium *et al.* (2006).
27. Originally discussed by Arnstein (1971), and more recently summarised and related to tourism by Pretty (1995) and France (1998).
28. For example Simmons (1994), Pearce (1994) and Connell (1997).
29. See for example Hitchcock's (1993) use in reference to the Ata Modo of Komodo Island.
30. lcweb2.loc.gov/frd/cs/profiles/Indonesia.pdf.
31. The imposition of Javanese territorial unit: the *desa*, a unified education curricula, the encouragement to convert to one of the monotheistic recognised religions, and the establishment of paddy as the major crop and rice as *the* valued carbohydrate have all worked to unify and homogenise the cultures in Indonesia.

Chapter 4
The Villages

In this chapter I will describe the villages. The intention is to provide enough detail for the reader to evoke life as it is experienced by the villagers. While the two villages share a similar social organisation and belief system, although only 12km apart, they differ substantially in terms of agriculture, livelihood and opportunities for education. Tourists visit the nucleated heart (*nua*) of the villages but the *nua* are part of a much wider region where the villagers have land and extended family members have homes. The first section provides the backdrop to the villagers' livelihood, social organisation and belief system. The villagers' involvement in the market economy, opportunities for education and social activities are then presented before a background to tourism.

Livelihood

Agriculture

Both Bena and Wogo are essentially agricultural villages. Farming is unmechanised (although a tractor is available to hire for ploughing in Wogo) and no pesticides or chemical fertilisers are used (except on wet rice and vanilla). However, as altitude, rainfall, topography and soil type between the two villages are different, their agriculture will be described separately. Wogo is higher (approximately 1100m[1]), wetter and flatter and supports significantly more intensive agriculture than Bena, which is lower (approximately 700m), and has much steeper sloping fields, which are more easily eroded and receive less rainfall. The land in Wogo supports a significantly denser population than Bena, 196 to 98 people per square kilometre respectively (*Ngada dalam angka*, 1996).

In Wogo, land holdings vary tremendously between households. On average a household will have usufruct rights over about half a hectare of land, which is planted with maize, inter-cropped with beans, twice a year. In the dry season, kidney beans are planted between the maize plants and in the wet season either kidney beans or soya beans. This half a hectare yields between a tonne and a tonne and a half of maize and four to five hundred kilogrammes of beans. Since this is more than enough to feed an average family, the surpluses are sold. The beans are largely sold to buy rice.

At most meals, the family will eat a mixture of maize and rice, often with a few beans mixed in. One aspect of change brought about by nationalism and state unity has been the establishment of paddy as the major crop and rice as *the* valued carbohydrate. As a result the villagers grow progressively smaller amounts of un-irrigated rice and other grains, such as millet and sorghum. Older members of the village referred to the seven grains that they used to grow. Two of these have totally disappeared and it is now not possible to buy the seeds. As less grain is grown, the sparrow problem is intensified as the birds scavenge on scarcer resources, thus those farmers who do grow grain have the arduous work of bird scaring for the entire time the grains are maturing. Furthermore, the sale of kidney and soya beans yields sufficient cash to buy rice. Unfortunately, the purchased rice is of poor quality and far less nutritious than the variety of grains that the villagers used to grow.

The villagers also have an average of half a hectare of land for tree crops. Coffee, which was introduced in the 1950s, is the most popular cash crop. Recently, vanilla has been introduced as a cash crop. Candlenuts (*Aleurites sp*), a native plant on Flores, whose commercial value has only recently been recognised, are increasingly important. Vegetables are grown on land around the house; the most important of these are root crops, which form an important part of the diet. An important vegetable is a type of gourd locally known as *labu jipan* (*Sechium edule*), of which both the fruit and young shoots are edible. This plant grows with almost no labour input and, together with cassava leaves and papaya leaves, represents the main green vegetable eaten by the villagers. Bananas, papayas and other fruit are also grown.

Around both houses and gardens, hairy palms (*Arenga saccarifera*)[2] are tapped for their juice. The tree sap is collected in bamboo tubes, where it ferments through the day or overnight. This slightly alcoholic drink was an important part of the villagers' diet and remains an essential element in rituals. The importance of this drink is underlined by the ritual process undertaken for the tapping of the trees.[3] Tapping hairy palms is highly skilled and few young men are learning the art and thus the ritual is now infrequently performed. Some fermented tree sap is distilled locally.

As the villagers of Wogo pointed out, they are blessed with fertile soil and no one goes hungry. With the minimum of work a balanced and varied diet is accessible to all those prepared to invest the effort. There have been increasing moves away from self-sufficiency as more rice is eaten and more of the villagers land is used for cash crops.

In Bena, a household will also have an average of half a hectare of annual crops. However, rather than their land being harvested twice in a year, it is often only harvested an average of once in every three years. Generally, the same patch will be cultivated for 2–3 years and then left fallow for 5–6 years. Maize and beans are important crops but Bena is much more dependent on root vegetables (*Dioscoreaceae sp.*, *Colocasia sp.* and *Manihot sp.*), which form a larger proportion of the diet. The villagers generally have more land under perennial crops and the government has provided incentives to reforest 400 hectares in the village with useful tree crops. Coffee is less suited to the soil and climate although some villagers have planted it with success. Cocoa, pepper and, recently, cashews have been planted. The prices for all these cash crops are unreliable and fluctuate in accordance with international markets. The situation is exacerbated by poor communications and restricted access to the market. The villagers of Bena do not collect the sap of the hairy palm: they purchase the distilled version from other villages.

As compared to villagers in Wogo, where wealth is considered a consequence of agricultural diligence, those in Bena are disenchanted with the results of their agricultural labour. In the case of cashew nuts, they receive a pittance for a crop whose use they are ignorant of. Tourists represent a potential market for cashews, but the villagers are unaware of how to process this crop.

Villagers keep water buffalo, horses, pigs, dogs and chickens. Buffalo are becoming less common as more land is cultivated but their slaughter is considered essential for some ritual occasions, such as a house building final ceremony (*Ka sa'o* Ng), and the funeral of an important person. Nearly all villagers keep pigs, either under or behind their houses. The constant exchange of pigs forms an essential part of ritual life and is essential in maintaining relations within and between villages. Horses form the traditional payment for house carving, divorce and other settlements. In recent years this payment is frequently made in the cash equivalent. Horses provide an additional source of meat at rituals, but are not offered to the ancestors. Although once an important form of transport and used for hunting, they are now frequently kept as a hobby for racing by young men. Dogs were also used for hunting, but are kept now as pets, as guards and for food. Villagers rarely eat their own dogs but buy and sell them for food. They are not offered to ancestors or used for ritual purposes, except when a new *ngadhu* is 'planted' with a live red puppy, piglet and chick. In 2000, nearly all dogs were killed due to a serious outbreak of rabies. Chickens are required for ritual purposes and are kept by villagers around and under houses. The high market value of chickens not only reflects their use in rituals but also the constant battle against an airborne virus called Newcastle's disease that sweeps through Flores on a regular basis, killing a large proportion of chickens.

Income and occupation outside agriculture is very different in the two villages. In Bena, weaving is the most important income generator outside agriculture. Most of the women are involved in the production of ikat cloth (see below). In Wogo, the Catholic Church is the biggest employer. Twenty members of the village work at either the local seminary or the convent. In Wogo and Bena, villagers also work as teachers in state schools and as merchants (who buy small amounts of cash crops from the villagers, until they have the bulk to sell them on to Chinese merchants in the local town). Both villages support two small shops, which sell sugar, cigarettes, sweets, cooking oil, dried fish and soap etc. In Wogo, there are several blacksmiths. They specialise in making the long knives (*parang*) used by all villagers and occasionally sold to tourists. Other villagers specialise in toddy (*moke* Ng) collection for sale to other villagers, some in distilling the liquid, and one man ploughs land with his buffalo. Another raises money through the use of his grinder. In Bena, one man and his son are wood carvers, contracted by villagers all over the area to carve house decorations. This specialist job is passed down through certain blood-lines.

Craft production

The difference in craft production is an important factor in Bena's greater dependence on tourism. Weaving is not only important for economic reasons but also by providing a 'traditional' industry for the tourists to gaze upon. Before examining the development of weaving and the sale of crafts to tourists, a brief examination of the weaving process is necessary.[4]

Fabrics in Bena are produced by the following method. The warp of a cloth is wound around a rectangular frame. Sections of the warp are then tied together before the warp is dyed. The sections that are tied together will resist the dye and retain the original colour of the warp. The dyed warp is then transferred onto a back-strap or body-tension loom for weaving. The tying process is inherited and passed from one weaver to another and is the preserve of only a few Ngadha villages. Any female can undertake the weaving process, once it is on a loom. In Bena, experienced, busy weavers tie the warp, dye it and thread up a loom, then they pass it on to other younger, less experienced women to complete the weaving for a fee.

Ritual dress in Ngadha is black with a white pattern (sometimes with gold threads). There are three different white patterns, one for each of the ranks (see p. 75 on social organisation). The smallest and simplest represents a chicken's foot, and is worn by the former slave rank. The commoners' design consists of the outline of a horse in a variety of different sizes.

The design for nobility is referred to as an elephant; the pattern is in fact the same as a horse but bigger and filled in. The warp threads that are tied together to create the patterns are always an odd number.[5] When women learn to ikat from an elder female relative, they begin with only the chicken's foot; as they progress, they make bigger and bigger horse designs. This progression from one level to another involves a ceremony where a chicken sacrifice is made. Only one woman in Bena is at the stage where she can produce the elephant pattern. Her traditional ikats are in demand. Other women who are capable of producing these designs would not do so. As they explained, 'it isn't appropriate to progress to that stage if you are under fifty', 'people who progress too quickly are punished by the ancestors, they get stiff hands or bad eyes and have to give up weaving altogether' and 'it's not worth it; we cannot make bigger designs without a ceremony or we will anger the ancestors'. As a result of this custom, the larger the design on an ikat the more expensive it will be. Other factors are how compact the weaving is and the complexity of the design and how well the design is 'matched up'. Tourists are unaware of the factors in the cost differential of cloths. They can get angry when a cloth in their preferred colour is more expensive. On one occasion a Dutch woman complained, 'I like that colour, it's the same size why should I pay more?' Then turning to her tour leader she said, 'When they know you want one they just put the price up.'

Bena is more dependent than Wogo on tourism revenue and this is mainly due to the sale of ikat. As has been pointed out, Bena is traditionally an ikat-weaving village, whereas Wogo never was. The only weaving in Wogo was plain or stripy cloth and none of the women now continue this craft. The tradition in Bena has been partly maintained due to tourism but also for two other reasons: initiatives by the Department of Industry and the adoption of traditional textiles as formal wear.

The Indonesian government has recognised the role played by handicrafts in regional development. The Department of Industry has worked through the family welfare programme (PKK) to develop home industries for women.[6] In 1983, before tourists started visiting the villages of Ngadha, an industry group[7] was created in Bena. This regional government initiative trained one woman from the village in group motivation and finance and gave the group a grant to buy equipment, such as large pans for dyeing, and a stock of dyes and thread. Women were encouraged to join the group and one day a week they would work together using the group's facilities. Men were also allowed to join so that looms and other equipment could be made and repaired. Each member who joined the group paid a small fee, so that the original capital was recouped and used for further purchases. Revenue from sales was shared out once a year.

When the annual revenue was shared out, women were able to invest in their own thread, dyes and pans and could produce their own ikats for sale. In fact, the group remains to this day and is an important part of the weavers' social life. Once a week, each member takes a small donation of food to be cooked communally for the midday meal. More experienced weavers are able to teach those with less experience. The women work together to thread the looms, a task that requires two people, and at the same time plenty of gossip can be exchanged. All the women in the group admitted that they no longer needed the group in terms of the facilities that it provided, but that they continued in the group for social reasons and because it was a source of loans in time of need. Group funds were loaned out as credit to members. This appeared to be the incentive for the men that had joined the group.

In 1994, the governor of East Nusa Tenggara, recognising the importance of ikat, decreed that the Thursday uniform for all government employees was ikat.[8] This rule included waistcoats for senior high school pupils. This decree not only created a demand for ikat but also sent out an important message that ikat was not primitive and outdated but was appropriate formal wear, worn at the highest level of government. In Bena, 50% of sales are to locals, much of which is to government employees in Bajawa. The remaining 50% is sold to tourists.

Long knives[9] are the villagers' basic tools, used both in agriculture and in the kitchen, as well as a weapon. Long knives are produced in Wogo, where the blades are forged from scrap iron on an anvil, handles are carved and sheaths made from wood and buffalo horn. The knives produced in Wogo are produced to order or sold at the local market in Mataloko. Tourists occasionally buy long knives. In Wogo this is usually the spontaneous purchase of the villagers tools. Villagers in Bena occasionally travel to Mataloko to buy a long knife or two for display and sale to tourists. However, due to their expense and unpredictable sales, many villagers are reluctant to invest in this business.

The traditional craft of weaving slithers of bamboo or other grasses to produce bags, mats and baskets is an important handicraft practised by some of the older women in both villages. A Ngadha woman's handbag consists of a multi-layered, box-shaped basket called a *bere*. It is used to carry their betel nut chewing paraphernalia, combs and money etc. Decorated baskets are worn as part of the traditional dress. Traditional meals are always served in an eating basket and four[10] different sized and shaped baskets are involved in the rice preparation process for rituals (see Plate 5). Baskets are also used in the house for storage of both sacred and profane objects.

Plate 5 Woman oversees baskets of rice collected for a feast

Basketry is a time-consuming craft and many women no longer make these items although they occasionally repair mats and baskets. Most of the young girls in both villages claimed either not to possess the skill or were ashamed by their poor ability because they could do only plain weaving and none of the decorative parts. Most women did not consider basketry as an income generation option. In Wogo, agriculture was preferred and in Bena basketry was considered to be too similar to weaving; the women wanted an option that was different and 'not all hands and eyes'. The old and disabled women who did maintain the craft in Wogo were able to sell all that they could produce. In a third village, an industry group for basketry has been set up. When, on one occasion, a group of tourists visited the village during a group activity, sales were considerable. If the women were pre-warned of group visits they could arrange group activities to coincide. As tour operators turn up unannounced the substantial sales to tourists on this occasion remains a one-off, a taste of what could be.

Other craft production in the villages includes: kitchen equipment, such as gourd bowls; wooden and coconut shell ladles, serving spoons and draining spoons; bowls and draining spoons made from coconut and bamboo. Of these, only coconut shell drinking vessels are already displayed and sold to tourists in Bena. In 1998 one man in Bena and one woman in Wogo made ceremonial bags from leather and white horse hair (as worn by the villager in Plate 14) and tourists occasionally bought these too. In 2001 the old man died. In 2005 a villager who had moved to Lombok visited the village. He was trying to sell 'traditional Ngadha' ceremonial bags, produced in Lombok to the villagers. The quality and materials (not real leather) was poor by comparison but white horse hair was still used. A villager said if she had had some spare cash she might have bought a couple to try and sell them to tourists.

Social Organisation

Ngadha social organisation is shaped by three conflicting sets of rules associated with the Indonesian state, the Catholic Church and customary law (*adat*). Since all of these impinge in some way on the local peoples' relations with tourists, it is necessary to clarify their essential features. This division is somewhat artificial since all these sets of rules exert an influence at the same time. The importance of these three forces and how they interact with tourism is discussed in detail in Chapter 9.

Administratively, the Indonesian Republic is divided into provinces (*propinsi*), which are further sub-divided first into regencies (*kabupaten*), then into districts (*kecamatan*), and further into villages (*desa*). The system is based on the Javanese model, which was introduced throughout the Dutch East Indies in colonial times. Villages are further sub-divided into hamlets (*dusun*), which are further sub-divided into neighbourhood organisations (*Rukun warga*, RW, and *Rukun tetangga*, RT). Each sub-division has a head and the smallest, the RT, consists of only 12 houses. The standardised village structure, making officials responsible for social, administrative and security matters of such small units, enabled the central government to maintain control over the smallest of remote settlements.

Despite only being 12km apart (as the crow flies), the two fall into different districts. Wogo is part of the administrative village (*desa*) of Ratogesa, Golewa district. Bena is part of Desa Tiworiwu in the Airmere district. It should be noted that an Indonesian administrative village can cover a large area (Ratogesa is over 8 sq. km and Tiworiwu is 11 sq. km) and the studies took place in one *nua* (traditional heart of a village, see below), at the centre of these administrative villages. In both cases, the administrative villages contained more than one *nua*. A *nua* is equivalent to a hamlet (*dusun*) in the administrative structure.

The Church's structure reflects the government structure (see Table 4.1). A parish (*paroke*) is in fact equivalent to a district, with a population of approximately 20,000. Each *paroke* is divided into stations (*stasi*), environments (*lingunan*) with the smallest sub-division consisting of prayer group (*kelompok doa*). Although the state and Church divisions are equivalent in terms of size, they do not necessarily coincide in terms of area covered.

Table 4.1 State and church administrative divisions

	Government division	*Church division*
District	*Kecamatan*	*Paroke*
Village	*Desa*	*Stasi*
Hamlet	*Dusun*	*Lingungan*
Neighbourhood	RW / RT	*kelompok doa*

The influence of the Church has varied from one village to another. Wogo is less than 2km from the mission at Mataloko, an important centre for the Catholic Church on Flores. Bena is, however, 1–2 hours walking time from a much smaller, less influential, parish church.

In accordance with custom, Ngadha society is organised around the following principles: social rank, membership of clans, Houses,[11] and *nua*.

Rank

In common with the societies of Eastern Indonesia, there are three ranks in Ngadha: the nobles (*gae*), the commoners (*gae kisah*), and slaves (*ho'o*).[12] Social rank is a traditional institution, which would appear to be decreasing in importance, under the influence of the Church and state. When I first visited Wogo, the villagers were keen to tell me their society was divided into three ranks. However, ten years later I was advised not to discuss rank[13] and few villagers would openly discuss the subject, except to claim it was antiquated, unimportant or not modern. One family in Wogo openly boasted their noble status and thought that rank was of great importance and a tradition that should be maintained. This is one of the ways tradition was articulated as a political strategy. In Bena, the villagers claimed only two ranks existed, there was nobody of slave rank in the *nua*, I was told.

For some of the villagers, rank is still important in relation to choice of spouse. However, there are a number of reasons why rank has lost its importance as an organising principle. Firstly, some of the villagers in both Bena and Wogo maintain that 'modern people' don't worry about rank. An elder from Bena told me that, with increasing education, educational level would in the future be more important than rank in spouse choice. Secondly, under the influence of the Catholic Church, some villagers feel rank is unimportant and claim: 'We are all equal in the eyes of God.' Thirdly, many of the villages believe that human rights considerations do not allow for people to be considered as slaves (*ho'o*).[14] Older women claimed that rank used to be obvious during rituals due to the different designs worn by the different ranks (see above). They told me, 'now they wear what they want, and we cannot admonish them or they say "You have not bought me, there are no slaves"'. Although those of slave rank were likely to dress as commoners, the commoners did not dress as nobility. Fourthly, for some villagers, the influence of status rules is less influential than economic standing. Finally, the principle may become less important because it is unsustainable (Smedal, 1998). According to the principles of hypergamy, men can marry down but women cannot. This leaves women at the top of the hierarchy unmarried and without available partners. There are a relatively large number of unmarried highborn women in Ngadha. According to the young people of Wogo, rank is still important in their choice of spouse. When asked about the risk of highborn women remaining unmarried, they claim that high-rank women will take a husband from outside the area, of no rank, and therefore will not lose rank through a wrong marriage (*la'a sala* Ng).

A single House belongs to people from more than one rank (usually all three). Houses are therefore not used as a means of differentiation between different ranks. Further, the social hierarchy in Ngadha society has not led to large buildings as it has in other Indonesian societies where the political power of nobility has led to impressive constructions (Waterson, 1990). Houses in Ngadha are all approximately equal in size and for the tourist there are no indications of the hierarchical nature of Ngadha society. Villagers appear equally poor.

Clans

The second customary organising principle is the clan (*woe* Ng) and each village is made up of a number of them.[15] Each clan is made up of a number of Houses and is represented in the village by a *bhaga* (house in miniature) and *ngadhu* (a sacrificial post). This pair of emblems represents the unity of clan members both past and present.

Bhaga are miniature houses, identical in construction with the inner sacred rooms of Houses. These emblems of founding female ancestors and clan unity are found in pairs with the *ngadhu*.[16] The *bhaga* are the responsibility of the clan's central House while the *ngadhu* is associated with the clan's second house. However, the *bhaga* is central in rituals involving the whole clan, revered as the clan's original womb.

Ngadhu[17] are a central feature of a *nua*, an important visible material element of Ngadha culture. These carved tree trunks, with three roots and conical thatched roofs, represent the original male ancestor of a clan. They indicate the coming into being of a clan and thereafter the unity of it. Not only are *ngadhu* important signifiers of clan unity and maleness, but they are also personified as male.[18] The *ngadhu* has become an ethnic marker, emblematic of Ngadha culture as it is represented to tourists (see Chapter 9), used in marketing material by the local government and in guidebooks.

Houses

Sa'o is a term used locally to refer simultaneously to the entire traditional house and its inner sacred room.[19] I will use House with a capital H to refer to entire Houses (see Figure 4.1). A true House has a name carried in a sacred dibbling stick belonging to the House. There are a number of traditional houses in Wogo and Bena that have no names and are therefore not Houses. Again, the tourist would be quite unaware of this as from the outside it is not apparent what stage of development a wooden house is at. Becoming a House is a long and expensive process. A house begins life as a small bamboo dwelling. It goes through a number of stages of rebuilding that can take several generations before it becomes a true named House.[20] A true named House (*sa'o ngaza* Ng) is built of lontar (*Borassus flabellifer*), and it has a name

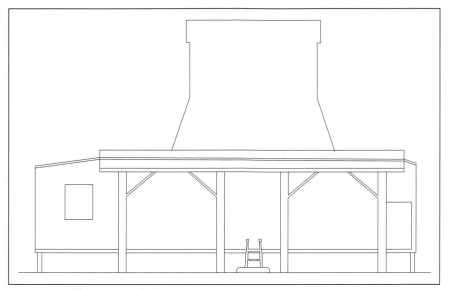

Figure 4.1 Elevation of a House

and a carved entry step (*a kaba pere* Ng) into the inner sacred room[21] (see Plate 6). The growth of a house into a true named House is likened to life from babyhood, through childhood and adolescence to adulthood and maturity. The House's layout (see Figure 4.2) and the way it is conceived reflects the same analogy, of growing up and going through life stages, as the process of houses maturing into true named Houses.[22]

The stones at the base of the step (*pali vai* Ng) lead to an open terrace (*tede moa* Ng) 'the childhood of the house' used during the daytime for children to play and for tasks undertaken at home such as shelling corn, threading looms, making baskets or weaving. A door leads to the main room (*tede one* Ng), which is likened to adolescence, where teenagers and guests sleep, where non-family guests eat and which also serves as an extension to the inner sacred room in times of need.

From the main room, there are steps leading over a carved threshold to a small door that opens into the inner sacred family room (*one sa'o* Ng). This part of the House is the only part that is sacred. In villages where concrete house have been constructed, this part of the original house may be kept behind a 'modern' house.

This sacred room is thought of as female, the womb of the house. The shape of the entry step is said to resemble a vagina. Carvings of horses with bucking legs pointing towards the door serve to remind men that

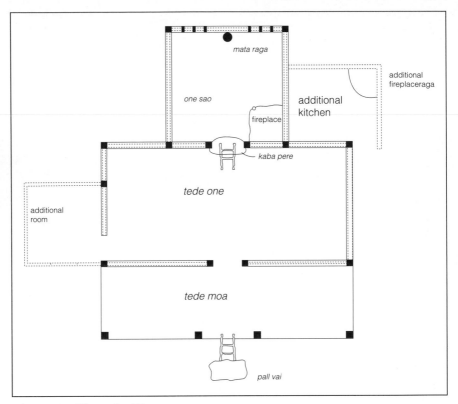

Figure 4.2 Plan of a House

misdemeanours would cost them a horse.[23] Children are born in the inner
sacred room and, after a period of segregation, have a symbolic second
birth.[24] Leaving the house's womb, the new mother and her baby sit on the
entrance step, while a female elder cuts a lock of the baby's hair. The baby
is then reborn, entering into the world of its gathered family, by being
passed into the central room.[25]

The doorway into the inner sacred room is small, requiring the entrant
to bend and bow in respect to the occupants. Elements of the life cycle
theme expressed in the construction of the house are also found here. The
difficult entrance was likened to the fraught passage of moving from being
a carefree teenager to becoming an adult. On a more pragmatic level, the
sliding door provides good security: from the inside the door is slid open
with the left hand, leaving the right to hold a weapon. An intruder attempting to enter is thus unable to open the door while holding a weapon in
their right hand.

Plate 6 A carved entry step to the inner sacred room of a named house

Once in the adult house, the space is differentiated on gender lines. The hearth, the female domain, is on the right of the door and women sit on this side of the room during rituals. Opposite the doorway is the centre of sacredness (*mata raga* Ng), where heirlooms[26] are hung, including the sacred dibbling stick, which carries the House's name. During rituals this is where the eldest male sits with the eldest female (often his sister) at his side.

The 'living nature' of Ngadha Houses is also reflected in how seniority, both in terms of age and rank, is reflected in the use of House space. Informants suggested that during the annual harvest ritual[27] (*Reba* Ng) people of low rank should sit on the terrace, commoners should sit in the main room, and only nobility should sit in the inner sacred room. This theory was not necessarily borne out in my observations but seniority, mainly through age but also through office, was displayed in seating arrangements.

Houses are not only symbolically living through indigenous cosmologies but they are given life force through rituals required for their construction (Waterson, 1990). Public ceremonies and rituals make up an important element in attracting cultural tourists and the selling of destinations for tourism. House construction rituals are still widely practised in Ngadha and play an important part in the villagers' lives on a number of levels:

(1) The house-based organisation of this society is continually reaffirmed when members of the House that live elsewhere collect in the House for the duration of ceremonies. The link between the living and the ancestors is maintained as the ancestors' approval is sought throughout the house building rituals.

(2) The mutual indebtedness and reciprocity (the glue of the society) through pig exchange is continued, as pigs are donated and repaid at most house construction ceremonies, and donations of pigs are frequently between Houses.

(3) A large part of disposable income is used for these ceremonies, underlining the importance that this society places on these rituals.

(4) Outsiders (state, Church and tourists) view of this society as 'traditional' is particularly prominent during rituals.

(5) Ethnic identity is celebrated through rituals whilst the House is a strong cultural symbol for defining identity.[28]

Traditional houses are one of the potent symbols of Ngadha society: the others are the *ngadhu* and *bhaga*.[29] Each symbolises an organising principle in this society and the interconnection between the two[30] is complex. Each clan will have a number of named Houses and these Houses have a hierarchy.[31] The central House, often referred to as such (*rumah pusat*), is called the *saka pu'u* (Ng literally root or trunk rider). This is the first house of the first female ancestor and house of direct line females and their families. In Bena, and many other villages, a miniature house (*ana-ye* Ng) on the roof indicates this central House. In opposition to this is the *saka lobo* (literally shoot rider). This, the second House in the hierarchy, has a miniature warrior on the roof.[32] Lower down the hierarchy are support Houses, known as *sa'o kaka* (Ng).[33]

Each House is headed by a *dongo sa'o* (keeper),[34] a woman chosen by her extended family. In theory, the eldest daughter of the present keeper will inherit her mother's position to remain in the House, look after it and its contents, i.e. family heirlooms. However, if the eldest daughter is unsuitable, another woman will be chosen. A *dongo sa'o* must smile easily, be a good cook, be hospitable, able to organise, able to take responsibility, and not get angry easily. They are special women, indeed. The fact that Houses in the *nua* are occupied by an extended family's most hospitable woman, who is used to comings and goings and acting as host, has an important bearing on tourism.

In Wogo, the task is considered burdensome but women chosen never refuse, as considerable honour goes with the task. Several women in Wogo admitted that they wish they had not been chosen and that they hoped the job would not fall on their daughters' shoulders. The reasons given by younger women were the responsibility, the costs that are not compensated for by the benefits, and the distance of the House from the gardens. The costs involve the taking of rice (and now sugar and coffee) to any other house that has any ceremony. They must entertain guests: any House member can arrive and expect to be fed and stay. Family members who live in the gardens should bring produce and share the burdens but not all do. In Wogo, many people still live in their gardens so House life is contrasted with living close to one's produce and not having a long walk carrying produce from the garden.

There are clear disadvantages to life in the *nua* but all women were keen to point out the advantages as well. Living close to one's neighbours means that life is very communal, very shared. It is normal to pop next door to ask for coffee or sugar or for embers to re-light a fire. There is always a friend close at hand to share some betel nut and have a chat. Children always have friends to play with and someone to comfort them. Help is always at hand.

In Bena, the same opinions were not expressed. Due to stronger government pressure villagers have been moved from remote garden locations to homes along the roadside to ease government administration. The alternative to life in the *nua* is roadside homes (*dena* Ng): both locations have the walk to and from home and gardens. Also, there are the advantages brought by tourism to offset some of the costs.

The *nua*

The *nua* (see Figure 4.3) combines all the traditional houses in a complex and gives the tourist a feeling of 'being enclosed in antiquity' (Cole, 1997a, 1997b). This provides an experience beyond visiting single traditional dwellings, which is the norm in other 'traditional villages' across the archipelago.[35]

The *nua* is a collection of houses belonging to between 2 and 15 clans, arranged in two parallel lines or along four sides of a rectangle.[36] They were traditionally built on the top of spurs overlooking the valley below, providing them with excellent security. All the members of a *nua*, as with the Houses, will not live permanently in the *nua*. Many villagers stay in houses in the gardens but are members of a *nua* just as they are members of a House, which is part of the *nua*. The central area or plaza should be kept free of weeds.[37] Social pressure is applied on villagers to keep the patch in front of their house free of weeds. In the centre of the plaza are the *ngadhu* and *bhaga* for each clan, facing one another in ordered pairs. Each pair is accompanied by a *peo*. These stones are used to tether buffalo before they are slaughtered. They are considered as the children[38] of the *ngadhu* and *bhaga*.

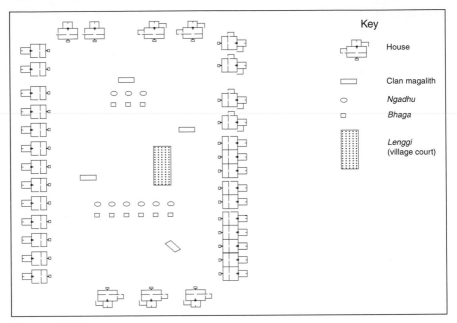

Figure 4.3 A *nua*

The *nua* across the region are hierarchically ordered. According to myth, this is based on the order in which they were settled. The first child or *ana wunga* (Ng) in a Ngadha family or the first to open land in a village is considered superior. The first child is referred to as *ie gae*, which means highest or supreme fruit. These children are also referred to as *tora koba*,[39] which implicitly means pioneer or initiator. 'First' thus has associations of supreme and pioneer: hence, the first *nua* to be settled is considered superior. This superiority is reaffirmed by the order in which each of the villages hold their annual harvest gathering. The primacy of Bena, the first village to have been settled, is particularly important and a controversy has arisen in relation to this (see Chapter 9). Bena is not only the 'eldest (first born) sibling' village but is also 'original'. 'Original' is an important concept in Ngadha (as in many Eastern Indonesian societies) associated with fundamental (or principle), strength and foundation. To stress the importance of original, the Ngadha make reference to both age (*olo* Ng) and *tedhe*, which has connotations of both steady and legitimate. Bena is original: it has always been on the same stunning site. Wogo, in contrast, moved to its present site in 1932. These important values are often articulated in reference to tourism: 'Bena was the first village to be visited by tourists', 'The government's decision to build village home-stays in Bena was partly because it 'is the first and original village.'

Each *nua* will have a first stone (*Watu wai* Ng) recognised as belonging to the founding clan. At the centre of the *nua* is an area made up of a number of flat stones and used as a meeting place to settle inter-clan disputes, often referred to as the village court (*lenggi* Ng).[40] Other stones found in the centre of *nua* include clan stones (*tureh ulu toli* Ng)[41], stones used to mark important members' graves and stones that form table-like formations.

Considering the romantic appeal of the term megalith (Waterson, 1990), it is not surprising that it has now been embraced by the local government, guidebooks and tourists alike in reference to the stones found in and around Ngadha villages. The word is printed in bold type in the 1999 *Rough Guide to Indonesia*. They form part of the attractiveness of these villages to tourists and are protected by law as historic/archaeological remains.[42] Some tourists visit the old site of Wogo without visiting the new site. The old site consists entirely of uninterpreted large stones in various arrangements. In Bena, the megaliths lie in the centre of the village, although many of these have been reconstructed and renovated in the past 15 years.[43] Villagers in Ngadha use the table-like structures to dry coffee beans or other products.[44] This profane use of these apparently sacred relics is a source of cultural confusion for tourists. The idea that heritage must be conserved without being used is challenged by the everyday lives of the villagers.

Megaliths found in Ngadha villages, as they are throughout South East Asia, are connected with religious life as a medium to connect the living with the dead. Terminological confusion arises from the borrowing of archaeological terms for the various stones. Constructions consist of flat stones (*dolmin*)[45] measuring about two metres by one metre, with a number of named upright stones (*menhir*).[46] The male–female symbolism is also used when discussing these village megaliths. Flat stones are female and uprights are male (see Plates 3 and 8). They are found together as couples, like husbands and wives. According to local myth, a giant called Dhake transported the megaliths found in Ngadha villages to their present sites.

All stones are referred to generally as *tureh* (Ng). However, village members know the names of important stones or collections of stones. Many of the stones mark the sites of important members' graves, assuring the occupant social immortality, the height of stones marking the relative importance of the individual. Gardens also have megaliths, as a place to lay offerings and as a mark of ownership. Further megaliths are found at the base of some palm juice trees as a place where men meet, drink and make plans. These *tureh loka* (Ng) are still occasionally used. Each clan has its own ancestral megalith, used for ceremonies.

Belief System

For some anthropologists (e.g. Needham, 1972), the notion of belief is not a discernible experience and therefore not a useful category. However, I am using belief as a literary convenience. I shy away from using religion because in Bahasa, Indonesia this has monotheistic connotations (see below). There are two central aspects to the villagers' belief system: Catholicism and ancestor worship/veneration.[47] The distinction is made locally, at least when speaking in Indonesian, ancestral respect and the complex of belief and rituals that go with it are referred to as *adat* and Catholicism as a religion (*agama*). These two aspects have to some extent been syncretised.[48] They also compete for importance in the villagers' lives. When I first visited Wogo, villagers were keen to point out that many aspects of *adat* were 'only remembering their ancestors'. 'Like you keep photographs of your grandparents we have our megaliths', I was told. In recent years, villagers have been keen to point out that they had a god (*ga'e dewa*[49]) before the missionaries came. In this sense the villagers are deliberately blurring the *adat*/religion distinction.[50]

The Indonesian word *adat* is usually used to refer to non-Muslim customs. In this Catholic society, it is the Indonesian translation of both *uku adha*,[51] rules of respect, and the longer fuller parallel poetic expression *epo po, nusi pera*,[52] the advice and teachings of the grandparents and great-grandparents. For the villagers *adat* is 'the way of the ancestors'. I use the pan-Indonesian expression not only as a shorthand but also because the use of the word has become incorporated into tourism discourse in Indonesia. For example, the villages in this study are frequently referred to as *kampung adat* (in which case *adat* can be translated as traditional).

The villagers are firm believers in God and are regular church-goers; most pray before meals and many make the sign of the cross before drinks are sipped. Alongside this most observant and punctilious Catholicism, the influence of the ancestors remains equally important.[53] The value of traditional beliefs for attracting tourists has only recently been recognised at an official level. Tourism is therefore one of the forces changing state attitudes, which in the past devalued the belief system and, together with the Church, have tried to curb sacrificial slaughter.

Feasting remains competitive, boasting about rituals relies on the number of animals slaughtered and the number of guests who attend. The distance guests travel is also important. This in part explains why tourists are welcome at rituals. Beyond this, tourists sometimes provide a source of photographs, entertainment and finance.

Families join together in their Houses for *Reba*, the villages' most auspicious festival. This annual ritual, an essential component of the villager's *adat*,[54] has become a matter for both the Church and the state. After *Reba*, the most important ceremonies surround House building and renovating. On average, two Houses in each village are renovated every year.

Rituals performed for rites of passage have been the most changed by Catholicism. Birth is celebrated with a traditional ritual performed particularly for the first born in the family. Baptism is important, but babies receive their *nua* name (*ngaza nua* Ng) at home before their Christian name in church. After baptism in the church, a family will sacrifice a pig and request acceptance into the family and good health, from the ancestors.

Several elders blamed the increasing frequency of teenage pregnancy on the lack of teeth filing ceremony, a female initiation ceremony banned by the Church. They also claim that skimpily clothed tourists, who cause arousal, are an additional factor.

Most people also get married in church, although it is not unusual for this to take place months or even years after a couple have been cohabiting. The customary ceremony, which theoretically takes place at the annual harvest festival, *Reba*, serves as the marker of when a couple can start cohabiting. In an attempt to cut down on excessive feasting, the Church has taken to marrying many couples on the same day at mass weddings. The plan does not appear to have been successful as continued feasting and pig exchange remains common for weddings. The format of weddings blends Catholic, Javanese and local elements. The groom wears a suit and his bride a long white dress and white gloves. Guests attend usually presenting a gift of money in an envelope and eat a Javanese style buffet meal. The music and dance that follows is always an eclectic mix of ballroom, Ngadha pop, and classics from the European charts. Tourists are invited to attend weddings because the young like to watch the latest dance moves, tourists provide part of the entertainment for the local guests.

It is during death rites that the syncretism of the villagers' past belief system and Catholicism are most clear. The nine-part ceremony takes four days and involves Catholic prayers as well as intricate rites to wish the dead a good journey to the second world and request that they do not return to bother the living. Like many Eastern Indonesians, the Ngadha distinguish between good and bad death each with their own distinct rituals (cf. Barnes, 1974).

For every major ritual, pigs will be donated by Houses, family and in-laws (see Plate 7). Pigs will be returned when the donors hold a similar ritual. In 1998, for a final House building ritual, 20 to 40 pigs were donated, and for funerals three to eight. Pigs are also donated for weddings but this is a new phenomenon, since marriages have taken place in the church at various times of the year, and not just during *Reba*. The donation of pigs depends on relationship and previous exchange but all houses in the *nua* take a hanging basket of rice (*bere eko* Ng) regardless of relationship. The constant exchange of pigs (*wado lima* Ng) is one of the ways family ties, both on the female and male side, are maintained. The hanging baskets of rice (and now sugar and coffee) maintain relations between the inhabitants of the *nua*.

Ritual life is costly but all the villagers were keen to point out that they have cut down on the number of animals slaughtered for sacrifices. Many villagers discussed the need to balance the demands of ritual slaughters with the costs of modern life. Whereas in the past many buffaloes would have been slaughtered for a final house building ceremony (*ka sa'o* Ng), nowadays it is common for only one to be sacrificed (together with 20–40 pigs). Many people slaughter only a handful of pigs rather than a buffalo for the final funeral rite (*ngeku mata* Ng). Levels of sacrifice are also dependent on the rise and fall in the fortunes of the hosting family and village and the amount of goodwill and relations they have built up. In 2005 I finally attended a triple house building (three branches of an extended family in one *nua* decided to hold their ritual at the same time). Many of the villagers had had a couple of successful vanilla harvests when the price of vanilla was particularly high. Seven buffalo and 50 pigs were donated. Younger members of the family expressed a combination of pride and worry – so much goodwill but also, as all donations will have to be returned, so much debt. As one said: 'My feelings of happiness are weighed against money thoughts, these donations must be remembered for seven generations.'

Villagers explain that their ancestors had only to think of *adat* (custom) whereas now there are competing expenses of school, tax, health and the Church. The villagers have been subject to significant pressure from the Church and state to cut down the number of animals slaughtered at major ceremonies. This was enforced through a punitive slaughter tax. The church insisted that poverty could only be alleviated by stopping excessive slaughter at ceremonies.[55]

Pig donating and receiving is an important public demonstration of relationships. Pigs are carried trussed up on bamboo poles and carried into a village for all villagers to inspect (see Plate 7), the bigger the pig the more important the relationship between donor and recipient. Pig jaws, donated for house building rituals, are kept and displayed above the door.

Plate 7 A family delivers a pig and baskets of rice for a ritual

The number and size of jaws signifies the number of relationships and amount of goodwill. Past ceremonies are remembered through the number of animals slaughtered.

Buffalo skulls and horns and pig jaws hanging outside houses form part of the tourists gaze. They confirm the 'primitive' picture that the tourists come to see. However tourists who do not attend a ritual often assume that they are relics of a past life and do not see them in the context of the villagers' present-day lives. Tourists who attended one of the rituals were much more confident that they had found the primitive people they had come to see.

Involvement in the Market Economy

The majority of villagers would call themselves *petani*, which could be translated as peasant or farmer. The former seems more appropriate due to the negative construction used by the villagers[56] and because they resemble peasants in the sense Redfield (1960)[57] and Scott (1976)[58] described. The agriculture is entirely unmechanised. The move from self-sufficiency to the commodification of time and the social construction of work, which only counts if it is paid for, is a recent phenomenon in these villages. As many villagers explained, the need for money for schools, health care, taxes and church 'tithes' are new demands. The need for cash and involvement in the market economy is an issue bemoaned by many villagers.

However, as many explained, it is still possible to live for long periods in Wogo without cash. Constant cropping of maize and vegetables keeps food on the table, hairy palms give sap for toddy without money and the bamboo in which it is collected is grown locally. Family members that need cash generally go and pick some produce, take it to market and sell it. A market is held in Mataloko only 2km from Wogo, twice a week. Villagers without paid work would sell between Rp10,000 and Rp40,000 (US$1–4) worth of produce a week. Sugar was the most frequently purchased commodity, followed by cooking oil. Petty merchants come to Wogo to sell fresh fish several times a week. This or dried fish is the villagers' source of animal protein between feasts. The village shops sell dried fish. Children's protein needs are supplemented by eating cicadas, crickets and other insects.

Villagers in Bena are more dependent on cash because their gardens are less productive. In the past, villagers used to collect firewood and sell it in Bajawa. As firewood has become scarcer and as townsfolk used more kerosene for cooking and the demand for woven cloth has increased, textile sales have become the villagers' most important source of income.

Although now peripherally involved in the market economy, the villagers are only weakly integrated into the cash economy. In most homes, hand-made hanging woven baskets of various sizes are used as containers for agricultural products, clothing and any possessions. Coconuts and dried gourd skins are still used as receptacles in the kitchen (although supplemented with plastic goods). Kitchen implements are made from bamboo and coconut shells. Rope is still produced with a local tool made in the village. Some villagers own a small amount of furniture but usually villagers sit and sleep on mats they make themselves. Many people in Bena wear sarongs made by women in the village. Many villagers, the young people included, claim that feelings are more important than economy; the costs of rituals and helping out relatives and neighbours are more important than material possessions. A popular material possession is a stereo system. Young males, in particular, aspire to possess one and compete to acquire larger and more powerful systems.

Many villagers own ceremonial costumes as prized possessions. Many villagers sold off these black ikats, with white (and sometimes gold) motifs, together with many other family heirlooms (*pusaka*) e.g. gold earrings (*bela* Ng) and chains (*rante* Ng) during the 1970s when the Church and state purged tradition. Since the traditional revival in the 1980s, villagers consider it important to possess at least one traditional dress.[59] Some men also have a headdress (*boku* Ng). However, these hand-spun naturally dyed 'scarves' are hard to find and costly to purchase. Women are very fond of beads and may have a string for ordinary days or Sundays. Long strings of beads are worn across the shoulder during rituals. Many villagers own accessories to the ceremonial costume, including bags and headbands. Villagers who do not own traditional dress hire them from other villagers for ceremonies. It is not permissible to dance in non-ceremonial clothes. On a number of occasions when I asked people why they were not participating in the dancing, they explained that it was because of a lack of appropriate dress.

One disabled woman in Wogo makes ceremonial bags that she hires out for ceremonies. Some villagers still have ivory bracelets; many others have fake ivory, white wood or plastic bracelets. House-based rituals are an opportunity for hosting houses to display any heirlooms. During the new Ngadhu ceremony in Bena (see Chapter 7 and Plate 13), several women wore their antique gold earrings and at a new entry step ritual in Wogo a man wore a long heavy gold chain.

Infrastructure

Wogo lies 2km from the trans-Flores highway. Public transport (buses and minibuses) is frequent down the busy highway, especially when there is a market in Mataloko. The branch road, which leads past the entrance to the *nua*, was a rough track in 1989 but has since been upgraded and tarmacked. Public transport (trucks and minibuses) goes past the *nua* entrance several times a day. Bena lies about 15km down a branch road. Although the road has been tarmacked, it is very steep in places and very windy and prone to landslides. It is not uncommon for it to become impassable during the rainy season. Bena is served by two trucks a day. They are nearly always filled to capacity and often leave villagers standing by the roadside as demand outstrips available space. The wear and tear on vehicles is such that it is not commercially viable to run minibuses on this route. However, minibuses are used to transport tourists.

Wogo has had electricity since 1991. The poles were erected following the shortest route, which was straight through the centre of the *nua*. Tourists, villagers and the Department of Tourism alike lament their position. Bena does not have any central electricity facilities. However, in 1998 two villagers had generators that supplied several houses each with electricity. In 2005 15 out of the 32 houses had their own generators. Most generate 650 watts, one generates 2 kilowatts and another 3 kilowatts. Diesel for the generators has to be purchased and transported from Bajawa, the regency town.

In 1998, in Wogo, water was available at two points behind houses that make up the *nua*. Water had to be queued for and collected for all household use. Bathing frequently took place at the river or at hot springs located a couple of kilometres from the *nua*. Water facilities in Bena were similar although the Department of Tourism has provided 'squat' toilets at two points in the *nua*. Water to both of these is unreliable and is not supposed to be for the use of the villagers. As can be seen from the section on the benefits of tourism (Chapter 7), the provision of water in both villages can be directly linked to tourism. In 2005 water provision had improved. In Wogo, pipes had been run to allow water to be distributed to some houses in the village. Several houses had their own 'bathrooms' and were using electric pumps to facilitate running water. In Bena, an NGO had funded water points every few houses and many villages had taken spurs off the pipe to facilitate direct supplies to the back of their houses.

Education

Children attend local primary schools from age 6 to 12.[60] Over the age of 12, education is far more accessible to the children of Wogo than Bena, and differences in educational levels between the two villages reflect this. Middle and high school children in Bena have to board (at parental expense) either in Bajawa or Jerebuu. This is not only an expense some parents cannot afford but it also removes the students from the informal schooling in the technical aspects of their local economy and ecology (Dove, 1988) and *adat*. Several high school students who returned to Bena bemoaned their lack of knowledge and said that they did not have the opportunity to sit around with elders to hear the narratives on customary matters. Furthermore, parents lose control over their children and are unsure what their children are getting up to. This was a constant source of worry for some parents. In Wogo, there is a choice of several middle and high schools within walking distance.

A very high value is placed on formal education and relatively large proportions of disposable income are used to educate students as far as their potential or will takes them. Daeng (1988) argues that villagers' resources have been concentrated on education since competitive feasting came under pressure from the government and the Church. In 1998, one member of Bena had a university degree and several were studying at tertiary level. In Wogo, there were eight graduates and several others who had tertiary education. In 2005 one villager was on a post-graduate scholarship in the UK and another was going to Australia. Educational opportunity is well balanced across gender lines. Whereas in other Indonesian societies boys are offered more educational opportunities than girls, in Ngadha mothers told me that 'boys will leave to join their wife's family; it is my daughters that are the future of this family so they must continue school as far as they can'. In Bena, many mothers wanted their daughters to weave but claimed that, if they showed potential at school, they would be supported to continue.

Social Activities

Music in the village is played on instruments made from bamboo and on iron gongs. Local music is very popular and it is common to hear the villagers spontaneously singing their own songs. Music and songs from House building ceremonies are recorded and frequently replayed on sound systems. The sound systems in Wogo are also used to play Indonesian and western music. In Bena, the young girls tend to sing the local songs whereas the boys sing Indonesian songs to the guitar.

Volleyball has been popular since the 1970s. It is played routinely in Bena every Sunday and also after communal work. During the warm-up, men and women play together; then the women play alone. Men then play and these games often involve gambling. Five hundred to a thousand Rupiah (5-10 US cents) is paid by each player to be split by the winning team. Men and women both play cards although more men play. Sundays, the day for relaxation, is the day most card games are played and also most gambling takes place. Women rarely gamble and many disapprove of the men doing it, mainly, it seemed, because the card playing would go on for longer if gambling was involved. In 2005 the police came under pressure to enforce the laws that made gambling illegal. This resulted in less card playing and volleyball matches.

Villagers take part in *arisan* (communal meals for savings groups). This method of saving and socialising is popular all over Indonesia and according to the villagers has local origins (*muvu* Ng). In Wogo, the Church uses it as a way to raise money. On Sundays, villagers meet in their prayer groups and share in a meal. Each member contributes to a fund, which one member wins, by drawing names from a hat. Once a member has won once, their name is not entered at the following sessions until all members have won. The winner hosts the next meal and has a sum of money sufficient to pay large church tithes, and maybe has some towards other needs. This formalised gambling allows the Church both to collect sums that would otherwise be difficult for villagers to raise, and to combine it with a social event. *Arisan* are not only held for the Church. The teachers hold an *arisan* once a month for teachers to get to know each other's families and to save for their own children's education. Clans also hold *arisan* on a monthly or tri-monthly basis. In the case of large, well-scattered clans, this is considered an important way for the different members to stay in touch. However, the costs of *arisan* are a financial burden to the villagers. Often a family would have more than one *arisan* to attend on a Sunday. The fees are variable from Rp2500 for a weekly *arisan* to Rp50,000 for a monthly meeting, to Rp300,000 for a tri-monthly meeting. The later would be raised collectively by members of a House. Sundays, as a day of leisure, are also a day to start drinking *moke* (palm toddy) in the morning, usually with a group of friends, while roasting corn.

Tourism

Occasional backpackers began visiting Wogo and Bena in the 1980s. When my company started taking tourists to Wogo in 1989, the villagers had seen a dozen or so tourists pass through the village. Table 4.2 provides figures for tourist numbers to Bena and Wogo through the 1990s. The Department of Education and Culture provided these figures and they are different from those provided by the Department of Tourism. The figures for Wogo are far less reliable than the Bena figures. For the latter, figures relate to ticket sales. In Wogo, not all tourists fill in the guest book, which is falling to pieces, torn, and used as notepaper. Neither department had records for 1999. A reorganisation of departments has meant that there is now a Department of Tourism and Culture. The figures they supplied for 2000 to 2005 illustrate more about the reporting and recording of tourist figures than about the actual numbers of tourists that visit.

Collecting statistical information about tourism in Ngadha was difficult. As discussed further in Chapter 6, until 2004 the visitor books belonged to the Department of Education and Culture, which is not interested in the nationality of tourists or group size. Furthermore, although in theory all tourists are requested to fill in visitor books, not all do. Frequently, only one of a couple would and on some occasions the guide would fill the book in once for a group of four or five. Even ticket sales in Bena do not provide an accurate base for tourist numbers as local guides are charged (and given tickets) on the basis of 'one per group free'. Thus, for example, a local guide would purchase four tickets for a group of five.[61]

As suggested in Chapter 2, tourism to Flores is subject to marked seasonal variation. The classic pattern for both villages is evident from Figure 4.4, which shows foreign visitor numbers each month to Bena. This figure is based on statistics provided by the Department of Education and Culture. The total does not, however, tally with those provided in table 4.2.

The nationality of tourists who visit Ngadha villages does not reflect those that visit Indonesia in general. Due to the difficulties noted above, there are no reliable data on the nationalities of tourists. Figure 4.5 is developed from counts from those that filled in the visitor books in September and October 1998. In several cases, it is known that a single tally represented a group (of unknown size). As the majority of groups are Dutch, the percentage for that nationality could have been even higher. However, the nationality of tourists had changed quite dramatically in 2004/2005. For example in July and August 2005 the French were the most dominant nationality making up 38% of independent tourists, followed by the Swiss who made up a further 17%. There were no Australians, only three British and one American.[62]

Table 4.2 Foreign tourist visits to Bena and Wogo

Year	Bena	Wogo
1991	3293	666
1992	4323	1318
1993	4228	980
1994	5729	900
1995	6456	1019
1996	6874	1100
1997	5949	966
1998	5121	1287

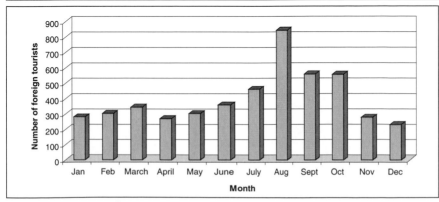

Figure 4.4 Seasonal visitor variations

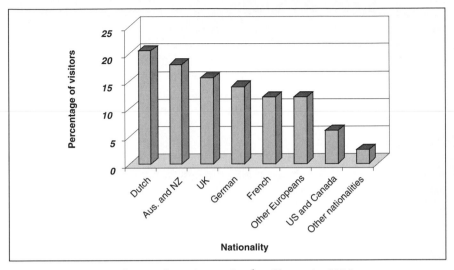

Figure 4.5 Nationalities of tourists to both villages in 1998

With a few exceptions, such as the tour groups I took to Wogo, tourists visit the villages as part of a day tour. The schematic map in Figure 4.6 shows the position of Wogo, Bena and other villages tourists visit in the Ngadha area. Most often, local guides take tourists to Bena via Bela and/or Luba and sometimes they continue to Nage in the morning. They return to Langga or Bajawa for lunch and then spend the afternoon at the hot springs near Soa. The standard day tour has started to change. As roads have improved guides are starting to take tourists to more remote villages.

On arrival in Bena, tourists or their guides buy tickets and are asked to fill out the visitors' book. In Wogo, if the caretaker or a member of his family spots them, they are asked to fill in the visitors' book and make a donation. The tourists then spend ten minutes to an hour or so wandering around the *nua* taking photographs of houses, *ngadhu*, *bhaga*, megaliths and people. Some give gifts to children and some attempt communication with the villagers. In Bena, they admire the weavings hanging outside many houses and walk up to the viewing post – a semi-circular concrete vantage point with a mock *ngadhu* and bench – to look at the spectacular scenery.

This chapter has provided an overview of the lives of the villagers central to this book. They are largely subsistence agriculturists who have recently been incorporated into the market economy. Social organisation in the villages shares much in common with other Eastern Indonesian societies. The house is the central organising principle. Collections of

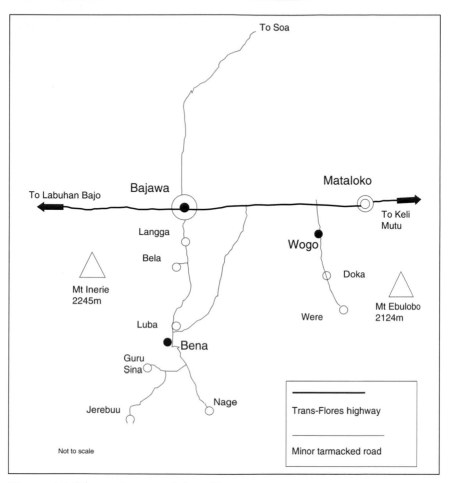

Figure 4.6 Schematic map of the villages

houses are found in *nua* together with *bhaga*, *ngadhu* and megaliths, providing a complex of attractions for tourists and a feeling of being enclosed in antiquity.

Although Catholics, the villagers' respect for their ancestors remains an important part of their lives. Considerable time and expense is dedicated to ceremonies, of which animal slaughter is an essential element. House-based rituals are not only important to reaffirm the house as the central organising principle in this society: they also attract tourists. Furthermore, the house is a strong cultural symbol defining identity and the rituals offer the opportunity to celebrate this identity.

Tourists began visiting the villages in the 1980s. Most visit as part of a day trip. Although the statistics are very unreliable, there is more seasonality in tourism in Ngadha than other parts of Indonesia. Also, the nationalities of the tourists who visit Ngadha do not reflect national statistics.

This chapter reveals some of the differences between Bena and Wogo. The former is more dependent on income from textile sales and tourism while the latter is more fertile and supports more intensive agriculture. Wogo lies closer to the Trans-Flores highway and the mission at Mataloko. This provides better access to markets, education and employment.

Notes

1.   Altitude is given for administrative villages, which cover a large area across which altitudes vary considerably, no indication of where the readings are taken is provided in the data.
2.   A number of palms are grown in Eastern Indonesia. The palm used for toddy in Wogo is a different genus from the palm used in Savu and Roti and the subject of Fox's (1977) book *Harvest of the Palm*. In coastal areas of Ngadha *Borassus* palms are tapped for their juice; this is locally known as *moke koli*.
3.   The first time a new tree is tapped, preserved pork must be eaten, the second time, a chicken is slaughtered, and the third time, a ceremony called *kolu keo* is performed. This involves three young but menstruating girls from the different ranks receiving fermented tree sap (*moke*) directly from the sap collector. Their position, one above the other, also serves to reaffirm their rank. Following this ceremony, rice is cooked in bamboo over an open fire.
4.   For a more in-depth discussion of ikat textile production in Indonesia, see Hitchcock (1991) and (1985).
5.   As among the Kedang, odd numbers are auspicious (cf. Barnes, 1974).
6.   The establishment of home industries for women is useful as such work can be combined with women's responsibilities of childcare, housework and seasonal activities (Hitchcock & Kerlogue, 2000).
7.   *Kelompok Industri.*
8.   All Indonesian government employees wear uniform and it is normal for these to vary with the day of the week and of the month.
9.   *Parang.*
10. *Wati, ripe, sole* and *bhodo*. (Ng).
11. House with a capital H is used to identify traditional houses that are named (see p. 76).
12. Some informants claim that originally four ranks existed but that the fourth has been combined with the slaves.
13. Adams (1995) also found that it was a sensitive subject among the Torajans.
14. Slavery was abolished under the government of Sukarno, the Republic's first president. The view that the slave rank was antiquated was frequently raised in 1998, partly due, no doubt, to the political climate at the time with frequent news reports about human rights.
15. Smedal (1998) challenges this common gloss because clan implies descent as the sole principle for recruitment and, in Ngadha, it is not the only principle.

In Ngadha, it is possible for a wealthy and powerful individual to create a clan. Invitations to potential members do not have to follow blood-lines. However, recruitment and organisation of these groups has little bearing on tourism development and the gloss is widely used, so I will continue with it.

16. A clan must have a *bhaga* before it can have a *ngadhu*, according to some villagers; others said they must come together.
17. Pronounced Madhu in Wogo, and frequently spelt without the 'h'.
18. Each clan will have a *ngadhu* and some will have two. Having two *ngadhu* can result either from wealth and numbers i.e. as a clan becomes large and can afford the costly ceremony, they may build a second *ngadhu*, as a major land owning clan (Ngate) in Wogo have done. In Bena clan Deru have two *ngadhu*; this is because a disagreement resulted in the clan splitting in two. They are referred to as clan Deru A and B and both strongly deny that there is any hierarchical order between them.
19. The inner sacred room is more formally called the *one sa'o*.
20. From the initial bamboo dwelling, if funds allow, a house is built partly of wood. Eventually a fully wooden house is built, though at this stage the type of wood is unimportant and the house is referred to as a *sao tede* (Ng). The next stage is a house of at least coconut wood with a small amount of carving. This is called a *sa'o bale* or *weti segere* (Ng).
21. According to some sources, each time it is renovated from this stage on it gets more and more carving. According to other sources, the carving remains the same as in the original *sa'o ngaza*.
22. The construction also reflects the three tiers common in Austronesian dwellings.
23. A horse is paid by a man to women in settlement if a relationship is begun but the couple do not get formally married.
24. In a ceremony that strongly resembles that of the Tetum (Hicks, 1976).
25. Both mother and father's kin attend this ceremony, underlying the bilineal nature of this society.
26. The *mata raga* is the place used to hang a *sua* (dibbing stick), *sau gae* (a sacred long knife), (*gala gae*) a sacred spear, and *bere kobho* (a hanging basket containing a special coconut shell and small basket with a lid).
27. And at other rituals according to some informants.
28. Taman Mini Indonesia Indah presents the diversity of Indonesian cultures through the construction of 'traditional' dwellings from the provinces.
29. The *bhaga* is inseparable from the *ngadhu* for the Ngadha people but less often used as a symbol by outsiders e.g. in tourism advertising.
30. As Howell (1995b) found among the Lio.
31. As they do among the Tana Wai (Lewis, 1988).
32. Waterson (1990) reports that Forth, in a personal communication, claimed that the Ngada had no explanation to offer for these symbols on house roofs. Waterson suggests that in other areas they are intended as resting places for ancestral spirits.
33. Also known as *saka die* (Ng), these Houses support first the central house and then the second house. In theory, each central House and its opposite will have two support Houses each. In reality, the main Houses have any number of support Houses according to the number of clan members and wealth.
34. *dongo* = to live for; *sa'o* = House.

35. Moni, central Flores, Tana Toraja, Lingga, near Berastagi, North Sumatra, Todo, Manggarai, Western Flores, all have traditional houses that attract tourists. Simanindo, on Samosir, North Sumatra is one village where the tourist is surrounded by traditional dwellings, in the same way as in Ngadha. However, this small village has now become a museum holding daily dance performances.

36. Originally two parallel lines, as they are described as such in older literature, e.g. Barnes (1972), but due to increased numbers of houses the two shorter sides of the rectangle have been filled.

37. '...thereby accentuating it as an ordered cultured space in contrast to wild natural spaces' (Waterson, 1990: 99).

38. Some informants claimed they were the original ancestors of the *ngadhu* and *bhaga*, not their child. A discussion about the symbolism of *peo*, as parents or child of *bhaga* and *ngadhu*, became heated. When the *ngadhu* was replaced in Bena (see p. 174) the *peo* also had to be replaced. A new father would mean a new child, I was told.

39. *Toro* = to cut down; *Koba* = dense forest.

40. *Lenggi* means to oil, the same synonym being used for peace-making as *kelaneo*, said to oil or cool ceremonies. The *lenggi* is referred to as the *lenggi jawa* or *lenggi nua* interchangeably. *Jawa* means peace according to some respondents.

41. *Tureh* = stone; *ulu* = head; *Toli* = death by murder.

42. UU No. 5 1992 Pemilihara Benda Cagar Budaya.

43. Their maintenance has consumed about 30% of the villagers' tourism income. It was one of the issues raised in discussions about the management of tourism.

44. Megaliths were also used for profane purposes in Nias (Suzuki, 1959), and Sumba (Hoskins, 1986).

45. *nabe* = Ngadha term.

46. *watu lewa* = Ngadha term.

47. Since the villagers are Catholics they prefer for their old beliefs to be described as respect or veneration rather than worship.

48. Reconciliation or fusion of differing systems of belief, as in philosophy or religion, especially when success is partial or the result is heterogeneous.

49. Literally supreme or highest God.

50. Cf. Forth (1998) who points out the same among the neighbouring Nage.

51. *Uku* = restriction/rule; *Adha* = showing respect

52. *Ebu* = grandparent; *Po* = advice; *Nusi* = great-grandparents; *Pera* = teachings.

53. Young people in focus groups were insistent that rituals for the ancestors remain an essential part of their lives and that, without them, the ancestors would cause harm, sickness and bad luck in their lives.

54. In discussions with the villagers, all named *Reba* as the most important ceremony and all mentioned *Reba* first when we discussed which aspects of *adat* would remain important in the future. The fact that discussions about *Reba* in Bena, a ritual held in December, had begun when I visited in September and became so heated serves to illustrate how important this ceremony is.

55. The poverty referred to by the Church was the economically determined poverty seen through western eyes. The people of Ngadha have very low net disposable incomes but they are very rich in culture and family relations. As

Dove (1988) points out, this myth of economic deprivation is also held by the state. As he notes, many have a better diet than in highly developed urban areas. However, if resources are used for ceremonial expenditure, they are not spent on purchases that would contribute to the income of the national entrepreneurial classes.

56. The villagers would say '*saya hanya petani saja*'. The use of double only (*hanya* and *saja*) indicates a negative connotation. 'I'm just a simple peasant'.

57. In *The Little Community and Peasant Society and Culture*, Redfield (1960) describes peasant society as one which has some field of economic activity that separates them from a primitive community. Peasants are small-scale agricultural producers organised into households that rely on a subsistence-orientated economy but one that is weakly or partially integrated into a larger state/world system.

58. In *The Moral Economy of the Peasant*, Scott (1976) suggests that the desire for subsistence security results in patterns of reciprocity, forced generosity and work sharing to ensure subsistence in rough times.

59. Male = *lue* (Ng); Female = *lavo* (Ng).

60. In Bena, two schools exist. As enrolment numbers are declining, some children have started school at five years old rather than the norm of six years old.

61. On three days, I kept my own record of tourist numbers and compared them with those recorded in the book. On 8 October 1998, there were 7 entries in the book but I counted 21 tourists. On 9 October, an out-of-area guide (see Chapter 5) filled in the book, including noting his impression, 'good', and his nationality, Indonesian, and did not note that he was accompanying eight Caucasian tourists. The following day, I noted five tourists but three were recorded in the book. The figures in Table 4.2 can therefore be regarded as low estimates of reality.

62. This may be partly due to the travel warnings issued by the governments of these countries.

Part 2

Perceptions, Priorities and Attitudes

Chapter 5

The Mediators of Tourism in Ngadha

As discussed in Chapter 2, tourism is a thoroughly mediated activity. A number of go-between actors or 'middlemen' structure and mediate tourists' experiences and their encounters with tourates. The first section of this chapter examines the role of the Indonesian state, specifically at the provincial and regency levels. As well as the actions of the government bodies, the data reveal the values, attitudes and priorities of these actors. It shows how the various layers of government hold differing, and at time competing, voices. In a state as centralised as Indonesia there are many bodies that influence the processes of tourism development at the village level, but few mechanisms for the voices of the villagers to feed back through the multi-layered state structures. The second section examines the role played by guidebooks as mediators of tourists' behaviour and experiences. The third part examines the work of guides, a key group of bridge actors who mediate between tourists and tourates. The final concluding section examines the role of mediators as both intentional and unwitting agents of change in tourism processes in Ngadha.

The Government and Tourism

Governments can play an important role in mediating tourists' perceptions and behaviour in tourism. From the issuing of visas, provision of infrastructure and marketing material, to the information provided by tourist information centres, governments are involved with attracting, directing and structuring the tourists' experience. Decisions about visas are made by the central government. As discussed in Chapter 3 the visa changes in 2003 and 2004 have had a profound effect on tourism to Ngadha. In combination with the actions of other governments through their travel advisories, the nationality and type of tourists has changed considerably (see Chapter 6). The highly centralised Indonesian state is sub-divided into provinces and these are further sub-divided into regencies. Both these levels of government have been important in the development of tourism in Ngadha. Furthermore, until 2003, tourism was covered partly by the Department of Education and Culture and partly by the Department of Tourism. In 2003 a restructuring of local government meant that a new department was created: the Department of Tourism and Culture. This followed a similar restructuring at the national level with the formation of a Ministry of Tourism and Culture, an interesting move that necessarily combines the two fields when developing policies (Salazar, 2005).

The area under consideration falls into the economically poorest regency, of one of the economically poorest provinces (Corner, 1989; Umbu Peku Djawang, 1991). It is important to stress the economic aspect of the poverty for two reasons. Firstly because the *raison d'être* for tourism development, from the government's point of view, is to reduce this poverty (Gunawan, 1999; Simpson & Wall, 1999; Sofield, 1995; Umbu Peku Djawang, 1991; Wiendu Nuryanti, 1998); and secondly, it is the *rich* culture of the region that attracts tourists. The distinction serves to underline that normative conceptions of poverty are framed in economic terms, and rarely consider other interpretations. However, in tourism (particularly in marketing literature) the richness of culture, wealth of biodiversity and so forth are used as selling points.

Views of the provincial level Department of Tourism, Kupang

Cultural tourism (*wisata budaya*) is one of three types of tourism that the provincial Department of Tourism claimed to be targeting (beach tourism and eco-tourism being the others). The Department also claimed to be specifically targeting backpackers, special interest tourists and eco-tourists as the most appropriate type of tourists to come to the province. These were indeed the types of tourist that visited Flores. While the Department might have claimed to be targeting backpackers this was at odds with perceived government policy, which has either tacitly ignored or actively discouraged backpackers (Erb, 2000; Hampton, 1998; Richter, 1993). Targeting backpackers will be even more difficult following the visa changes in 2003/2004 which have resulted in a dramatic decline in the number of young, long-term, backpackers.

The Department's staff firmly believed that culture could be sold for tourism. The head of the Department actually used the words '*kebudayaan bisa dijual*' (culture can be sold) and his staff made numerous references to people and their culture as tourist attractions (*obyek parawisata*):

> 'Tourists are interested in ceremonies, customs and everyday activities that have been passed down for generations and the villagers are happy for the tourists to come because they know tourists don't bring any problems.' 'The negative side-effects of tourists can be dealt with; guides are trained to handle tourists and communication with the villagers. We can stop the youngsters from becoming westernised (*ke-barat-barat-an* Ind) through education programmes. For example,

tourists like to put holes in their ears. For boys to do this is against our culture, so schools have refused to accept boys with pierced ears. This will stop the young people copying the tourists'.

The Department's attitude reflected the view that the culture of the province, and specifically Ngadha, is a commodity to be sold. Further, ways could be found to deal with negative impacts, mainly regarded as westernisation as a result of the 'demonstration effect'.

Other negative impacts of tourism were considered to be 'price wars of handicrafts between villagers and/or villages', which could be dealt with by 'the department fixing prices'; and 'information provision by tour operators or unscrupulous guides that was incorrect and offensive'. This could be dealt with by 'insisting that tour operators use licensed guides and by these guides discussing the official version of culture with the villagers. The information provided could then be true, correct, clear and be based on a source' (*benar, tetap, jelas dan bersumber*).

The Department of Tourism commissioned a tourism development masterplan for the province, which was undertaken by the Institute Tecknologi Bandung (ITB) and published in 1995.[1] The report itemises assets in terms of existing accommodation, restaurants and attractions, and details possible areas for expansion. As the document deals with the entire province, cultural tourism in Ngadha is given very little space. The north coast of the Ngada regency received much more detailed attention. It had just been designated a natural tourist park (*kawasan wisata alam*), as several of the 17 islands off the coast are home to large monitor lizards[2] and the reef is fairly intact. The north-west of the regency has since been designated an economic development zone and there are plans for a large airport and major luxury hotel construction along the coast.

Bajawa, the regency capital, is listed as a town that should be developed as a resting-place, due to its location between Labuhan Bajo (gateway to Komodo National Park) and Ende (gateway for Keli-Mutu National Park). The report notes that 'besides its luck of location, it has the additional attraction of the traditional village of Bena'. From reading the report, one would imagine that there are only two traditional villages in Ngada, and only Bena in the Ngadha area.[3] Members of the Department explained that, due to budget limitations, their efforts had been concentrated in one village, Bena. This village development was to act as a showcase for other villages to learn from. The development plan had two central elements: the building of the homestays and the 'development'[4] of the villagers.

In 1993, the Provincial Tourism Department funded the building of three traditional style houses as homestays and another as a souvenir shop, a concrete viewing post at the top of the village, next to the villager's shrine, and two toilets. Through negotiations with the village headman, a ticket system was introduced. The receipts are divided as follows: 5% to the ticket seller and of the remainder, 30% to the Department of Tourism, 50% to the administrative village and 20% to the *nua*.

Since the opening of a Tourism Department office in Bajawa, in 1996, the responsibilities had been delegated. The Department had hoped that the success of the homestays in Bena could serve as a model for other villages, which would be able to get loans for building similar facilities once the success of those in Bena had been proved. The Department indicated a range of possibilities for sources of credit including private banks and government funding for small tourism projects.[5] They were unaware of any problems and claimed that the guesthouses were functioning under the management group.

The homestays in Bena were not used for tourists but became temporary homes for village members. The failure of the homestays provides a useful example for reflecting on the government's mismanagement of Ngadha tourism development. Firstly, the Department of Tourism worked with the elected village headman, rather than the elders, on a project that affected the *nua*. All issues that affect the *nua* should involve an open meeting (*musyawarah* Ind)[6] with the village elders (and any 'listeners' who wish to take part). Secondly, the traditional style houses were not built using labour from the *nua*. This led to early resentment of the project. Thirdly, no interior furnishings or kitchen equipment were provided so the homestays were not ready for use. Fourthly, no training was provided for the villagers. Some claimed not to even understand what homestays were or their purpose. Fifthly, the fact that there were three homestays, each able to accommodate eight or more guests, implies that they were for groups to use, but no links were made with tour operators to inform them of the homestays. If individuals or couples were to overnight in the village, then the villagers would find it easier to accommodate them in their own homes. If women had been involved in the decision-making, they could have explained the potential difficulty of cooking in two places at once. Finally, the question needs to be asked whether homestays would provide the authentic back-stage focused social interaction sought by the kind of tourists who wish to stay in Ngadha villages.

The viewing post that was built has been important in the structuring of the tourists' experience in Bena. The viewing post is at the far end of the village. Beyond being a vantage point from which to view the spectacular landscape (see Plate 8), it gives tourists a bird's-eye view of the village (see Plate 9). It also gives them a place to head for, a place to rest and a place from which tourees can be observed from a distance. The viewing post structures the tourists' visit as it encourages them to walk up along one side of the village and back down the other. The viewing point, therefore, gives them a purpose beyond gazing on tourees. There was no indication from the Department of Tourism that this structuring of the tourists' visit was deliberate. The post was built to make a safe place from which to view the spectacular scenery.

The Department's staff were keen to point out how tourism would be beneficial for the villagers: 'It would provide an outlet for their handicrafts, specialist regional foods and vegetables, eggs and chickens.' However, to date there has been no help for the villagers in making these linkages. Souvenirs and village sales are a potential area that has yet to be exploited in the villagers' favour. The Department was also keen to point out that cultural tourism (*wisata budaya* Ind) was dependent on the villagers 'maintaining their traditions'.[7] The Department had worked with village 'cultural officers' (*penilik kebudayaan* Ind) in the hope that these local people would 'cultivate and develop' the villagers' culture. Village cultural officers, appointed by the Department of Education and Culture, are responsible for recording local culture, such as noting the position of megaliths, recording local songs and listing traditional buildings. The Department met with these officers and asked them to transmit the importance of the villages' cultural assets to the villagers and ensure that it is not eroded.

When I asked the staff if and how they had ascertained the views of the villagers for the guesthouses and other plans, they said that they had worked with the head of custom (*ketua adat*). However, such a position does not exist in Ngadha customary social organisation. They were in fact working with the administrative head of the village, who created, and appointed himself to, the position of *ketua adat*. The lack of village-level agreement lies at the centre of the non-use of the homestays. The villages of Ngadha have many elders (*tua tua adat*), not a single head, who understand customary matters (*adat*). This misunderstanding (deliberate or not) of the local culture was an essential flaw in the provincial development plan for their show cultural village.

The provincial Department of Tourism suggested the creation of a tourism management group (*kelompok pengolah* Ind) in Bena. This was done and has had significant success. Although the initial set-up of the group was organised by the provincial Tourism Department through official village structures, the make-up and organisation of the management

Plate 8 Views over Flores from the viewing point

Plate 9 Bird's-eye view of Bena from the viewing point

group was decided by the villagers. They decided that it would be made up of one representative chosen by each clan. The group then elected the various officials such as security, cleanliness, chair, secretary, accountant and so forth. These posts are unpaid. The group is entrusted with the authority to make decisions concerning tourism and the allocation of tourism income. As a group, they have a powerful voice in the village and have taken problems of corruption to the regency.

Regency-level perspectives

This local level of government is based in the regency capital of Bajawa. The head of a regency is a Bupati or regent. Bupati was a Javanese title, extended by the Dutch across the archipelago. These 'little kings' had extensive personal and feudal bonds and the power to control rural areas (Van Niel, 1979). Under the New Order government, these men were increasingly recruited from the military (Crouch, 1979). Since the fall of Suharo, the title of Bupati has been dropped, and the people have demo-cratically elected what are now referred to as *Kepala Dareah* (area head). Their power remains substantial.

Great importance is attached to tourism at the regency level as it is Ngada's second most important industry after agriculture. This is espe-cially the case since the regency possesses limited natural resources and has land that is hard to cultivate intensively. Tourism is then seen as a key to economic diversification.

When, in 1997, the north of the regency was designated an economic development zone, tourism development was a major part of the plan. In theory the capital of the regency was to move from Bajawa to Mbay on the north coast where there is room for urban expansion, including an airport. However, the move of an old mountain town in one cultural area to a new coastal location in a different cultural area raised a lot of friction but very little actual movement of the administrative buildings.

In 2005 the regency was considering splitting in two. The neighbouring regency, Manggarai, chose to split in two and many in Ngada felt that ethnic divisions would force a split there too. There were no further actions on a move to Mbay and no start had been made on the airport. The build-ing of an airport closer to the area of study would have an impact on visitor numbers. Plans also include luxury hotel developments on the north coast, which, in combination with better road links, could result in the future in the villages of Ngadha becoming excursion attractions for mass tourism.

Ngada opened its first Department of Tourism's office in Bajawa in 1996. As a consequence it is senior members of the Department of Education and Culture who have been involved with the development of tourism since it began in the 1980s. Efforts to preserve the villages' material culture resulted from this Department's initiatives, as did the appointment of village caretakers (*juru kunci*) and the use of visitors' books, all of which are essential in the understanding of tourism development in Ngadha villages.

As a senior member of the Department of Education and Culture explained, the original culture of the area and its material symbols were considered pagan and irreligious by the Catholic Church, and were not preserved or maintained and therefore began to disappear. Villagers were encouraged to move out of their traditional homes, as these were considered unhealthy. Villagers who cleaned and maintained *ngadhu* and *bhaga* were considered infidels. But, as he went on to explain, the symbols of the ancestors had important bearings on customary social organisation. Without them, status in society was unclear: conflict over rights, responsibilities and ownership resulted from blurred clan make-up. The Department of Education and Culture felt that conflicts in the villages were due to the lack of observance of custom, and that the preservation of the remaining material symbols could help prevent further conflict.

In 1982, the Department of Education and Culture began its restoration programme. This involved appointing village cultural officers (*penilik kebudayaan*) to record and report on the cultural assets of the villages and the appointment of caretakers (*juru kunci*) in selected *nua*. One of the cultural officers, when recording local songs, managed to persuade villagers to set up a cultural studio and obtained government sponsorship. This group has since played at provincial and international music festivals (held in Bali) and for tourists. Their recent success has been limited, as discussed in Chapter 7.

The job of the caretaker is twofold: firstly, to organise the preservation of the villages' material cultural assets i.e. the megaliths, *ngadhu*, *bhaga* and houses, and, secondly, to be responsible for the visitors' book. Caretaker appointments were made according to three criteria: completed primary education, rights in the village (i.e. born to a woman in the village, not married into it, so that they would feel the responsibilities and have the authority) and ability to motivate other villagers. Not all *nua* had caretakers. It is a paid position and the Department could only afford to appoint a limited number of caretakers. This is recognised as a problem by the Department.

The restoration programme was initiated for the benefit of the villagers but it was quickly realised that it was also of benefit to researchers and visitors. It was for this reason that the caretakers were issued with visitors' books. Visitors entered their name, occupation, origin and purpose of visit and could also make a donation towards the restoration of the village. The mutuality of restoration and visitor attraction is well understood by the Department of Education and Culture. The only village that received financial help for its restoration programme was Bena. This was because, as discussed in Chapter 4, Bena is considered the 'eldest sibling' village and has priority as a result. Furthermore there was only a small amount of restoration needed, access was relatively easy[8] and funds were extremely limited.

The Department has never concerned itself with the funds the villages receive. As one representative told me: 'The funds are for the villagers to use as they see fit and their allocation should be decided by village elders (*tua tua adat*).' Conflict has arisen in both villages as a result of fund allocation. In Bena, the conflict is over the allocation of funds from tickets and corruption at the administrative village level. The Department of Education and Culture approved of tickets: 'Tickets mean that, although less money may go into the village, it is clear how much there is and there is less potential for conflict.' However, members of the Department of Education and Culture thought that the percentage allocated to the administrative village in Bena did not reflect what had been spent in the *nua* and was bound to cause ill-feeling.

In Wogo, the caretaker appointed initially came into conflict with a man who considers himself the landlord of Wogo. The caretaker felt 'powerless to carry out his task' and that his job 'led to too much bad feeling ... so it was easier to give it up'. The self-appointed landlord took over as caretaker and has collected all the donations from tourists but has not redistributed them. The Department of Education and Culture was aware of the problems in Wogo but felt 'it is a matter that needs to be dealt with further up'. Deference to higher forms of authority is a common way to avoid dealing with issues. Placing responsibility for thorny decisions in the hands of a higher authority avoids the possibility of being blamed for making the wrong decision.

Data on visits to the villages were derived from the Department of Education and Culture visitors' books. Although the Department of Tourism could ascertain the number of visits in Bena (and Bela) from the number of tickets sold, they could not obtain this information from other villages that did not use tickets. Further, other information that should be useful for the Department of Tourism, such as tourists' origins, was collected in the visitors' books but not analysed or used by the Department of Education and Culture. The management group in Bena were requested to break down visitors by country of origin for the Department of Tourism, but, as they pointed out, 'they give us nothing so why should we do that for them?' The caretaker, appointed by the Department of Education and Culture, is paid an honorarium and is therefore willing to collect and provide visitor information requested by that Department. However, the analysis is limited to total numbers of foreign and domestic tourists as the Department of Education and Culture is not interested in a breakdown by nationality.

The staff at the Department of Education and Culture have been personally engaged with tourism on an ad hoc basis but have no formal training. They are well aware of what is going on at village level and, through experience, have useful insights into the working of tourism in the area. However, when the Ngada regency opened its own Department of Tourism, this was no longer their area of responsibility.

A Department of Tourism opened in Ngadha in 1996. The head of the Department was given an intensive two-week training course in tourism. Neither he, or his staff, had much idea of the dynamics of tourism, rarely visited the villages, and had little rapport with the villagers. For example, it was their opinion that 'all the villagers want is for tourists to come and pay the ticket fee. The villagers are not interested in tourism beyond this.' 'I have never heard of any problems about driver-guides from Labuhan Bajo [see below]. Perhaps this is a problem because it means lost opportunities for local guides.' It is clear from these statements that the Department of Tourism staff lack a full understanding of the situation.

The Department of Tourism has vacancies but government departments do not appoint their own staff. Thus, they were unable to appoint a young woman from Nage who had just returned from university in Java with a first class honours degree in tourism from a prestigious institution. She had wanted to work in tourism as she saw this as the best potential for her village's development. It is reasonable to assume that the lack of expertise in the Department will negatively impact on tourism development in the villages, especially when we consider how the villagers look up to authority and have been directed from above for so long. In 2004 one member of staff returned from Java where he had been sponsored to study tourism at master's level. His knowledge and empathy with the villagers' plight was evident but while apologising for the apparent contradictions between rhetoric and reality in the department's action he said: 'The problem is the "bureaucracy ethic", ideas have to come from above, and those in charge have no idea about tourism.'

The centralised system of government in Indonesia meant that the head of the Department felt bound to above authorities and lacked autonomy to take locally appropriate decisions. He was issued with instructions from Kupang (the provincial capital) and was obliged to carry them out. 'Following instructions from Kupang' was frequently given as the rationale for the Department's actions. Thus the guides' training course, which the Department ran in its first year of operation, included half a day on immigration and quarantine matters, of importance only where there is an international air or sea port. As Ngada has neither, the information was largely irrelevant for the trainee guides. 'But,' said the head of Depart█████ 'we were told to include it. Something about local culture might have█ useful but we only had two weeks and there was so much we were t█ cover.'

In its first two years, the Department ran education programmes for local guides and for the villagers of Bena. The villagers' education programme followed a provincial instruction to 'develop the villagers'[9] through the tourism awareness campaign (*sadar wisata*). Tourism awareness was a training programme initiated by the Minister of Tourism in 1989–1990. At the heart of the programme was a seven-point formula to be disseminated through government departments, community groups and youth organisations (Joop Ave, n.d.). The seven-point formula (*sapta persona*) consisted of 'security, orderliness, cleanliness, comfort, natural beauty, friendliness and memories' (Joop Ave, n.d.: 46).

The training programme consisted of a presentation given by the regency tourist office to the villagers of Bena in 1996. The material presented included an explanation of what tourism is, how it benefits the area and its potential negative impacts,[10] how far tourism had come in the last national five-year plan, and the above seven-point formula for successful tourism. The presentation was open to all the villagers, but initially was so badly attended that elders, members of the management team and others were persuaded to attend. The programme provided an overview of the reasons why tourists visit their village and why preservation of both material and non-material culture would serve to develop economic rewards.

As I have discussed elsewhere (Cole, 2005), such public education schemes may seem laudable but their content raise ethical questions. Are such training programmes educating communities or training them for quality subservience? The primary function of training for local participation is to develop the political skills of local people to actively take part in decisions about tourism development, (Goodwin, 1995).

To date, the government programmes in Ngada have emphasized quality service provision i.e. providing for the needs of the tourists. They have attempted to get support for tourism but have not educated residents about tourism development issues or developed their confidence and skills for empowerment.

In 2000, another training programme was organised. Three members each from four villages were invited to attend one and half day's training in Bajawa, the regency town. Each was paid expenses. Three members of the Bena tourism management group attended. 'The same again, just like what they said last time, protection of culture, preservation of our material assets, be good hosts. Nothing new, no help, we did not learn anything' is how the head of the management group described it to me.

Following the success of the ticket system in Bena, the Department of Tourism is keen to introduce a similar system in Wogo 'that would ensure accountability and would be the right way to begin development'. They wrote two letters to the caretaker in Wogo and tried to visit him three times in a matter of months. Having failed to make contact or get a response from the caretaker, a member at the Department said, 'We do not know how to deal with someone who rules like they did in feudal times.' In a similar vein to the Department of Education and Culture, they claimed: 'The only way this can be resolved is if it is sorted out above us.' Again, the Department used deference to a higher level in the Indonesian bureaucracy as an excuse for inaction.

Government and marketing

Marketing and tourist information are two of the major roles of a government tourism department. In this case the government has produced very little marketing material, and what is produced is not well distributed. Information for tourists is virtually non-existent. I was given two booklets produced by the provincial Department, a photocopy of a third and one produced by the Regency Department. One of those produced by the province was clearly aimed at local investors. Entirely in Indonesian, it provides 'basic data' (*data dasar*) on six tourist regions in the province including Riung in the north of Ngada. Bena is included as an *'obyek'* in the area with great potential – a photograph accompanies a sentence of commentary: 'A beautiful panorama, customs and culture make a deeply enjoyable tourist attraction'[11] (Dinas Parawisata Prop. Dati1 NTT, 1998: 12). No mention is made of any other villages in the text. In the list of events, *Reba* in many villages is included. In the list of attractions, megaliths and traditional houses in several villages are included.

The second brochure from the province entitled 'Flores and Alor' (no publisher or date but co-ordinated by the head of the Manggarai Tourism Department) is a 32-page glossy booklet. Four pages are dedicated to Ngadha. The information, which is incomplete and incorrect,[12] again only gives details of Bena as a traditional village in the Ngadha region. The limited text is interspersed with photographs. At the back of the booklet, along with town maps is a section on practical information. A sub-section, travellers' tips, says, 'Conservative dress and behaviour are an expression of courtesy here' and 'Be prepared for a lot of attention and remember tourists are welcome.' Until the code of conduct was distributed in 2005, this was the extent of government initiative to educate tourists about appropriate behaviour or dress when visiting Ngadha villages.

One leaflet claims 'the name Ngada can also be found in the Urdu language of India. Faith in a Supreme Being still exists among the Ngada people although the majority professes to be Catholics ... Most of the inhabitants use primitive farming methods.' The local crafts of weaving and 'making bags from plaited straw' are mentioned. Again, under the list of interesting places Bena is included to the exclusion of other villages. The wording in the leaflets glorifies the simple nature of the villagers' lives. It makes links with their history and points to their pre-Catholic faith despite the fact that the government has actively discouraged it.

Although I managed to acquire copies of these brochures, I never saw any tourists with them. The Department of Tourism in Bajawa does not act as a tourist information centre, although increasingly tourists expect it to. They visit the office expecting it to function as a 'Tourist Information Centre', to provide them with maps, transport information and brochures. Some leave disappointed, as one said, 'What is that place? I have never been to such a useless tourist office anyway in the world.' Others engage with staff from the office who enjoy the opportunity to practise their rusty English conversation skills. The office is not set up to be, or regarded locally as, a tourist information office but is evolving as it responds to visits from tourists who expect a 'Tourist Office' to provide information. A space has been created where tourists can be received, consisting of a desk placed near the entrance behind which a map and some photographs have been arranged. There are no leaflets, postcards, maps or books for the tourists to look at or buy. The lack of promotional material and information for tourists indicates an area in which the government could do much more to mediate the tourists' experiences in Ngadha. Furthermore, the marketing material that has been produced to date illustrates just how Bena is marketed to the exclusion of other villages. This has feed inter-village jealousies and rivalries, one of the conflicts discussed in Chapter Eight.

Guidebooks

As discussed in Chapter 2, guidebooks mediate tourists' experience. They act as a bridge between tourists and destinations, and between tourists and tourates. They are powerful tools that direct the tourists gaze and can make or break local businesses. The authors of guidebooks, who are often reliant on information supplied by tourists, may be regarded as distant actors who influence events locally. Lonely Planet guides were the most common guidebooks to be used by tourists visiting Ngadha. Lonely Planet publishes three relevant guidebooks: one to South East Asia, one on Indonesia and, since 1998, one specifically on Indonesia's Eastern Isles. They all follow the same format. Aimed at the backpacker, they provide a wealth of information on routes between islands, towns and attractions, together with listings of places to stay, places to eat, and things to do and see.

Covering a large area, the Lonely Planet guide to South East Asia deals with Ngadha in a couple of hundred words. Following about 60 words on the geographical setting and 100 words on *bhaga* and *ngadhu*, the guide states that Bena is '19km north[13] of Bajawa' and 'one of the most interesting and traditional villages'. Four other villages, including Wogo, are listed as 'worth visiting' (Taylor, 1997: 321).

The Lonely Planet Indonesia guide and Eastern Isles guide have virtually the same background to Ngada (*sic*: incorrectly spelt without the 'h' see page 3). Approximately 800 words are used to provide details of history, tradition, the importance of the *bhaga* and *ngadhu* and the preservation of animistic beliefs.

As Anderson (2000) discusses, Lonely Planet guidebooks encourage a highly frugal mentality in the visitor. The 1990 edition of their guide to Indonesia advises travellers to negotiate about entrance fees and bring gifts of cigarettes 'to start off on a friendlier, less commercial footing' (Wheeler, 1990: 615). General advice about responsible behaviour is limited but it is possible to discern a slight improvement when comparing the various guides Lonely Planet has produced during the 1990s. In their 1990 edition to Indonesia, advice on conduct was hidden within the 36 pages of 'facts for visitors'. Tourists were advised to take photographs with discretion and women were advised to dress modestly. The section on time is about time differences and there is no mention of different perceptions of time. There is also no mention of begging. The 1997 South East Asia guide has a specific section titled 'society and conduct' but the information given in 400 words is still extremely limited when compared with other guidebooks e.g. Bill Dalton's *Indonesia Handbook*. Lonely Planet's 1998 guide to Indonesia's Eastern Isles makes one specific but important reference to conduct in its section on Ngadha. 'Taking photos is usually not a problem, but ask and remember entering a village is like entering someone's home' (Turner, 1998: 247).

Guidebooks do little to educate tourists about their behaviour in Ngadha villages because they do not give specific advice to tourists and the general advice (presented in the introductory chapters and possibly read many weeks earlier) is too general and very limited. However, there are a number of ways in which guidebooks direct the tourists' experiences. Firstly, the listings influence where tourists stay, where they eat, where they visit, and in some cases which guides they use. As the manager of the Anggrek guesthouse in Bajawa explained:

> We used to be the top *losmen* (guesthouse); we were always full of tourists. Then we installed a TV. Some guests, including some tourists, like to watch the television, but it also for our staff who live here. When someone from Lonely Planet came to check out the hotels, there must have been something popular on and someone might have turned the volume up. In the next edition we were described as 'very noisy' and tourists started going to the Elizabeth or the Kornia.

The drop in popularity of the Anggrek had an effect on the business of two guides that are based at this establishment. For a few years the Anggrek remained one of the few places in town tourists ate, and the guides approached tourists that ate there. But as one of them told me: 'It was much easier when they stayed here, we could help them out, and have a little time to get a bit friendly before talking about the tour.'

Some guidebooks e.g. *The Rough Guide to Indonesia* (Backshall *et al.*, 1999), Periplus' *East of Bali* (Muller, 1991) and Bill Dalton's (1995) *Indonesia Handbook* recommend particular guides. This can have an impact on guides' work and put those not mentioned at a disadvantage. The most used guidebooks – those produced by Lonely Planet – do not mention specific guides. The Eastern Isles edition suggests 'a guide is well worth it – instead of awkwardly fronting up yourself at a village, a good guide will provide an introduction, explanations of local custom and give insight into village life' (Turner, 1998: 247).

Guidebooks are likely to determine where tourists visit. As discussed, Bena has been given precedence in tourism development and marketing by the government. The guides were also more likely to take tourists to Bena (and other villages) than Wogo. The question must be asked how much impact the guidebooks have on the continued preference for Bena over Wogo and other villages. All the guidebooks mention both, but all mention Bena before Wogo (although the lists are not in alphabetical or geographical order). Bena is given at least twice as much space as Wogo and other villages. Bena is variously described as the most beautiful, traditional and even the best. The *Rough Guide* suggests that it is the ritual centre of the area and the place to see festivals. The Lonely Planet guides imply that *Reba* is only held in Bena. It is therefore no surprise that tourists ask their guides to take them to Bena. As one guide told me: 'They believe what they read in the guidebooks, they all want to see Bena for themselves. Transport is too expensive and it takes too long to go to Wogo as well. Most tourists have made up their mind from what the guidebooks say.'

In decisions for my tour company, I was influenced by the guidebooks. In our search for a village to take tourists to, I asked our contact to take us to a village but specified that we did not want Bena. As Bena was in all the guidebooks, it was on 'the beaten track' and our tours were sold to clients as 'off the beaten track'. For a few tourists (and some tour operators), guidebooks serve to delineate the 'beaten track' and serve to specify where not to go. However, for the majority of tourists that visit Ngadha, this is not the case.

The local guides also read guidebooks. We must question, therefore, whether the guidebooks get their narrative from the guides or vice versa. For example, the Lonely Planet's 1998 guide to Indonesia's Eastern Isles states that the model houses and small warrior statues (*ana ye*) represent 'the female and male clan houses respectively' (Turner, 1998: 249). This was also heard as part of the guides' narrative to tourists. These symbols serve to indicate a clan's first and second house respectively, the house of the clan's founding female and founding male respectively. Some tourists I chatted with were confused about seeing men in 'women's houses' and women in 'men's houses' and thought this meant that the villagers were no longer sticking to tradition. Furthermore, could it be that the view expressed by some guides, that Bena receives enough tourists in the high season, has influenced or been influenced by Lonely Planet's 1998 guidebook, which states, 'Bena is far and away the most visited village … It is touristy … and it can be crowded' (Turner, 1998: 249).

Both the guides and Tourism Department employees expressed the view that the electricity poles in Wogo spoil it. Does this come from the reading the guidebooks? The Periplus guide specifically mentions how 'the district's best set of *ngadhu* and *bhaga* sit amidst bright green electricity poles' (Muller, 1991:151), others mention which villages do not have electricity yet. As I have discussed elsewhere (Cole, 2004a) this implied celebration of pre-electricity has worked against other villages getting electricity (see Chapter 8).

Guides

As discussed in Chapter 2, guides, despite their vital role, are a poorly researched stakeholder in the tourism development literature. With a few exceptions (Bras, 2000; Cohen, 1985; Salazar, 2005) they have been treated as a largely homogeneous group. As this section discusses, the guides who bring tourists to the villages of Ngadha are not a homogeneous group. In order to better understand these important actors I have sub-divided them into local Ngadha guides, out-of-area guides, driver guides and tour leaders. Nearly 90% of tourists that visit the villages of Ngadha do so with a guide.

Local guides

I use the term local guide to refer to guides who come from the Ngadha region and work in the villages. Although there are 30 members of the regency guiding association (HPI[14])[15] only 15 were working as guides. Ten of these were working in the villages. None of these guides came from the tourist villages. They originated either in the town of Bajawa or a large village close to the town, called Langga.[16] The association meets on an ad hoc basis about three times a year; usually when there is information to be disseminated from the regency Department of Tourism.

In theory to become a member of the association a guide must be licensed. A licence is issued on completion of a training course, open only to high school graduates. In practice, not all members are licensed or high school graduates. Neither of these factors appeared to have a significant impact on the guides' skills. One of the well-regarded guides was disabled and had dropped out of school at the end of his primary education. As the head of the Tourism Department felt sorry for him he was allowed to attend the training course regardless of the fact he did not have a high school certificate. One of the trained guides who had a high school certificate was one of the guides most regularly complained about. The guiding courses run at regency and provincial level are discussed below.

All the guides are self-employed, working as much or as little as they please and often combining guiding with agricultural or other work. They take as few as 1 tourist and as many as 20 in a group in the high season. On average, they take 4 to 8 tourists and charge US$4 (Rp40,000)[17] per person. The rate was not standard or fixed and they would try for more if they could. From their fee, they would pay for transport and entrance tickets. This could earn a guide a very good salary in local terms if they could find work every day or even be sure of work three times a week. However, the tourist season is short. None of the guides could survive year round on their guiding income. Most had supplementary incomes and combined their work with agriculture.

The local guides resemble the network specialists described by Bras (2000). Representing a transitional position between Cohen's (1985) path-finder and mentor, many had much more than a smattering of a foreign language. One of them spoke fluent English, Dutch and German, and some Japanese. Most had attended a guide training course at the regency level and several had attended an advanced training course at the provincial level. They would offer more than the facts and figures of a professional guide and flavour their tour with a personal touch and interpretations of the local culture. They were freelancers who would make contact with tourists at their points of arrival. Formerly, they used to wait at the bus station for tourists but, more recently, due to the tourists' increased use of hired vehicles, they usually approached them in the guesthouses and restaurants in Bajawa. Their work involved guiding tourists who often formed temporary groups in order to keep costs down. As the groups are very transient, and with the guide only for a day, tension management and group interaction[18] were not important roles played by these guides. Some of the Ngadha guides worked alongside European tour leaders, accompanying the day tour in the Ngadha region. In these circumstances, the guides would often be responsible for local administrative tasks, such as hotel bookings and meal payments.

Most of the guides' work involved taking tourists on a day 'package' from Bajawa. This would include visiting between one and three villages in the morning, lunch, either with relatives, or at a restaurant in town, and a visit to the hot springs north of Bajawa in the afternoon. Some guides worked as 'path-breakers', leading tourists to villages with no vehicular access and not normally visited by tourists. Villages that were just off a road became increasing popular. A new periphery to this peripheral tourist area was therefore being created over time. Working as path-finders on hikes made up a very small proportion of the guides' employment since few tourists enjoyed the arduous walking, in the heat, which was involved. Occasionally tourists would hire a local guide to lead them up the volcano. Few of the guides enjoyed this type of work. Expressing a common view, one guide said: 'It is too hard and tiring. We have to set off at 4am. It is exhausting, and tourists do not pay that much.'

Nearly all guides offer very similar standardised day tours. They have both co-operative and competitive relations with each other. They compete for the tourists but, in a similar way to the guides of Lombok and Yogyakarta, 'they use each other's resources, pass on jobs to each other, share each other's income. In this way they establish ties of reciprocity' (Dahles & Bras, 1999: 276). They share profits with family and friends instead of reinvesting them. The guides discussed the problems of working in such observable work. 'My family or friends can see if I have tourists, they know when I have a big group, they know I will have cash. Someone in the family always has some kind of pressing need, it's impossible to refuse'. Few of the guides appeared to be amassing any wealth from their profession due to family obligations and pressures to redistribute wealth. The one guide that withstands redistribution pressures is unpopular as a consequence. Work satisfaction was as important as financial reasons for their choice of occupation. Being able to practise their language skills was another important reason for their choice of work. One learnt English through listening to the BBC World Service; he then worked as a guide while he was at high school to practise his skills. This has enabled him to get a job with an international organisation – the United Nations High Commission for Refugees (UNHCR) and to go on to get a scholarship to undertake post-graduate studies in the UK. Several other young men who have worked as guides have gone on to use their language skills to get work with international organisations (e.g. AUSAID). They have left Ngadha to experience life in Jakarta and beyond. They have used their relations with tourists and other westerners to help finance the education of their siblings. They have become agents of change in their communities. Their jobs with westerners have not only brought them economic benefits but also respect. They have been able to use their influence on house, clan and *nua* decisions.

Strategic relations with the drivers of private vehicles are central to the success of Ngadha guides. Public transport to Bena, on the back of trucks, is irregular and hard for tourists to access, and they rarely wish to walk. The Ngadha guides work with drivers to facilitate access to the most popular villages. Rarely would a tourist be able to access transport to Bena without paying for guiding services. One of the guides arranges transport for tour groups on the trucks. This, he said, gave them a more authentic experience. However, transport to Bena and other villages on this route is exceedingly limited and use by tourists could cause resentment among villagers. In 2004 both Suzuki and Honda opened sales outlets in Bajawa. Motorbikes were offered on credit with very small down payment requirements. The number of motorcycle taxis (*ojeg*) exploded and a new form of transport was open to tourists. In 2005 one guide regularly took individuals by motorbike and some tourists were renting motorbikes to visit villages without a guide.

Although there were many similarities between Ngadha guides and those analysed by Bras and Dahles, tourism on Flores is less well developed than on Java or Lombok and differs in several fundamental ways. The 'gigolo scene', for example, does not exist in Ngadha, so it is normal for tourists to be taken to the guide's home, usually for meals, with little suspicion developing from friends and family. Ngadha guides, though not tainted as gigolos, are marginalised and deemed untrustworthy by more conservative members of their community: their western hairstyles, clothes, friendly relations with female tourists and tour leaders set them apart. Some guides have moved away to avoid this prejudice.

Ngadha guides mediate between the villagers and the tourists and organise services for the tourists. The communication component of a guide's work can be divided into selection, interpretation, information and fabrication (Cohen, 1985). As already noted, the guides did little by way of selection for two reasons. The tourists had pre-selected where they wanted to go from the guidebooks and the guides generally provided a fairly standardised product. It is the area of information provision and interpretation that was important according to all the stakeholders. The work of Ngadha guides is principally concerned with cultural issues. They provide information about the livelihoods, rituals, social organisation and arts of the villages. Like anthropologists, they translate the strangeness of a foreign culture into a cultural idiom familiar to the audience. Consequently, cultural knowledge was required and disseminated by the guides. The guide as go-between has the role of bridging the cultural gap between tourist and tourate to prevent misunderstandings and conflict. From the villagers' perspective, the responsibilities of the guides fall into two areas: the dissemination of the correct information, and the management of tourist behaviour.

Guides' knowledge and narratives

The villagers thought the guides' cultural knowledge of Ngadha was insufficient and / or 'guides are not interested in telling the "right" narratives, only in getting money'. The worst offence was caused when a guide claimed that a *ngadhu* was for chickens to roost in and a *bhaga* was a child's playhouse! These are extreme examples but I became aware of a variety of different narratives about various features of the village, while eavesdropping on guides' narratives.

There were clear differences in how certain aspects of Ngadha culture are explained to tourists. The meaning of miniature houses (*ana ye*) on the roofs of some houses provides a good example. Some guides thought it identified 'the women's house', some thought it was 'a spirit house' and some suggested, correctly, that 'it served to identify a clan's central house'. There are however elements of truth in all three responses: miniature houses are associated with women,[19] and the central house is responsible for the *bhaga*, a female symbol. The ancestors are considered to reside in a number of places in clan houses, including the *ana ye*, so a rough translation could lead to it being referred to as a spirit house. The guides blame the variation in their narratives on the lack of a published book on the culture of Ngadha and the lack of dissemination of cultural information at the guides' training course.

The guides agreed that their knowledge of their own culture was insufficient to accurately answer all the tourists' questions. However, these guides could not admit to their clients that they did not know: it would cause them loss of face (*malu*). In order to avoid this, the guide's solution lay between 'keying' (Goffman, 1974: 45ff) and fabrication. Keying, the overemphasis of some aspects at the expense of others, was used to enhance the guide's narratives. Aware that tourists are attracted to the villages because of their difference from the tourists' own culture, guides would emphasise differences. For example, they would talk about family size using examples from the adult generation to point out large family size instead of pointing out the smaller size of many families in the present generation. Guides would talk about the large number of buffaloes slaughtered at rituals when pointing out horns displayed on houses. However, few of them would point out that usually a far smaller number of buffalo are now slaughtered at rituals. Focusing on aspects of culture that are particularly different from tourists' own was also a role adopted by the guides studied by Salazar (2005). However, unlike them, none of the Ngadha guides had been to Europe or attended courses in European culture; the Ngadha guides had all learnt on the job.

Falsification and fabrication were used less frequently. Tourists were unaware of either. One tourist I met in Labuhan Bajo read from his diary what he had written about Ngadha culture, as learnt from his guide. He had had 'a fantastic day' and thought he had learnt so much, and found it 'hard to believe that such a primitive society still existed'. He recounted much false cultural detail that his guide had told him e.g. 'annual festivals where scores of buffalo are slaughtered'. Clearly some guides falsify their cultural narratives more than others do. In many cases, tourists expressed greater satisfaction with a guide who had provided an enjoyable day (even if it was full of falsification of which they were unaware), than with a guide who lectured them on Ngadha culture beyond their capacity to enjoy it.

The guides' work as culture-brokers involves translating the villagers' culture to the tourists. The villagers' culture is complex and tourists' level of understanding and desire to learn is variable. As Crick (1992) discusses, guides have the insight to read a social situation, and the Ngadha guides, like those in Yogyakarta, 'subtly adapt the depth of their information' and pitch their narratives at 'the average intellectual level of the group' (Salazar, 2005: 639). A continuum exists between the guide as entertainer and guide as educator. Part of the role of a guide is to assess their clients quickly and adapt their pitch, communicative talents and performance skills accordingly. Dealing with transient groups of tourists, who had a variety of demand levels, challenged the best guides' attempts to provide accuracy and entertainment.

Managing tourists' behaviour

The second element of the guide's responsibility that is central to the role as go-between or bridge actor is that of managing tourists' behaviour. All the Ngadha guides agreed that they should prevent their tourists kissing in public but, beyond this, at the time of my long fieldwork, there was little agreement on how to go about managing tourist behaviour. There was a far greater consensus after I had shared the results of my fieldwork and the guides joined in the production of the codes of conduct for tourists.

Although they all claimed to agree that guides are responsible for telling tourists what clothes are appropriate,[20] in practice this does not happen. Tourists reported that they were not told, even if they asked. The guides explained the gap between theory and practice in the difficulty they had in expressing anything to the tourists that might put them off. If they were to become authoritarian in any way, they feared it would result in a bad reputation and fewer clients. They did not feel that they had the appropriate language to explain the concept of 'conservative dress' to tourists and were uneasy about pointing out the problems they had with women's clothing. Tourists would be offended, embarrassed or angry, they thought, if they pointed out that, according to the local culture, they were revealing 'too much flesh' or 'private body parts', including navels. Just as they avoided loss of face (*malu*) themselves, by keying, they should not cause a tourist to lose face. It is not culturally acceptable to chastise someone in public in case they are caused to feel *malu*. It is very unlikely that the guides would have an opportunity to mention such subjects in private with female tourists.

The guides in Ngadha agreed that the situation would be aided by the display of codes of conduct in the guesthouses in Bajawa. In this way, rules could be established and the codes of conduct could be pointed out, without any potential for causing offence. The guides took an active part in the initial drafting of a code of conduct – what tourists should know before visiting the villages. They were also keen to scrutinise it and suggest changes to the language after it was piloted. The guides thought the code of conduct was working. On one occasion in 2005, two tourists were seen with their sarongs wrapped around bare shoulders and over the top of shorts. One the guides said to me, 'see it works', making reference to the code of conduct. The guides also discussed ways to improve the dissemination and display of the codes. Several guides thought that more guesthouses would be willing to display the code if it looked official; it needed to have government approval or an official stamp to carry weight locally.

Guide training courses

The guides' training course provides an official certificate: 'an outward measure or symbol of achievement, [and] the essential foundation of a certificate is education' (Pond, 1993: 98). However, the guides believe that they learn on the job and that the training course is purely a formality, as it does not provide them with the necessary education. Certainly, there is no examination or summarative assessment in order to measure the education gained. Unlike in Lombok, there was no examination for extensions to guides' licences (Bras, 2000). According to Pond (1993), guide training requires two essential elements: subject and skills. As will be seen from the analysis of the training programme these guides attended, the course falls short in both these elements.

When the Department of Tourism office was established in Ngada, one of the first things the head of the Department did was to run Ngada's first guide training course. Some of the guides were already working at this time. In order for the course to be seen as a success, students that attended were paid by the Department. This resulted in some people attending to receive the payment rather than the course material and licence. According to national legislation, only high school graduates are allowed to attend these courses. This ruled out several of the active guides.

The course lasted ten days and covered 22 subject areas. Subject matter included aspects of law, the history of Indonesia, state philosophy and the constitution, national consciousness, quarantine for animals and plants, earth science, safety and hygiene. With such a variety of subject areas, little depth was given to any. A lecture was given by the Department of Education and Culture but the terms of reference were (1) Indonesian culture; and (2) the laws pertaining to the preservation of historic monuments. The most thorough coverage was on guiding technique from the perspective of guides as ambassadors (cf. Bras, 2000). It covered the importance of guides, as the first and often most influential Indonesian tourists will meet, and the need to be prompt, polite and friendly.

The guiding course made no reference to the importance of a guide as translator of culture, i.e. as a go-between. As Steege *et al.* researching guide training in Lombok found, 'the local community is ignored …. Being a 'bridge actor' … is not regarded as important in government courses.' (1999: 124). As Gurung *et al.* note, in reference to Nepal, 'the prime focus of guide training is meeting the needs of clients rather than safeguarding the resource base' (1996: 125). As tourism is a service industry, priority is given to clients' needs.

The management of tourist behaviour was considered by the villagers to be a very important role for guides and a contentious issue by the guides themselves. If the guide training course is representative of the official government view, management of tourists' behaviour is conspicuous by its absence. There was no mention of the responsibility of the guide to educate and inform the tourists about appropriate behaviour and clothing when visiting the villages. It did not include the need for a guide to introduce himself, and the tourists, to the villagers nor the importance of polite and friendly relations with the local people (Cole, 1997b). Many guides bemoaned the lack of information about local culture in the course. Further, no training was given to further the guides' business management or entrepreneurial skills.

Six of the Ngadha guides had a provincial licence, issued in Kupang by the provincial government. The guides who attended reported it was little different from the regency course. 'No different, the same boring nonsense, with more about immigration rules' is how one guide described the course on his return. The course was even further removed from the guide's needs. It dealt, for example, with issues of immigration, which may be useful for a guide working in a town with an international airport, but not for those whose work is confined to Ngadha. Guides who hold a provincial licence are allowed to work as guides anywhere in the province. This allows guides from further afield to work in the Ngadha area.

Out-of-area guides

These guides fall on a continuum between amateurs and professionals with typical out-of-area guides lying between the two. Out-of-area guides cause more ill-feeling with villagers than local guides. The descriptions below illustrate three types of out-of-area guides.

La'a dulu [21] (Ng) / *'The Cowboy' guide* [22]

Many tourists begin their trip through the Eastern Islands in Bali or Lombok where they may, especially if they are younger women, find a local companion (cf. Dahles & Bras, 1999). These men then lead their new-found friends through the islands. These men would not admit to not knowing about the local culture. They are, however, frequently less knowledgeable than western tourists and they are keen to imitate western behaviour. It is these 'guides' who have been known to kiss in front of *bhaga*, to hold hands in public and to demean local cultural values as primitive.

A second trip may be made once they 'know' the Eastern Islands well enough to sell themselves to tourists who are 'fed up with the hassle' of Bali and Lombok. The self-appointed 'cowboy' guide wants little more than to cover his costs. He takes a large bag of sweets for the children and cigarettes for the men so that the villagers will be friendly. When I have suggested to such guides that they could engage locals as guides, and translate for the tourists, they stated that the locals are 'too primitive' and that there were no signs indicating that such local guides were available.

The 'typical' guide

The 'typical' guide could be characterised as a male in his twenties with a high school education and perhaps a semester or two at college. They can converse in English and/or another foreign language. They work for national tour operators such as Ramayana or Mega Buana and have probably entered the profession through a relative or close family friend. Their clients arrive at either Maumere or Labuhan Bajo and travel to the other end of Flores via Keli Mutu in between three and six days. These guides will readily admit their shortcomings and are embarrassed by their own lack of knowledge. They successfully hide this from the tourists, who expect little else from their 'third world' guide. Some are less self-effacing and, as one informed me, 'I'm native Flores, so I know.' However, I frequently heard flawed accounts given by these guides.

The 'professional' guide

'Professional' guides do exist on Flores. These guides have excellent language skills and take large groups of tourists, and thus fulfil the criteria set by Cohen (1985). However, the tourist type that they guide, and particularly the schedule they are working to, leads to its own set of problems. They don't explain the weaving process in Bena:[23] The tourists are told that 'it is the same as in Maumere'.[24] They don't use a local to explain the culture because 'they take too long. We must stick to the schedule.' They concentrated on the fluent operation of the whole tour to the detriment of detailed interpretation of local phenomena or developing relations with villagers. One such guide, who called himself an activist, is a member of Contours and a follower of Tourism Concern on the Internet. He said: 'I'm ruining the culture, but I have to separate idealism from reality. I earn my living doing this.' Professional guides may be indistinguishable from Indonesian tour leaders. Some accompany tours that visit a variety of destinations and some work alongside local guides or site-specific guides.

Driver guides

These men are strictly speaking not guides and many will tell you: 'I'm not a guide, I'm just a driver.' Indeed, many work purely as drivers, together with guides from any of the above categories. However, increasingly, and particularly since the economic crisis, tourists form groups and hire a car and driver in Labuhan Bajo or Maumere to take them across the island. The drivers become familiar with the tourist routes and deliver the tourists to the villages. Many park at the entrance and remain in their cars (or the shop in Bena) and leave the tourists to walk around. Their English is limited and their cultural knowledge likewise. They were rarely heard providing false information to tourists but the villagers and guides dislike them. The guides lose business because of them and the tourists wander around on their own without any interpretation at all. The villagers are most perplexed by these tourists who show little respect for the villagers' way of life. Villagers frequently asked me: 'Why do they come? They know nothing from just looking. What do they want?'

Driver guides are not licensed to guide tourists around the villages. However, as members of the management team in Bena said: 'How do we know if he has a provincial licence? He could get angry if he has.' Or: 'He could be a local tourist if he buys a ticket. How do we know he is a "wild guide" (*guide liar* Ind)?' When a driver was new, the villagers were unable to distinguish if he was a provincial guide, a domestic tourist, or an unofficial (wild) guide. Due to the collectivisist nature of Indonesian culture, the desire for harmony and the avoidance of conflict, the villagers were unlikely to confront the drivers in case a dispute ensued. Driver guides that came regularly rarely attempted to guide tourists around the villages. However, they frequently dropped off poorly dressed groups of tourists who were unaware that their dress and 'horseplay' were causing offence.

Tour leaders

Tour leaders also work to mediate the tourists' experiences and behaviour in Ngadha villages. They differ from guides in that they are usually staff from countries where tourists originate or are Indonesians leading tours to a variety of provinces. In many cases, they work alongside local guides. I worked as a tour leader taking tours to Ngadha for six years. I also had long chats, over dinner, with the tour leader of a Dutch-based tour company that brings the most groups to Ngadha and a Danish couple who were planning to operate tours in the area. Only my own company and one other (see below) arranged for tourists to stay in the villagers' homes. All the other tour operators stay overnight in Bajawa and take excursions to the villages.

The tour leader from the most used tour operator works alongside a local guide. The tour follows the same path that the local guides take. The leader told me: 'We try to visit villages that do not receive many tourists. We still go to Bena but we spend much more time in Bela, Luba and Nage.' My own company also thought it was important to stay in a less visited village. However, the Danish couple thought it was important to 'consider the capacity of a village to take tourism pressure'.

On the subject of managing the tourists' behaviour, the leader from the Dutch-based company said: 'We certainly do not allow our guests to give out sweets to kids or wear inappropriate clothing.' The Danish couple has meetings with clients in Denmark in winter: 'They are more about instructions than information and we provide a 50-page booklet which includes general and specific dos and donts.'

One of the successes of my own tour company was that both a western and an Indonesian tour leader accompanied tours. When we first visited Wogo, the villagers stressed to my Indonesian partner the importance of the tourists being correctly dressed, if they were to stay in the village. As a western female, I was able to be strict with the groups and strongly direct what clothing should be worn, in a way that an Indonesian would consider to be causing offence.

When I suggested to one of our Indonesian employees that he should take a very small group alone, he said: 'Yeah, but I cannot possibly explain to tourists what clothes are unacceptable the way you do. What happens if on a village visit they dress in a mini skirt? We always get some clients who like exposing themselves.' When I suggested it was his duty to explain he stared at me – surely I knew – 'for an Indonesian it's too difficult'.

On their exploratory trip, the Danish couple used a local guide. They did not think he was informative and thought that local guide improvement was essential for upgrading tourism in the region. 'They need to provide more deep information, more stories from the local people. I don't think we would use one except perhaps for translation.'

Not all foreign tour operators had the responsible attitudes of those described. An Austrian company takes groups of 8 to 18 tourists once a month through the high season. They stay for one night, usually in Bena. I have met them on several occasions over the years. In 1998 while stopping to view Wogo on route to Bena, they became aware of preparations for a ritual. They spontaneously changed their plans and stayed in Wogo (see Chapter 7). They failed to show up in Bena, where preparations had been made for their stay. In 2005 the same tour leader arrived in Bena with a group. They brought their own picnic including bottles of beer, and palm spirit (*arak*) from Bali. While several of the tourists said they would have delighted in the chance to taste local food the tour leader told me, 'I cant take the risk my group wont like the food, anyway what kind of food could a village like this possibly offer us?' The local shop in Bena sells beer, and the *arak* from Ngadha is one of the most prized brews in Indonesia. Since the beer the Austrians brought had become warm (from being transported on their bus all day) they asked to swap it for the slightly colder beer from the village shop. Their tour leader then asked Om Alo for the blankets he keeps in his house. He brought them in 1996 and told Om Alo not to use them but to look after them, for the exclusive use of his tourists. When I asked why he didn't bring blankets and donate them to the various houses his tourists stayed in he said: 'That means I'd have to buy them each time, its easier to keep a stock here.' Om Alo said to me: 'We wouldn't have use for blankets as bad as these.'[25]

As in the case with my tours, the Austrian tourists were distributed around a number of houses, which receive a donation for putting up three or four tourists. In order for houses to equitably share in the few tourists that come to stay, the village agreement is for the hosting to rotate around the village. When the tour leader asked to use the same, closest houses, for the second visit on the trot Om Alo tried to explain the village agreement but his words fell on deaf ears. He thought the Austrian maybe didn't understand and asked me to explain in English. I was told: 'I don't need your help, I can speak Indonesian quite well enough. I want my clients to stay at this end of the village, it is too far to carry their bags up there'.

A tour group of this nature puts some villagers to considerable inconvenience (for example, moving children out to neighbouring houses to make room for the tourists to stay) but minimal economic benefit. The donations amounted to a tenth of the cost of staying in a guesthouse in town. Furthermore, interactions with the villagers were minimal. After arrival the tourists settled down to their picnic in front of the village shop. Following distribution to the various houses where beds were prepared, the group reconvened for a night walk to the local hot springs. By the time they returned most villagers had turned in but their hosts waited to see them settled and wish them good night. In the morning the tourists were served tea and coffee and exchanged a few words with their hosts before meeting together at the viewing post for a talk from their tour leader. They then returned through the village to their bus and departed for their next destination. None of the tourists purchased any souvenirs. I was told this was typical. It would appear that the village was used as little more than a cheap (and exotic) overnight resting place.

High school trainee guides

When 180 tourism students, many of whom hoped to become guides, came to overnight in Wogo some common issues were highlighted. According to the school's headteacher, the field trip was organised 'in order for the students to know the local traditional culture'. However, following a long journey, and a party that lasted until dawn there was little time to learn about local traditional culture, even if these non-Ngadha students were so inclined.

Their enthusiasm to use English, 'the language of tourism', led to misunderstandings that I heard repeated by guides, time and time again. For example, translating the local Ngadha term *woe* as 'ethnic group' led to guides telling tourists 'there are nine ethnic groups in Wogo'. It was clear from the type of questions that the students asked that they did not have any deep interest in the local culture. All they really wanted were soundbites that would impress tourists, culture rendered into a few memorable phrases that could be regurgitated when passing through the area.

The headteacher was keen that data were collected: 'it is important that someone goes to the hot spring and gets the data on what's there so we know what "objects" there are in this area'. The term for tourist attraction in Indonesian is *obyek parawisata* (tourist objects). All attractions are recorded and listed: a lake, a view, a traditional house, a traditional village and so on. The headteacher's data collection reiterated and reconfirmed the objectification of attractions in Indonesia. The field trip served to reinforce the village (and its occupants) as objects that could be explained in a few memorable English phrases. The local culture was essentialised so it could be reproduced in a simple standardised narrative.

Mediators and Change

This chapter has examined the actors that mediate tourism in Ngadha. The actions (and inaction) of government departments, the narrative in guidebooks, and the words and deeds of guides influence the way tourists and villagers experience tourism in Ngadha. Over the years they have been both intentional agents of change and have also unwittingly been party to the processes that have lead to change and, in some cases, the lack of it.

Overall, it can be seen that the government's perceptions of tourism follows a well-documented pattern of tourism in less economically developed countries. Tourism is seen as important to generate income and diversify the economy. As with other highly centralised new nation-states, power from the centre comes down through the bureaucratic structures.

There is little or no co-operation between departments and few mechanisms for the flow of information from the bottom upwards. Those lower down the structure are fearful of authority and not empowered to act on their own initiative. State structures are one of the barriers to bottom-up entrepreneurial change.

The provincial government has provided physical structures in Bena. The homestays and souvenir shop, which are not used for their original purposes, serve to illustrate how not to manage tourism in Ngadha. The viewing post is used daily and is important in structuring the tourists' experience in the *nua*. The creation of the tourism management group and the use of tickets in Bena have been important actions in the management of tourism in Bena. The sale of tickets has been part of the commodification of this village, a process, which as we will see, is negative according to many tourists. The government's minimal marketing efforts have marketed Bena to the exclusion of other villages.

The appointments of caretakers and cultural officers have encouraged the preservation of the outward signs of the villagers' culture and have thus been important aspects of tourism development. However, as we shall see, by ascribing heritage status to the villagers' material culture it has consigned it to the past, removed it from context, and disconnected it from the living culture.

The Department of Tourism ran educational programmes for guides and villagers. These attempts to professionalise tourism in the area have had limited success. In 2003 a local government reorganisation placed Tourism and Culture in the same department. The new department better reflects local needs and should result in fewer gaps and reduced duplication of responsibilities and less competition over limited resources.

Guidebooks influence where tourists stay and which villages they visit but do little to influence tourists' behaviour in the villages. Guidebooks contain incorrect information, inaccuracies and myths. As tourist numbers have increased so has the amount of information about Ngadha in most of the guidebooks. However, they continue to exoticize and glorify the culture and lives of the villagers and fail to relay any information about the contemporary lives, poverty and problems the villagers face. Some of the information feeds back into the local communities and may directly or indirectly influence the guides and the government, as well as the tourists.

Guides are the most visible bridge-actors or go-betweens in Ngadha tourism. There is a variety of different types of guides. The local self-employed guides offer a standardised day package. They take more tourists to Bena than Wogo because the former has a reputation and tourists want to go there. The guides' work as culture-brokers requires translating the strange culture of the village into an idiom familiar to a range of tourists. Many guides did not feel they had the cultural knowledge to satisfy the demands of some tourists. As the number of tourists has increased over the years so has the number and type of guides. As the local guides face competition with a variety of types of out-of-area guides and drivers delivering tourists to the most visited village, they take tourists further a field. As tourists still want to visit the famous village of Bena they visit this and other villages. As a consequence tourists spend less time in Bena. Local guides also face competition from motorcycle taxis that have multiplied rapidly in recent years. Individual tourists and couples can rent motorcycles with (or very occasionally without) drivers to take tours of the villages. This makes it harder for local guides to form a group to hire a minibus for their tours.

Several local guides have developed long-term relationships with foreigners and foreign organisations. They have developed knowledge and contacts and been able to make strategic use of personal and economic resources. As a result guides have become important agents of change within Ngadha communities. Despite increased competition and a shorter season, guides have consistently praised their vocation. Their reasons: making use of their skills, the autonomy of self-employment, being valued by tourists and villagers, and their links with foreigners, have remained unchanged over the years.

Governments, guidebooks and guides have all been agents in the objectification and essentialisation of the villagers' culture. The life of this marginal community is romanticised and presented as exotic. The realities of the villagers' everyday lives are excluded from the narratives presented in guidebooks, government marketing material and the guides' stories. The guides overemphasise some aspects of Ngadha culture. Markers relating to the material aspects of tradition (e.g. megaliths and traditional houses) and the past (e.g. large families and large numbers of buffalo slaughtered) presenting a romantic, frozen, unchanging image of culture are used at the expense of explaining contemporary aspects of the villagers' lives.

Notes

1. Rencana Induk Pengembangan parawisata Dareah NTT. Laporan akhir (1995) Bandung: Pusat Penelitian Keparawisataan ITB.
2. These may be the same species as Komodo dragons (*Veranus komodensis*) or may be a different species.
3. The other traditional village that is noted is Soa, a village known for its hot springs and traditional boxing matches that attract tourists. However, this

village lies to the north of Bajawa and does not fall into the cultural area under consideration here.

4. *Membina* = to develop or cultivate (Echols & Shadily, 1989).
5. IDT Instruksi Desa Tertinggal: finances for the least developed villages in Indonesia was considered a good source of credit by both this Department and the regency Department. Funds are allocated per head to villages in the poorest areas of Indonesia for villagers' projects. A lot of the funds go unused, I was told.
6. Ngadha term = *utu bhuo*.
7. *Budaya harus dipertahankan*.
8. In comparison with Nage but not with Wogo.
9. *Membina masyrakat* (Ind).
10. *dampak negatif* (Ind).
11. *Panorama alam yang indah, adat istiadat dan kebudayaan yang merupakan obyek wisata yang dapat dinikmati*.
12. For example, 'Bena has three tiers of *bamboo* houses'.
13. Bena is south of Bajawa.
14. Himpunan Pramuwisata Indonesia, a local branch of a pan-Indonesian professional association.
15. For a discussion on the development and politics of this organisation see Dahles (2002).
16. This is important because of the way the guides are talked about by the villagers and it also indicates how identity is drawn and redrawn. The guides from Ngadha are less disliked than guides from further afield, but they come from a different village and local people say, 'they cannot really know our culture'.
17. Average exchange rate in 1998.
18. The social components within the leadership sphere in Cohen's model.
19. The clan's second house has a small warrior on top.
20. Because they knew that it was one of my 'pet' subjects, I suspect.
21. *La'a* = travel; *dulu* = together. The expression implies only together for their travels.
22. Term frequently used by local guides when speaking in English and 'Cowboy' has entered Indonesian colloquial language.
23. Bena women are aware that sales are greater when guides make the effort to explain the process. They claim to know that tourists ask for information about the weaving and are unhappy that explanations are not forthcoming. They also claim that guides do not quote the correct prices, or warn the tourists that Bena ikats are expensive without pointing out the reasons why.
24. The principle of ikat is the same all over the Eastern Islands of Indonesia. The motifs, colours and yarns are quite different.
25. '*Kita juga tidak ada pakai kain panas sejelek ini*'. While in 1996 it was very difficult to get soft warm blankets they are now much easier to find and relatively cheaper (although still a considerable expense for most villagers).

Chapter 6

The Tourists and their Perceptions of Tourism in Ngadha

This chapter explores tourism in Ngadha from the perspective of the tourists. The tourists' values, attitudes and behaviour are not homogeneous. Although they are all cultural tourists, seeking the exotic Other, they vary in a number of fundamental ways. Following an examination of their variation, I discuss the factors that affect the tourists' perceptions. Their attitudes to commercialisation and attending rituals are then discussed before I examine the tourists' varying desires for social interaction and the factors affecting their behaviour management. The final section examines how the tourists have changed over the years I have been visiting the villages.

Some Tourists in Ngadha

Margaret

Margaret was in the first group I took to Wogo. She was an experienced tourist in her late fifties. Despite the problems she reports in her diary, she described her stay in Wogo as 'the best bit' of her 'most fantastic trip'. She suggested that we rename Wogo as something else in our marketing material so that no one else finds it. 'It's such a special place it would be terrible if it was spoilt by tourists'.

> Immediately surrounded by youngsters, we rather hesitantly got off the bus. With great ceremony we were ushered to sit on mats on the terrace of one of their splendid houses … Sitting like royalty on the platform ever increasing numbers of children and adults packed the compound in front of us. Fingers started pointing at cameras and then back at themselves. Having sought permission from Stroma we began to take photos. The youngsters clapped and cheered with delight every time the flash went off. Tea and coffee were made and passed around (eventually without sugar!!) They were amazed we don't like sugar.

> I was longing to spend a penny but did not know where to go. The welcome speeches were going on and on. As we sat cross-legged on the floor we thought our legs would go numb.

We had to bed down on a wide woven mat on the wooden floorboards. Our hosts watched as we prepared for bed. Staying dressed and donning jumpers we were most uncomfortable and freezing! Huge wafts of cold air rose through the slatted floor. It was impossible to sleep, with our hosts chatting and rustling noises in the rafters. Jane said she saw a rat run along the rafter above her head!

Extracts from Margaret's diary (1989)

Bernard

Bernard, a 31-year-old German, was travelling across Flores as part of his six-month travels. He wanted to go to Bena because it was in his guide-book (*South East Asia on a Shoestring*) and joined a group with a guide mainly to facilitate transport to Bena. With his local guide, he had visited Bela, Luba and Bena. They had returned to the guide's house in Langga for lunch and spent the afternoon at the hot springs in Soa. Bernard thought that the trip visited too many places in too little time. He had wanted to leave earlier in the morning and spend more time in one village. 'You need to spend more time in one village to have a good cultural experience. I took photographs of the people, they didn't mind, but it would be better if I could have communicated with them. My guide didn't help us talk to the people.'

The guide did not advise the group about clothing and Bernard was uncomfortable about how some of the tourists were dressed. 'Maybe in Bali it's OK to dress like some fashion show but I think the people respect you better if you wear a bit more', he said. Bernard had already spent three months in Indonesia but rated his stay in Ngadha highly: 'It is a fascinating culture, the way they mix animism and Catholicism. I would like to have learnt more about the way they live and how they interact with nature.'

Steve's group

A driver dropped off Sophie, Katy, Steve and another couple. They paid for their tickets but complained about paying the parking charge ($0.05) for their minibus. They filled in the visitors' book and wrote comments ('great') on their initial impressions. Steve, a British man in his thirties, described himself to me as a 'post-traveller tourist – I'm not a traveller – that's "poncey". I'm here [in Indonesia] because it's cheap, the beer, the fags – it's great. I'm learning the language. I love it here! We're on our way to Labuhan, where I'll hang out till my visa runs out again'

While Steve and I chatted, Sophie and Katy walked up one side of the village to the viewing post and back down the other. Both were wearing shorts and vests. Sophie's vest was short and tight stopping some inches above her shorts. Katy's was baggy displaying her bra underneath. Twenty minutes later they returned and sat in front of the shop, smoking, sunning themselves and chatting while they waited for the other couple to return. As a villager entered the shop, he attempted to greet them '*Selamat pagi* (Ind)' (good morning) but they did not respond.

The other couple was taking photographs of the villagers' graves when a few children began edging towards them. While rummaging through their bag, the tourists began trying to communicate with the children 'What's your name?' 'How old are you?' The exchange was concluded with the passing round of lollipops. The couple examined some ikat cloth but negotiations did not result in a sale. They were going to buy a drink before continuing their journey but said: 'We can't stand warm Sprite, we'll wait till we get back to Bajawa.'

A Typology of Tourists in Ngadha

The tourists that visit Ngadha are of a hardy type (Erb, 2000). Their nationalities do not reflect national statistics, as exceedingly few Asians visit Flores, but they dominate visitation at the national level. While many tourists in Ngadha could be classified as backpackers, this term is too general to deliver a deep understanding of the variety of tourists, their perceptions and their behaviour. As discussed in Chapter 2, the segmentation of tourists into types has been used as an analytical device to better comprehend tourists and their behaviour. While a multitude of tourist types have been developed, Fennell quoted Boyd as identifying 90 types (1999: 54), very few deal with tourists' behaviour and adaptation to local norms. One notable exception is Smith's (1978) typology, which built on Cohen's (1974). I have used this often-quoted and familiar typology as a basis for the typology of tourists visiting Ngadha (see Table 6.1).

In 1999 the segmentation proved to be a powerful instrument (Dann, 1981) to examine which behaviour was attributable to which groups and to explore the reasons. In 2003/2004 the type of tourists travelling to Ngadha changed, for the reasons examined in Chapter 3. As the new type most closely resembles the elite, they have been added to this group. The changes and consequences are discussed further below.

Tourists' sources of knowledge and previous travel experience were important factors in their behaviour, so these have been incorporated into the typology. The level of knowledge indicated in the typology was ascertained in three ways. Firstly, from pre-visit questions put to tourists; secondly, from questions tourists asked me when we met in the villages (these frequently demonstrated whether or not they had an understanding of the villagers' livelihood and culture); and thirdly, from post-visit questions.

Adaptation to local norms is indicated for each of the tourist types. This judgement is made according to the clothing worn and behaviour displayed by tourists and how it accords with villagers' values. To facilitate the categorisation, the villagers were asked to indicate if tourists were polite, impolite (or indecent) or rude (or offensive).[1]

Where appropriate, Smith's (1978) categories are maintained: elite, incipient mass and mass. Unlike in Smith's typology, the order of the groups does not reflect the volume of tourists, although the elite tourists were fewest in numbers in 1998/1999, by 2003/2004 this group was the most numerous. Until 2003/2004 shoestring tourists are the most frequent tourists to Ngadha. I have divided this group in two according to direction of travel, eastbound and westbound, as there were differences in their perceptions, behaviour and adaptability to local norms. There are no self-drive cars for hire on Flores so if a tourist used a car they also had a driver (see p. 128 on driver guides).

Elite tourists have travelled extensively in less developed countries and have often visited Indonesia on more than one occasion. Usually travelling as individuals, in couples or in family groups, this type of tourist often used more than one guidebook and had high levels of knowledge. While nearly all of them used a car, some also used local guides. Most of these tourists adapted well and I met two who were repeat visitors to the village. Many of the tourists in the elite category would classify themselves as backpackers. Many were backpackers in their youth but have become what Pursall (2005) calls 'Flash packers' and Cochrane refers to as 'backpacker plus' (2005). In Bajawa they stayed in the best available guesthouse. Whilst this meant paying twice the average room rate, accommodation was still basic by international standards.

In Smith's original typology (1978: 9) the independent or backpacker tourist fell into one category – the 'off-beat' tourists. This type of traveller has become increasingly common. This large group is then sub-divided into eastbound and westbound shoestring tourists, and Bali-Lombok strays. Flores falls on a well-worn track for Europeans heading to Australia and back often as part of a 'gap year' before or after university.[2] Shoestring tourists were longer-term travellers than Bali-Lombok strays. The former were travelling for three months or more.

The eastbound shoestring tourists had travelled through West Indonesia and/or Sulawesi before arriving in Flores. They had visited other villages and 'knew what to expect'. However, as Flores was often at the end of their travels they were running out of visa time and in a hurry. Many were travel-weary and looking forward to home comforts. They 'couldn't wait to get back to civilisation' and some were not inclined to make the same effort to integrate with the villagers as they had been earlier in their travels.

Although eastbound shoestring tourists often used the most general guidebook – Lonely Planet's *South East Asia on a Shoestring*, they had a reasonable understanding of village life in Indonesia and many adapted well. This type of tourist nearly always travelled by public buses before the economic crisis, but since then they have increasingly formed groups in Labuhan Bajo and hired cars.

The westbound shoestring tourists were travelling from Australia. They had little previous experience of visiting villages in Indonesia and some were still suffering from culture shock because their visit to Ngadha fell into their first week of travelling in a less developed country. Most used buses, either because they did not know how economical it was to hire a car or because arduous bus journeys were still a novelty. With the help of local guides they formed a group for the day. This type of tourist lacked the knowledge to adapt but was more likely to prolong their stay or adapt their travel plans to include attending a ritual.

The Bali-Lombok strays were usually on long holidays rather than career breaks or gap years. Usually travelling for between three and six weeks this group includes young backpackers 'doing Indonesia'. They often did not intend to get further east than Bali or Lombok. In fact several Bali-Lombok strays were 'doing Bali and Lombok' but 'got irritated by the hassles' or 'tempted by the Lombok–Labuhan boat'.[3] Frequently they had formed a group on the boat and then used a driver guide to travel to Keli Mutu. This group includes women travelling with companion guides. Many of these tourists use Lonely Planet's *Indonesia on a Shoestring* guidebook. Most had poor levels of knowledge and did not adapt well.

The special interest tourists' category comprises largely of small groups of middle-aged tourists but also includes school and college groups from Australia.[4] The tour leaders or teachers of these groups had high levels of knowledge, which they shared with their clients or students. These tourists adapted their clothing and behaviour accordingly.

In Smith's (1978) typology the incipient mass are a 'steady flow'; in Ngadha they are more like a trickle. Travelling with national operators and their guides these large (15 plus) groups do not carry guidebooks. They spent the least time in the villages and it was difficult to have more than a two-minute conversation with them, so it was hard to gauge their level of knowledge. However, they were not only disappointed that there were no postcards for sale, but considered this epitomised the 'villagers' backwardness'.

There is no 'continuous influx of visitors' as Smith's typology suggests of mass tourism. However, in 1997 a German ship carrying 202 passengers used 16 buses to get to Bena. Although to date this has only occurred once, the potential exists for a more massive form of tourism in the area, without any great infrastructure changes.

Table 6.1 Types of tourists in Ngadha

Elite	Older age group, make return visits. Travel as individuals, couples or as family groups. Usually use a car and driver. Sometimes use local guides, but frequently travel without a guide, may speak Indonesian. Often carry more than one guidebook. High levels of knowledge. Most adapt well.
Eastbound shoestring tourists	Young, travelling long term (three months or more), often en-route to Australia. Form groups to share a local guide, or employ a driver guide. Have visited other Indonesian villages. Use Lonely Planet's *South East Asia on a Shoestring* guidebook. Reasonable levels of knowledge. Adapt reasonably well.
Westbound shoestring tourists	As above: young, long-term travellers but heading west from Australia. Form groups and use local guides Use Lonely Planet's *South East Asia on a Shoestring* guidebook. Have very little previous experience, some still culture-shocked. Poor level of knowledge. Do not adapt well.
Bali-Lombok strays	Includes young backpackers 'doing Indonesia'. Frequently have formed a group on a boat and use a driver guide, or are travelling with a 'companion guide' from Yogyakarta, Bali or Lombok. Use Lonely Planet's *Indonesia on a Shoestring* guidebook Poor levels of knowledge. Do not adapt well.

Special tourists interest	Usually middle-aged tourists, but also includes school and college groups from Australia. Travel in small groups (8–20 people) with 'concerned' operators. Have a tour leader or teacher but some use a local guide as well. Have a good level of knowledge. Most adapt reasonably well/very well.
Incipient mass	Mostly middle-aged. Travelling in groups of 15 plus, with companies that have offices in Labuhan Bajo and Maumere. Use national or out-of-area guides. Do not use guidebooks. Little knowledge. Adaptation variable.
Mass	In 1997 a German ship carrying 202 passengers used 16 buses to get to Bena. A one-off that indicates the potential for a more massive form of tourism in the area.

General Perceptions of Ngadha Villages

The tourists thought 'the villages were beautiful', 'the people were friendly' and many commented that 'the children were nice'. They frequently made comments that the villagers should keep their villages as they were and their traditions alive. Tourists had favourable impressions of their experiences. Some thought that the trip was a highlight of their travels, 'worth coming all the way to Flores for', 'the most beautiful villages we have visited in Indonesia', 'the least spoilt villages we have seen', and 'the most traditional culture' they had observed. Beyond these general comments, tourists' perspectives of their experiences were dependent on a number of factors and differed in relation to which village(s) they visited. The factors affecting tourists' impressions will be examined first, before an analysis of issues that underlie their perceptions.

Factors affecting tourists' perceptions

As discussed earlier, the guidebooks used by tourists affected where they stayed and which villages their visited. The guidebooks are also likely to have affected their pre-trip images and what tourists focused their gaze upon in the villages. As the majority of tourists used similar guidebooks, or were presented with very similar information about

Ngadha, it is unlikely that guidebooks can account for the differences in tourists' perceptions. Shoestring tourists, who used a single guidebook for all of South East Asia, were furnished with the least detailed information to form their pre-trip images. The major factors in determining the different perceptions held by the different types of tourists were previous experience of Indonesian (or possibly other South East Asian) villages, the variable amounts of human activity in villages from one day to another, and the use of guides.

Previous experience of Indonesian villages

If tourists had not visited other traditional villages in Indonesia (or other places in South East Asia) such as in Tanah Toraja, Nias or Toba, the villages seemed 'too good to be true', 'too perfect', 'unreal' or model-like. Tourists who had visited other villages in Ngadha that contained both concrete and wooden houses with a mix of both tin roofs and thatched roofs were more inclined to voice the opinion that Bena and Wogo were 'alive only for tourism' 'like walking into a show' 'like a picture postcard'. For some tourists, these views were expressed about Wogo because 'there was nobody around, it was dead, alive only for tourism'. For others, the same views were expressed about Bena. Due to the sales made to tourists, the village appeared 'unnatural, a model for tourists'.

Tourists' pre-trip perceptions of cultural villages varied according to previous experiences. Eastbound shoestring tourists expected the villages to be less well preserved. They had visited other parts of Indonesia and were more likely to compare Ngadha villages with other similar experiences. Westbound shoestring tourists, in contrast, had little previous experience on which to base their expectations.

Experience from other villages in Indonesia prepared tourists for the mix of Catholic and pre-Catholic symbols in the villages, as this is common in a variety of areas across the archipelago. The westbound, inexperienced tourists knew little about the syncretism of Indonesian belief systems and were confused about the existence of Catholic and pre-Catholic belief system symbols. They were confused about Catholic graves alongside megaliths (see Plate 15) and concluded that the latter were preserved for the tourists' sake or, in the case of one tourist, that the Catholic graves were put in the village for show.

The tourists that were new to Indonesia were more likely to conclude that the villages were preserved for tourists. They did not believe that what they were seeing were real authentic living villages. These tourists denied or doubted the authenticity of the villages.

Variation in visible human activity from one day to another

Sometimes, when tourists visited the villages, there were few people around; on other occasions, the tourists arrived in the middle of a major ritual and the villages were full of people and activity. Wogo is more dependent on agriculture, so during the day, when tourists visit, villagers are often in the fields, and the *nua* is frequently devoid of villagers (except a few very old and very young). 'There was nobody there. I've seen the houses and megaliths in other villages. It was like walking around a museum .....' 'It felt weird, walking around but there were no people, just one old lady ....' 'It's much better when you can see how the people live, just seeing their houses doesn't give you much of an impression.' 'We really like to meet the people; that's why we hired a guide – hopefully he will help to translate'. On viewing a seemingly unoccupied village, the tourists were at once disappointed and quick to conclude that the village is 'a dying village, preserved for tourists'.

In Bena, tourists frequently viewed women on their terraces weaving. However, this was not always the case. When a ritual was being prepared, women stopped weaving in order to participate in community activities, some of which tourists could observe. On Sundays, although there were no weavers to observe, the village volleyball matches that took place in the *nua* would provide a focus for the tourists' gaze. On a few occasions, such as when there was a funeral in the neighbourhood and a large proportion of the villagers attended, tourists found, as in Wogo, a largely unoccupied village. For the greatest proportion of days, there was much more human activity to be viewed in Bena than in Wogo.

Tourists want to view human activity as part of village life. The number of villagers present in the *nua* during a tourist's visit affected their perceptions. To see the stage without the actors did not fulfil their expectations of a cultural village visit. With the exception of the incipient mass tourists, authenticity, beyond the physical props and touristic spaces, was sought. The desire for focused social interaction suggested by other authors (for example Cohen, 1989; Hughes, 1995; Moscardo & Pearce, 1999) is discussed further below.

Guides' impact on perceptions

The vast majority of tourists visit the villages of Ngadha with guides. Local guides accompany some elite, some shoestring and some special interest tourists. Local guides manipulate their good relations with the villagers in Bena to facilitate understanding of the villagers' lives for tourists. For example, on a quiet day, a guide used a few handfuls of macadamia nuts, left to dry on a stone, as an entry point into an explanation of the villagers' livelihood. Having offered the tourists a taste, the guide entered into a conversation with a villager about how much he could earn from the crop and then translated this for tourists. Frequently an old man, who sat on a terrace producing *lega* (bags worn by men at ceremonies), was used as an entry point to discuss a variety of rituals in the village. Guides would ask him, and translate to tourists, how long it took to make the bag, how much he would sell it for and the significance of the bag worn in ceremonies. As the guides did this on a regular basis, they were not asking the man to learn for themselves, but to provide a bridge to a form of focused social interaction – to give the tourists an opportunity to communicate with the villagers. Some guides would use the example of washing being dried on megaliths to explain that this does not reduce the sanctity of the stones, that the villagers use the stones for profane as well as sacred purposes.

Through the explanations provided by guides, tourists would have a better understanding of the villages. The megaliths for example, would be understood, not as relics of a pre-Catholic past preserved for tourism, but as part of the villages ongoing belief system. The guides could explain the apparently empty village and the few villagers that remained could be engaged in conversation. Tourists that use local guides are subject to less cultural confusion and were less inclined to view the villages as 'models for tourists'. The Bali-Lombok strays and some shoestring tourists (more often eastbound) that used 'driver guides' were less likely to be provided with the necessary narratives or to be accompanied on their walk around the villages. They were, therefore, more likely to view the villages as 'unreal'.

Perceptions of Commercialisation

Many tourists, usually from the elite, shoestring or specialist groups, described Bena as 'spoilt', 'a bit spoilt' or, as one put it, having 'a veneer of commercialism'. The reasons given for these opinions were the ticket sales, the Coca-Cola sales, the large number of houses displaying ikats for sale, the fact that children asked for sweets, and the requests for money to take photographs (especially when they were asked for money to photograph the new *ngadhu*).

Tourists' views about the sale of tickets to visit Ngadha villages were expressed as follows: 'Paying for tickets feels like a set-up', 'It's fake to pay for something so beautiful', 'We would pay more if we knew where the money was going.' Tourists thought it was unreasonable to charge for entry for what they considered to be public spaces.[5]

These comments reveal that tourists see the sale of tickets as the commercialisation of culture, spoiling a village by making it 'touristy'. When a village uses tickets, it indicates that it is used to tourists, and is on the beaten track. Shoestring tourists who strive to stay 'off the beaten track' view this form of commercialisation particularly negatively. For this reason, many tourists preferred Nage, a village that does not sell tickets (but was planning to). Specialist tour groups also wish to avoid villages spoilt by tourism. As the tour leader said: 'Our company wants to visit villages that don't have tourists.' My own company stopped visiting Wogo when guides brought tourists to see performances we had sponsored. We moved to a remoter village in the hope that our clients would have a unique experience, exclusive to our group, unspoilt by the presence of other tourists.

Tourists claimed that they preferred to make voluntary donations. As local guides paid entrance fees, many tourists were unaware of the ticket price paid in Bena. When I told them, tourists were surprised how little they cost – US$0.25 in 1998.[6] The tourists did not feel over-charged but viewed the use of tickets negatively. I asked tourists how much they would have paid if making a voluntary donation (before telling them the ticket price). Indeed, many would have paid more than the ticket price. In Wogo, as elsewhere, the amount tourists donate is recorded in the guest book. Frequently, the donation was more than the ticket price in Bena. In 1998, the average was US$0.50. Following the example of previous visitors, a standard is developed.[7] When a couple in Wogo donated US$0.50, they said that larger donations were pointed out to them, as if to suggest they should pay more: 'He [referring to the caretaker] subtly applied pressure to give him some more, but we didn't. We knew [from a visit the previous day] that in Bena tourists pay US$0.25 each, so we thought our donation was fair.' A standard ticket price clearly affected these tourists' perceptions about what was a fair price to pay.

Several tourists suggested that they would be happier to pay if they knew what the money was for and some said that they would pay more if they were donating to a specific project. Contributions by my own clients towards the water project in Wogo were 25 times the going rate for donations to visit the village. This in part reflects the socio-economic class of specialist group tourists and it cannot be assumed that shoestring tourists would be so generous. However, further information about the economic situation of the villagers and specific projects for tourists to donate to, are likely to raise more revenue from tourism than the standard ticket sales. Although tourists believed that the 'villagers should keep their traditions' and 'preserve their culture', many explicitly commented that it was the government's role to provide the necessary finance.

The sales of other products meant Bena was 'touristy', according to many tourists. The sale of Coca-Cola is clearly tourist-related, as is the sale of bottled water. Tourists also sometimes purchase biscuits sold at the shop. The villages' shop that sells these products is at the village entrance, so all the tourists pass it. It is here that vehicles are parked and tourists convene to continue their journey. The shop doubles as the 'bus stop' where guides, driver guides and villagers wait. Some guides have a late breakfast of noodles while their clients walk around the village.

Many houses in the village display ikat cloth for sale to tourists (see Plate 10). Although the fabric is hand-made, bright synthetic yarn is used. The colours do not correspond to the tourists' notion of 'traditional and primitive' and the fabrics are therefore considered inauthentic. The cloth frequently failed to fulfil the desires for a memento of the tourists' visit to an exotic and 'primitive' village. The villagers are aware of this and have tried to incorporate more browns and reds as primitive colours. However, the synthetic browns and reds do not correspond to the tourists' expectations either.[8]

Plate 10 Tourists examine 'ikats' hanging in Bena

Westbound tourists and elite tourists who have visited parts of NTT may well have visited places that still use vegetable dyes e.g Watu Belapi, near Maumere and Jompu near Ende. The ikats that result are less bright and more fitting with tourists' expectations. Several tourists made comparisons, and some that had not already bought an ikat were regretful that they had not bought a nicer one further east. Westbound tourists were also often aware of more authentically coloured ikats from the galleries in Bali and wanted to buy an ikat memento that better met their expectations.

The bright colours were popular with the Australian high school tourists. It may have been coincidental that the colours popular in the village, purple and green, were also fashionable at the time, or, perhaps this group of tourists had fewer preconceptions of ikats that would serve as souvenirs.

A few houses also display other souvenirs such as coconut shell bowls and woven baskets and long knives. Bena was considered spoilt because villagers appeared to be money-minded. As one tour leader said: 'In Bena, they are economically minded. When they know I can speak Indonesian, they ask me to suggest to my clients that they buy an ikat.' As a tourist said: 'They want our money in this village. Look, nearly all the houses are trying to sell ikats.' 'These people have become money-minded because of tourism.' In comparing Bena with other villages, tourists pointed out: 'Nobody tried to sell us ikats in Nage', 'Bela and Luba are less spoilt. The villagers are not selling to tourists.'

The view that the villagers in Bena are more economically minded than in other villages needs to be questioned. The villagers of Nage do not produce ikats and therefore do not sell them. When the women of Nage helped me to buy coconut oil and palm spirit produced in the village, they added a small profit margin for their efforts. The economic necessities of life in Ngadha villages mean that villagers seek opportunities to make money. As Bena receives large numbers of tourists (relative to the other villages), they use this as an opportunity to gain an income.

According to the incipient mass tourists, the villagers were not economically minded enough. 'They do not sell postcards? Really? Everyone sells postcards!' one woman exclaimed. When one incipient mass tourist asked how much one of Mama Mia's ikat cloths was, Mama Mia replied 'eight-five' (meaning Rp85,000), showing eight fingers and then five. 'Very expensive', retorted the tourist. But her friend asked: 'Is that in guilders or dollars?' Seeing Mama Mia's face contort with incomprehension, I could not help intervening and explaining that the cloths cost about eight dollars. The tourists bought three of the four Mama Mia was displaying.

It is common in many parts of the developing world that children ask tourists for sweets and pens. It is a clear sign that tourists have been before.

Although I was asked for sweets by children in all the Ngadha villages and in the town of Bajawa, tourists used this as an example of why Bena was spoilt. Although tourists viewed requests for sweets from children negatively, many tourists and out-of-area guides did give children sweets. Several tourists pointed out that the children in Bena were not offensive when their requests were unfulfilled, unlike their experiences in other areas of Indonesia e.g. Tanah Toraja and Nias.

Many elite, shoestring and specialist tourists visited more than one Ngadha village. They usually preferred villages that were less used to tourists and made little attempt to make money from tourism. Authenticity is a value sought by cultural tourists to Ngadha villages, and commercialisation was equated with the loss of authenticity. Villages that were less commercialised were preferred. Further, tourists preferred villages that appeared economically poorer, e.g. Nage and Bela. In seeking experiences as far removed from their own lifestyle, tourists seek 'primitive' culture. Poverty is related to primitive in the minds of tourists, as is not being 'economically minded'. Although I did not investigate these views specifically it would appear that tourists preferred poorer villages as these were considered the most primitive and therefore the most authentic.

Tourists' Perceptions of Rituals

Tourism to Ngadha is seasonal. The August peak season coincides with many house building rituals. It is therefore common for tourists to see villagers preparing for, or engaged in, rituals. Most tourists only spend one day (two nights) in the area. When they hear of a ritual happening the day they have planned to leave they experience stress and anxiety. They are torn between taking in some other sites or prolonging their stay to witness a ritual. Tourists do not want to feel they have missed something but many have ambitious and inflexible travel plans. Elite and westbound shoestring tourists were the most likely to change their travel plans to attend a ritual.

Negotiating changes to travel plans with other members of temporarily formed groups and drivers led to additional stress. Sometimes, eastbound shoestring tourists would try to attend a ritual in the morning and continue their journey to Moni in the afternoon. This meant that they were clock-watching and became anxious when rituals did not begin at the times they had expected. The fact that tourists are anxious and stressed not only affected their own enjoyment but also their interactions with villagers.

At rituals, just as the slaughter is the highlight for the villagers, so is it for the tourists. Tourists commented: 'It's great to see their real culture',

'We used to do this: it's amazing to be somewhere it still happens', 'I feel so privileged to see true tradition.' Some tourists (more often women) clearly have a dilemma of whether or not to watch a slaughter. The majority do choose to watch. As male villagers crowd around the beast to be slaughtered, tourists who want a good view compete for 'front row' positions. Female villagers do not attempt to get close. Slaughters of buffalo are considered dangerous, as a buffalo could get away and run amok. Women remain on terraces with the children. Many female tourists join their male companions close to the slaughter action. At the Robo Keri ritual in Doka (see p. 174), I was told that I should remain on a terrace. A number of male villagers offered to take photographs for me so that I could get photographs without transgressing norms and upsetting the villagers. I was asked to tell the tourists, which I did. One woman said she was glad because she was unsure if she wanted to watch anyway. Another said that she had come all this way, wanted the photographs and did not trust the villagers with her camera. The third initially stayed back on the terrace. However, when all attention was on the slaughter, she edged closer to watch over the heads of the villagers only to turn her head away after the lethal blow. Women on the terrace nudged me and tutted. Turning away or burying their faces was behaviour displayed by a number of (usually female) tourists who had thought they wanted to watch but at the last minute were unable to.[9]

Women tourists, having decided to watch, take up 'male-space' close to the slaughter. Some were unaware of the gendered division of space, others did not think it applied to them as tourists, and many used photography as an excuse to transgress local norms. The body language of the tourist that turned away expressed shock and upset at an occasion intended to be proud and happy (see Plate 11). Tourists, lacking appreciation of the villagers' emotions associated with slaughter, transgress norms by displaying opposing emotions. One young villager expressed the difference between tourists, and villagers, views: 'We are full of pride and happy when we see an animal slaughtered. Tourists are sad mixed with frightened, especially the girls, but they still want to watch.'

Although most westerners would not choose to witness an animal being butchered in their home environment, on holiday in Ngadha they make particular effort to see animals being slaughtered. Regarding holidays as taking place in sacred time (Graburn, 1978), the reversal of normality can be explained, following Turner's notion of *liminas*. The normality of shunning direct observation of animal slaughter when at home in the western world is overturned in the tourists' betwixt and between state, during their sacred holiday time.

Plate 11 Women tourists turn away and express shock and disgust at the the slaughter of buffalo

Observing rituals adds to the authenticity tourists strive to experience. Visiting a village allows the tourist to stand on the stage of the exotic culture. Visiting a village during a ritual allows the tourists to stand shoulder to shoulder with the actors, to be extras in the play. Most tourists, like many villagers, do no more than observe the slaughter. In this point in the ritual, observation is part of the action, and some tourists are able to share the sense of excitement, and perhaps even partake in the villagers' *communitas*.

Observing ritual slaughters performed by (preferably) a single blow to a buffalo's throat, or pig's skull, the tourists' confirm their view that the villagers are primitive. The crude, unsanitised slaying of numerous beasts in public, which are then rapidly and roughly chopped up with long knives, on leaves on the ground, contrasts with the modern, hygienic preparations of meat in their home lives. Tourists who observed rituals did not think that the villages were preserved for tourists. The rituals served as proof that the villagers were primitive and their villages were authentic.

Tourists' Desire for Social Interaction

Tourists spend as little as five minutes and as much as 44 hours (in the case of our clients) in Ngadha villages. Tourists usually spend more time in Bena (average one hour[10]) than in Wogo (average 20 minutes). During this time they wander around looking at the obvious cultural manifestations: Houses, *ngadhu*, *bhaga* and megaliths; they take photographs; some play with the children and give gifts of sweets and pens to them; some, with or without the help of guides, enter into conversations with the villagers. In Bena, they may additionally examine and negotiate to buy ikat fabrics and other souvenirs, rest at the viewing post to take in the scenery, rest at the shop and buy drinks and biscuits.

From the observed behaviour of tourists in the villages, only playing with children, negotiating for souvenirs and conversations with villagers involve focused social interaction. Some tourist types – the Bali-Lombok strays, the more travel-weary eastbound shoestring tourists and the incipient mass – entered into the least social interaction and were content with unfocused social interaction. The Bali-Lombok strays used their visits to gaze and as a means of socialising or sharing experiences with other travellers. Learning from other travellers was as important as learning about Ngadha villages. After 20 minutes looking around Bena they would lie in the sun and chat to fellow travellers for an hour or more. The cultural village was a backdrop for a conversation that could have taken place anywhere in the world. In these cases, their consumption of cultural tourism fulfilled a focus of interaction with other tourists rather than the experiential characteristics (Sharpley, 2000) frequently associated with cultural (ethnic) tourism (Harron & Weiler, 1992; Wood, 1984).

Frequently, it was observed that elite tourists, some shoestring tourists and specialist tourists wanted to engage in focused social interaction with villagers. In Wogo especially, if tourists just looked at the village, the visit was over too quickly. If they lingered in the centre of the *nua*, the tourists were exposed and uncomfortable (and in direct tropical sun). Tourists employed strategies to prolong their stay. Some would sit, uninvited, on empty terraces, in which case they might be approached and communication may ensue. More often, tourists would approach children or communicate with children who approached them. They could use their basic Indonesian with less embarrassment with children. Giving out sweets, pens or balloons was frequently a strategy employed to open exchanges with children. Animals such as chicks or kittens were often the objects of the gaze of tourists travelling with their children. Attempting to pick them up or stroke them was a strategy used for entry into conversation. Using basic Indonesian tourists were able to ask how old the animal was, how many chicks were there etc.

Tourists who used local guides, either experienced more focused social interaction, facilitated by the guide, or at least hoped to. As one tourist, working as a volunteer English teacher on Java, said: 'Although I can speak some Indonesian, I employed a guide because I thought he would introduce me to the villagers, to make communication easier, to feel less awkward. I thought he would tell me where to go and where not to go and what not to do.' His disgruntled partner interrupted: 'He doesn't. He's ripping us off: all Indonesians do. They charged us Rp40, 000 to hire a car to get here.'[11]

A Dutch couple met an elderly man in Bena who could speak reasonable Dutch.[12] In their language, he explained much about the culture of Bena. The tourists could have got similar information from a guide but, as they explained: 'It's incredible to be able to talk to the villagers about their lives; it made the visit really special. Getting to know local people is important for us when we travel. It's not just seeing places, but meeting people, that makes travelling like this worthwhile.'

The different types of tourists exhibited different levels of desire for social interaction and different levels of cultural capital they could employ. The westbound shoestring tourists were keen for social interaction but some were still in a state of culture shock and most lacked the cultural capital, built up from Indonesian village visits, which the eastbound shoestring tourists had. Of this latter group, some were travel-weary and, having met villagers in other areas, were no longer keen to invest their energies. Those that were less jaded had built up tools and skills, transferable from other village visits. They knew how to answer banal questions – questions, to which the answers are obvious, but are commonly used to open conversation, (see Chapter 7) – or were prepared for the questions of socio-cultural location in order to enter into communication with villagers. Elite tourists, likewise, had enough experience to facilitate a high level of social interaction if they so desired.

As Iso-Ahola (1982) suggests, the fear of embarrassment or incompetence is a limiting factor for some tourists who desire social interaction in an unfamiliar culture. This is especially acute for tourists who were new to Indonesia and still experiencing aspects of culture shock. Although fascinated with the new culture, they faced greater barriers as the signs and symbols of social intercourse are so unfamiliar (Furnham, 1984). Without the facilities of a competent guide, tourists were unsure of how to engage with adults. Communication with children was used as a substitute for more meaningful social interaction with adults. Children were easier to approach and attempts at conversations with them were less threatening than potentially embarrassing exchanges with their parents.

Tourists' Knowledge and Adaptation

As I have suggested, some tourists adapted to the villagers' culture better than others. Those who had previous experience of cultural tourism in Indonesia and had visited other villages were more likely to have the cultural capital required to adapt. Those who travelled with a local guide (or some tour leaders) were furnished with the knowledge that helped them adapt.

Those least able to adapt were tourists new to Indonesia, not travelling with a local guide. Many of these were westbound shoestring tourists who were very keen to learn about the local culture. Many would not have made social faux pas if they had known the correct behaviour. The inappropriate behaviour they displayed was a result of ignorance.

Those travelling with a local guide were usually given some information that prevented some behaviour that villagers found offensive. For example, guides warned tourists that villagers dislike public displays of amorous relations. However, local guides did not provide information on dress codes and sweet-giving. Table 6.2 below summarises the inter-play of cultural capital built up from previous village visits and guides as a source of information on behaviour management and the different tourist types.

Table 6.2 Sources of knowledge leading to behaviour management of different tourist types

| | | *Cultural capital accumulated from previous village visits* | |
		Yes	*No*
Information gained through using local guides	*Yes*	Elite and some eastbound shoestring tourists	Some westbound shoestring tourists and specialist groups
	No	Eastbound shoestring tourists that use driver guides	Bali-Lombok strays and westbound shoestring tourists using driver guides

Although knowledge was important for a tourist to be able to adapt his or her behaviour in the villages, it was clear that not all tourists adapted their behaviour even when they had the knowledge. Tourists were observed pushing away ritual food even after their guide had told them it was impolite to refuse it and that it was diplomatic to accept a token amount. In this case the guide provided the tourists with the information but they chose to ignore it. Tourists were also observed pushing villagers out of the way in order to get their desired photographs.

From observation and talking to tourists it appeared that the majority of behaviour that caused offence to villagers arose out of ignorance. If tourists were provided with more information, much offensive behaviour could be avoided. However, some tourist behaviour is caused by attitudes that could perhaps be more accurately described as arrogance. As Pearce explains while some rule breaking by tourists is unintentional, cultural arrogance is 'disregarding the sensitivities and reactions of the local community … behaviours which *knowingly* break moral, religious and social codes' (1995: 144; my emphasis).

On two occasions, tourists refused to pay for their tickets or make a donation. Their view was that the *nua* was a public space and anyone could walk through it. In 1994 two women tourists who refused to pay for their tickets in Bena ended up in a physical fight when villagers tried to prevent their entry due to the non-payment. Although I did not witness the fight, I met these women some days later, on a ferry to Sulawesi. Both were badly bruised. One woman's nose appeared broken and she had a black eye. The other woman's shoulder was severely swollen and she thought she might have broken her collarbone. Despite the apparent severity of their injuries, they chose not to seek medical advice and were in a hurry to leave Flores. The only common aspects between the villagers' and the women's story was that the fight occurred in Bena and was provoked by the women's refusal to pay for their tickets. After this occurrence, in order to prevent disagreements escalating into violence, villagers ignored tourists that refuse to pay for tickets. Following the incident the villagers requested a security officer or village policeman. They had hoped that a member of the village would be given a paid position. Ten years later a village policemen was appointed. He was an immigrant from neighbouring Sumba. He worked out of the 'souvenir shop' (built by the provincial Department of Tourism but never used as a souvenir shop, see Chapter 5). The villagers were disappointed that a villager had not been assigned the role but were pleased to be provided with the security they had requested.

Differences in the Consumption of Tourism in Wogo and Bena

Physical differences between Bena and Wogo result in differences in the way tourists gaze in the two villages. As suggested, the viewing post provides a structure for tourists' visits in Bena. It provides an end-point and a place to make for, giving tourists a purpose to their walk. It also provides a vantage-point so that tourists can gaze on the villagers without their knowledge.

The bench outside the village shop, where tickets are sold, provides tourists with a second place to sit and view village life. Although it is a poor vantage-point for the *nua*, this neutral space was regularly used by tourists to take some views of exotic life. A woman balancing large bundles of vegetables or animal fodder on her head as she walks past, a pig trussed up on bamboo poles or children returning from school in their tenth-hand uniform held together with safety pins are examples of village life that were noteworthy for tourists.

By comparison, Wogo does not have any neutral safe spaces. Tourists must either walk, stand in the *nua* or sit on a villagers' terrace. As indicated, by walking around the *nua*, the visit is concluded too quickly. There is no endpoint or place to make for in Wogo. Tourists can view one similar house after another but there are no ikat fabrics to examine and compare from one house to another. Standing in the village leaves tourists feeling exposed (and hot). While many tourists used the camera to hide behind, all photography was overt with very limited opportunity for concealed shots. Sitting on a villager's terrace clearly involves 'invading another's private space'. Eastbound tourists who have built up the cultural knowledge to know that Indonesians do not have the same views on private space and thus do not regard sitting on their terrace as an 'invasion' and have learnt enough Indonesian to sit and chat could turn this into an opportunity for social interaction. Many tourists, however, felt too awkward and vulnerable to sit on a villager's terrace uninvited.

The tourists' experience in Bena is therefore easier. There is more to look at and there are two places, the viewing post and the bench, where tourists can absorb the exotic at a safe distance, with little need for social interaction and resultant feelings of inadequacy.

Changes over Time

As destinations develop, the type of tourists who visit also tend to change. Although, there has been relatively little development in Ngadha, changes in the types of tourists who visit have been discernible. In 1984 there was no complete road across the island of Flores and only the most intrepid of travellers attempted to make the journey from Maumere to Labuhan Bajo – it took ten days. There was no network of guesthouses and visitors had to be prepared to sleep on mats in villagers' homes and stay at missions. By 1989, when I took my first tour group, only a dozen foreign tourists had ever visited Wogo. In the early 1990s there were no guesthouses or restaurants that specifically catered to tourists needs in Bajawa, accommodation was basic and nearly all the tourists were hardy backpackers.

As tourism to Indonesia boomed in the mid-1990 new guesthouses appeared that specifically targeted foreign tourists and the first 'tourist restaurant' in Bajawa opened. While the majority of tourists were long-term shoestring tourists, other groups began to emerge. As journey times from Labuhan Bajo to Maumere (the gateways) decreased over time, Bali-Lombok strays and tour groups arrived in greater numbers. Whereas in the early 1990s tourists would say, 'You need a week or ten days *to do* Flores', ten years later tourists said, 'You can do Flores in three days, but four or five is better.' In 2005, tour companies in Bali were selling 'Flores overland 5 days 4 nights ex Denpasar'. As more comfortable accommodation has developed, groups with older clients and families have ventured to the region. Despite the improvements, however, travelling on Flores remains a 'fairly strenuous and enormously time consuming ... destination for the relatively adventurous type' (Erb, 2000: 143).

The biggest change in tourist type resulted from the foreign government travel advice, following the 2002 Bali bombings and the change in visa arrangements in 2003/2004. The nationality of the tourists changed. The effect of the travel warnings can be seen in the change in the nationalities of tourists between data collected in 1998/1999 and 2005. In 1998/1999 tourists from Australia made up 17% of tourists, and the UK market made up a further 15%, tourists from France represented 11%, and those from the USA and Canada 5%. In 2005 the French were the most dominant nationality making up 38% of independent tourists, followed by the Swiss who made up a further 17%.[13] There were few Australians, British or Americans.

The type and age also changed. In 1998/1999 the majority of independent tourists were young backpackers – shoestring tourists – travelling on long overland trips, frequently to or from Australia. In 2005 the majority were adventurous holidaymakers taking a three- to four-week trip combining Bali with the Eastern Isles. There was a significant increase in the number of people travelling with children. No families were observed in the eight months of research in 1998/1999 whereas six families visited one of the villages during one week in 2005. The average age of adult tourists had increased from 29.4 in 1998/1999 to 35.7 in 2005.

Tourists rated their visits to Ngadha villages highly. The *nua*, houses, *bhaga*, *ngadhu* and megaliths provided the tourists with a feeling of being enclosed in antiquity, a 'primitive' stage to stand on. There were usually more actors on the stage in Bena providing more activity to be viewed and gazed upon by the tourists. For some tourists, the villages were too unreal and felt like a model rather than a real village. The authenticity of a tourism setting is not a tangible asset but a judgement or value placed upon it by the observers (Moscardo & Pearce, 1999). The perceived authenticity of the villages was affected by a number of factors. Tourists who had little experience of Indonesian (or other South East Asian) villages doubted their authenticity. When tourists visited an empty village, it was considered to be just a model for tourists. Tourists travelling without local guides were also more likely to deny the villages' authenticity.[14]

The villages were, however, perceived as authentic if the tourists' visit coincided with a ritual. Not only was the 'primitive' stage full of actors but it also gave the tourists an opportunity to share an experience with them. The tourists' behaviour at rituals expressed *liminas* and inversion as they chose to observe the slaying of pigs and buffaloes.

Attempts by the villagers to make money are viewed negatively by tourists. Villages that sell tickets are 'touristy' and therefore less authentic. Although some tourists want to drink chilled bottled drinks, for many the sale of such drinks indicates modernity and therefore inauthenticity. While some tourists wanted to buy postcards, most saw villagers' attempts to make sales to tourists as signifiers of 'being spoilt'. In seeking a contrast with their own culture (Rojek, 1997), tourists have notions of how the villages should be: rural, poor, primitive, dirty and traditional in contrast with their urban, rich, sophisticated, clean and modern lives. In the case of the Ngadha villages, judgements by tourists of authenticity were related to poverty, lack of obvious evidence that the villagers were interested in deriving economic benefit from tourism, lack of begging children and evidence of traditional culture without it being too well preserved.

Some tourists, in particular the Bali-Lombok strays, the incipient mass and the travel-weary eastbound shoestring tourists, wanted unfocused social interaction. They were happy to gaze, take photographs and share experiences with other travellers. The other tourists displayed the experiential characteristics of cultural tourists and wanted focused social interaction. Sometimes local guides facilitated this. Sometimes the tourists used children as entry into conversation. For tourists who sought focused social interaction, their visit to the villages was over too quickly if it just involved looking, especially in Wogo, where there is less to look at. When tourists got the social interaction they desired, for example, sharing in the villagers' excitement at a ritual or being able to communicate with the villagers or joining in a volleyball match, this was a highlight of their visit.

In order to develop a deeper understanding of the tourists, a typology was developed. Although Smith's (1978) typology was a useful basis for understanding which tourists adapted best in the villages, sources of knowledge and previous experience were considered important factors and were therefore incorporated into the model. An important difference was found between eastbound and westbound shoestring tourists. The analysis of the tourists' knowledge and adaptation to the villagers' culture also revealed that the majority of inappropriate behaviour was due to tourists' ignorance. However, sometimes, when the tourists knew of how to behave appropriately, but did not, their transgressions were perhaps caused by arrogance.

The type of tourists who visit Ngadha has changed over time. This change was in line with changes that would be expected as a destination 'develops'. As roads are improved, and accommodation and restaurants catering to tourists' tastes are opened, a broader range of tourists are attracted. However, the greatest change in tourists occurred as a result of external influences – foreign government travel advice and changes to visa arrangements meant long-term backpackers were replaced by adventurous holidaymakers. As a consequence, the 2005 season was the shortest and most concentrated the region had ever experienced.

Notes

1. *Sopan, kurang sopan, tidak sopan* (Ind).
2. Many fly to and from Indonesia out of Bali and miss out the on Indonesia's Eastern Isles.
3. A four-day boat trip from Lombok to Labuhan Bajo via Komodo and other islands.
4. I met one school group and one college group in 1998 and was told a few such groups visit each year.
5. The same unwillingness to pay for public space is expressed with regard to the use of the British countryside (Sharpely, 1993).
6. The exchange rate was particularly favourable for tourists at this time.
7. Erb (1998) observes the same phenomena in Manggarai.
8. Forshee discusses how Balinese design galleries refused cloths that were 'too chemical in appearance' (2001: 170).
9. One vegetarian woman turned away from watching a buffalo slaughter, only to accidentally witness a horse being killed by a single blow to the head. She

fainted and the villagers' attention was immediately turned away from their ritual to the well being of their guest.

10. The time of arrival and departure for all tourists in each village was recorded for several days to establish these approximate averages.

11. This was US$4 for a private charter 25km return on a bad road. The locals would have paid US$3.50.

12. He had lived most of his life in Java but had returned to his village for his old age.

13. These figures relate only to a four-week period in July/August. However there were virtually no tourists in the preceding weeks. Some friends stayed in Ngadha for a week in April and saw no other tourists!

14. Similar doubts were expressed by 'young authenticity-seeking tourists' in Northern Thailand (Cohen, 1979: 27).

Chapter 7
The Villagers' Perceptions of Tourism

This chapter examines the villagers' perceptions of tourism. As discussed in the previous chapters, Bena is not only more economically dependent on tourism than Wogo but it has also been subject to more state intervention, more changes, and is more 'touristy'. As a result, perceptions of tourists and tourism differ between the villages. However, as this chapter discusses, there are more similarities than differences. Following a brief description of tourist–villager interaction, I will evaluate the overwhelmingly positive attitudes towards tourists before discussing the problems villagers have with some tourists and tourism. The final sections of the chapter examines the perceptions of tourism in the socio-political context and how tourism reflects the political disquiet and disillusionment with the local political system; and how the villagers perceptions have changed in the years I have been visiting.

Tourist–Villager Interaction

Villagers usually see and meet tourists when tourists visit the villages. Some villagers also see tourists when they are in Bajawa. In Bena, the vehicles hired by tourists pull up next to the village shop. When more than one vehicle arrives at once they park in an area created for parking at the bottom of the steps leading to the village. Local guides often let tourists enjoy the gentle walk down hill from the neighbouring *nua* of Luba, in which case the tourists arrive on foot. Either sighting transport pulling up at the shop or tourists walking down the hill is a cue for the villagers to hang out their ikats and put other souvenirs on display.

Tourists climb the steps and 'enter' the *nua*. They walk around, take photographs, examine and sometimes purchase ikat and other souvenirs, occasionally engaging in dialogue as they pass the villagers' homes. They make their way to the viewing post at the far end of Bena and take in the spectacular views of the surrounding scenery and look down on Bena.

Nearly all tourists arrive in Wogo by car; a very small number walk from the Trans-Flores highway. The cars park at the entrance to the village where tourists disembark. They then wander around the village in the same way as in Bena. However, there were no souvenirs on display (until 2005 when two women were sometimes displaying a few purses and baskets on chairs on their terrace). Whereas in Bena souvenirs provide an opening for conversation, this opportunity does not exist in Wogo. The viewing post in Bena gives the tourists a place to head for and thus a structure to their visit. In Wogo, visits aree less structured. Sometimes, half the way down Wogo tourists cross the *nua* and return to their vehicle. Villagers sometimes try to engage with tourists through greeting and banal questions. Often tourists begin their communication with children.

This pattern of tourist–villager encounter is a typical version of the majority of tourists' visits in the villages. The villagers' perceptions of tourists and tourism are largely based on these short (ten minutes to one hour) visits. The tourists I took, as explained in the introduction, spent two days in Wogo. This represents the other extreme – the rare longer stay. Two or three times a year, a single tourist or a couple request to stay overnight in Bena or Wogo.[1] Only one other tour company has made arrangements to stay in the villages (see Chapter 5). Furthermore, some groups do turn up and make spontaneous arrangements, for example a group of Austrians arrived in Wogo and arranged to stay as a *kabe pare* (entry step) ritual was under way (see below).

'We Like Tourists'

There are six general reasons why both Wogo and Bena villagers like tourists and tourism. Tourists make the villages lively; they provide entertainment, information and status. Tourists help strengthen cultural values, provide a window on the world, bring development (or have the potential to do so) and have led to the improvement of village facilities. The variations that exist between the perceptions of villagers in Wogo and Bena are examined under each of the general headings.

Just more guests

All the villagers living in *nua* are used to playing host. As the occupants of Houses, the villagers are constantly receiving friends and relatives to stay, from the gardens. Having been used to constant visitors from birth, the villagers like guests and see tourists as an extension of this. Like most Indonesians, 'the villagers like life to be noisy, crowded and lively' (*ramai*) (Just, 2001: 55).[2]

As discussed in Chapter 4, the House hostess (*Dongo Sa'o*) is chosen for her hosting skills and is therefore the perfect person to deal with the constant stream of visitors. Her sense of duty is extended to tourists. They are not family members with rights to be in the house, but they are '*tamu negara*' (guests of the nation). It is a duty to the state to show them the utmost in hospitality.[3] It is unusual for members of the village not to extend hospitality to tourists. All members claim to like tourists, not to be bored with tourists, to want more tourists and wish to strengthen and extend their hospitality to tourists. A tourist visit that results in a conversation provides a break from the ordinary, a fresh face for a different conversation, and a story to tell. Resoundingly, most tourists are liked because more visitors make life more crowded, noisy and lively.

Tourists as entertainment (*Hiburan*)

In Wogo, the term *tamu* (guest) is normally used to refer to tourists. In Bena, tourists are usually referred to as tourists (*turis*), which according to Hughes-Freeland 'is coming to replace the formerly ubiquitous *londo* [Dutch person] as something to yell at Caucasian foreigners' (1993: 140). It was the women of Bena who pointed out that tourists provide them with entertainment (*hiburan*), something to look at and gossip about. All guests' comings and goings in the *nua* were noted and talked about and tourists are no exception. In 1998, the women of Bena were not bored with seeing tourists. Hairstyles, dress and body shape combined with the tourists' origins and which guide they were with (if known), provided eternal conversation starters. On numerous occasions, anyone (including me) sitting on the terrace would be persuaded to stand up and stare at 'such a fat', 'such an old' or 'such a strange' tourist.[4] Villagers that visited the *nua* could be entertained on and off all day by the coming and goings of tourists. In 2005, one of the guides said he thought that people in Bena were bored with tourists and that they were not as enthusiastic anymore.[5] He took his tourists to another, more remote, village where the kids still shriek 'hello mister' and the villagers were more modest. Although by 2005 a few villagers, in both villages, had bought televisions, the majority of villagers did not watch television, and few owned any books, thus tourists provided a precious source of entertainment.

The people of Ngadha have no aversion to being stared at or to staring. On one occasion, I joined the weaving group. As I helped thread a loom, I was not only watched by tourists, but local men and boys passing by stopped and stared at me. Some made comments such as 'look a tourist can weave' or 'see that *bule* [albino, white skinned person], can they ikat too?' Most just stood and stared. I felt very uncomfortable and asked the local women how they felt when tourists stared at them. The women disagreed: they felt privileged to be stared at, staring was equated with admiration; it was positive. Furthermore, when tourists stared at them they felt excited and filled with anticipation that they might make a sale.

'Tourism will strengthen our cultural values'

In Wogo, liking tourists is linked with increased pride of cultural heritage. They say tourists make them feel proud that their culture is known to outsiders, (*'kami bangga adat istiadat dikenal oleh orang luar'*). The villagers believe that tourism is strengthening cultural values (*'mentebalkan adat istiadat'*) and that the children in the village will have the importance of village custom reconfirmed by seeing tourists come from afar to see it. 'If our culture is worth coming all the way from England to see, it is worthy of preservation', one informant told me. The villagers believe that their reverence and respect of the ancestors can only be helped and not eroded by tourism. Traditions will be maintained because they are a tourist attraction and hence the younger generation will appreciate the belief system. By contrast, in Bena such views were not articulated. Villagers saw no connection between the preservation of custom and tourism. They told me that custom would be preserved regardless of tourism.

The revitalisation of tradition has been recognised in other areas of Indonesia. Considering the government's cultural policy, the villagers of Wogo could have been articulating well-absorbed national discourse. However, the inference from the villagers was that this view was learnt from experience rather than repeated nationalist dogma. Elders used tourism as an excuse to preserve symbols of the ancestors and also claimed that the cultural values would be strengthened by tourists' visits.

Tourists provide a window on the world

The mass media available to the villagers are limited. In 1998 there were no televisions in Bena and those in the *nua* of Wogo have such bad reception they are rarely watched. By 2000 many children in Wogo would watch satellite television in friends' homes close to the *nua*. In 2005 several houses in Bena had televisions. Villagers owning radios listen to them only sporadically due to the relatively high cost of batteries. Newspapers are not easily available. A few villagers read *Pos Kupang* (the newspaper is East Nusa Tenggara) but this does not cover international issues. The villagers like tourists, especially those who can converse in Indonesian, or who are prepared to converse through willing guides, because they provide *kakangai otaola*, 'a window on the world.'[6] This important benefit of tourism is often expressed by explaining that through tourists it is possible to get messages from another world (*Tuku mumu, nunga lema*).[7] Through conversations with tourists, the villagers learn what goes on outside the area. Most villagers have not been outside Flores – some have not been even as far as Bajawa – and are interested to know what goes on beyond. 'We can learn about the world from tourists' was a more commonly cited reason for liking tourists in Wogo than Bena.

A villager's status is raised if they can boast a friend from afar. Just knowing a tourist's name, age and origins will make them a friend and thus a story to be recounted. Increased status due to contact with the outside world is common in Indonesia. 'As in Java, guests signify a host's superior status, the greater distances travelled reflect a greater drawing power' (Volkman, 1987: 167).

The villagers liked the idea that they could exchange ideas with people from far afield and reiterated the pan-Indonesian saying: 'many friends bring good fortune' ('*banyak teman, banyak rejeki*'). There are two local expressions, both in 'paired parallel poetic language' (cf. Forth, 1996): 'many friends much luck, few friends little luck' (*Hoga woe woso n'oe, hoga woe dhoso n'oe*) and 'good friends bring much luck, bad friends bring misfortune' (*Hoga woe modhe ngawu kono one, hoga woe ngesa ngawu ili lema*). A desire for contact with the wider world combined with a wish for their culture to be known to the world strengthens the villagers' like for tourists.

The findings from the villagers were reiterated in a discussion with third-year senior high school students studying English. Of class members who wanted to become guides, the reasons given included opportunities to learn about other countries and the opportunity to meet other people from different backgrounds.[8] A further reason for a desire for contact with foreigners comes from their hopes and dreams. Some, especially young people, want to associate with tourists as they might 'adopt them', pay for their education outside of Flores, or even take them back to Europe (cf. Dahles, 1999; Erb, 2000)

As with many societies in the region, travel is valued because it leads to knowledge and respect. This is summed up in another local expression: 'wander away, seek knowledge; travel far, seek wisdom' (*la'a ezo, gae go be'o; la'a dada, gae go magha*). In some societies, this is institutionalised, as among the Minangkabau of West Sumatra, whose men leave to *merantau*,[9] and among the Iban of Kalimantan who *bejalai*, a journey to get profit and prestige. As Caslake (1993) discusses, the tradition that a much-journeyed man can command considerable social prestige provides a base for relations with travellers. Tourists are foreigners on *bejalai*.

Economic importance

Being an agriculturally poorer village, Bena's greater dependence on the economic benefits brought by tourists clearly inter-plays with their liking of tourists. Hence, economic importance was the second reason Bena villagers gave for liking tourists. Tourists represent an 'outlet for sales' (*pintu jual*) for ikat fabric, and, as tourists walk through the village, women become excited at the prospect of a sale. However, in 1998, women in Wogo would not consider hanging out their wares in front of their houses. 'This is a *sa'o*, not a market, I would be ashamed (*malu*) to hang my baskets (*bere*) outside like a shop', one woman in Wogo told me. Instead, she asked guides if any of their guests needed a basket, and brought them out if requested to do so. In 2005 this woman and her neighbour sometimes put their baskets on a chair on their terrace. The 'display' was so informal that it was not obvious to tourists that the baskets were for sale. The women were facing a dilemma, economic needs were such that making a sale was important but they didn't want to desacralise their houses.

By contrast, such feelings of shame clearly do not exist for the women of Bena, nearly all of whom display their wares outside, on their terraces. These are mainly ikats but increasingly include other items such as long knives, and carved coconut shell bowls. The women of Bena were keen to point out that sales began when tourists started requesting purchases from items hanging on villagers' washing lines and not by women initially offering ikat cloths for sale. Further, the Department of Tourism has provided a souvenir shop so that 'all ikat cloths can be hung in one place and not all over the place, as if the village is a market', as a representative from the provincial Department of Tourism said.

Facilities

Both Wogo and Bena have gained improved facilities either directly or indirectly as a result of tourism. Tourism has brought piped water closer to the villagers' homes. In the case of Bena, voluntary donations from tourists, before the onset of ticket sales, were used to pipe water to the village. More recently an aid agency match funded[10] further water distribution, the villagers used tourism revenue as their share. In Wogo, my tour company provided the materials, and the villagers the labour, to bring water and build containers for it, close to the village. Tourism was a factor in the government's decision to improve the road to Bena. This meant more and better transport for the villagers and thus eased access to markets in Bajawa and further afield. These fringe benefits have clearly made up part of the villagers' positive view of tourism.

Understanding Tourists and Tourism

Alongside the villagers' positive view of tourism is a feeling of bemusement. Frequently I was asked by villagers in Wogo, 'Why do they come?',

'What do they want?', 'They don't ask anything; they don't learn anything; that one didn't even take any photographs', 'They just look and take photographs; they do not understand the meanings.' Villagers thought I should know why tourists came, looked, took photographs and departed. Similarly, villagers in Bena expressed their lack of understanding of tourists. They are unclear why tourists come and what they want. Villagers in both Bena and Wogo bemoaned their lack of understanding of tourism.

The villagers of Bena had a pragmatic view about their lack of knowledge inasmuch as they felt it was the government's duty to educate them. The villagers' lack of knowledge and confidence in understanding tourists is further reflected in their lack of knowledge of the tourism process.

The villagers' knowledge of tourism processes had been learnt from three sources: the government's tourism awareness campaign (*sadar wisata*), communication with guides and their own experience. The government's campaign taught them, in vague terms, that tourists have come to see the beauty of their village, to see somewhere so different from what can be found elsewhere and that is why it must be preserved. As Adams discusses, the campaign encouraged remote villages to recognise their uniqueness and 'to consider their own touristic charms and attracting powers' (1997: 158).

Through communication with guides, villagers have learnt that tourists do not like children 'begging' (see Chapter 8) and disapprove of villagers asking for money if a tourist wants to take photographs of them. Guides have taught the villagers not to surround tourists or invade their personal space and that some tourists feel nervous when villagers get too close.

From their experiences, the villagers are able to discuss a range of tourist types that visit the villages. Villagers identify three groups: the young, dirty, low spenders;[11] the older, fat, high spenders, an increasingly frequent type; and those who want to understand. They know that tourists do not have much time and are, by local standards, impatient; some said increasingly so.

The villagers lacked knowledge about issues of carrying capacity. Several villagers suggested that each of the provincial homestays could accommodate 30 tourists. This was based on their own Houses accommodating in excess of 30 House members at major rituals. However, it is unlikely any tourists would be prepared to sleep in such cramped conditions. Although each homestay could reasonably accommodate 8 tourists, only one toilet was provided for all three houses, seriously restricting potential occupancy levels.

Arguably, the psychological carrying capacity of the village of Bena is reaching saturation point during the peak season. Tourists stated dissatisfaction due to too many other tourists. On one day in August 1998, tourists had to queue to get up and down the steps to some of the village's terraces. However, all the villagers but one said they wanted more tourists, including in the high season. Only the chair of the tourism management group suggested that on peak days in August Bena was crowded enough. The environmental carrying capacity also needs to be considered as stone features show increasing signs of wear and tear, for example steps are so worn as to be dangerous in places.

Tourism and Economic Development

Most villagers in both Bena and Wogo live close to or below the poverty line by international standards however, in the opinion of the villagers, in Wogo, the land can supply enough food and cash for their needs. Villagers said that all that prevented them from earning and producing more was the will to work harder.[12] Most claimed they are happy and satisfied with what they have already (*puas dengan apa adanya*). However, they are aware that in the next generation shortages will occur and therefore view tourism as a potential vehicle for further economic development. Only 50% of women in Wogo used non-natural[13] family planning and clearly if the population continues to expand at present rates, the land will not meet the needs of future generations to the same extent as it does now. Birth control is much more widely used in Bena (90% use non-natural contraception).

In Bena, tourism has become part of the economic fabric of the village and the villagers are keen to extend this. As in Wogo, all villagers felt that tourism had the potential to bring further development to the village. Underlying the lack of development in Wogo and the slow pace of development in Bena are a number of similar factors. While the external factors were explored in Chapter 3, the internal factors are discussed in turn below: the restriction of entrepreneurial behaviour caused by the importance of community over individuals; the history of outside authority; and the absence of an active marketing strategy.

Entrepreneurial spirit in individuals is frowned upon because it can lead to envy and bad feeling. Villagers find it hard to rise above the majority. In such a closely knit community, wealth is known and there is great pressure to share it. This was borne out on numerous occasions in conversations and comments from the villagers. 'Don't grind too much coffee, or someone will see it and ask for some', 'There's no point in having a motor bike because everyone would use it', 'There are differences in wealth but we should not allow them to be seen.' The villagers in Wogo claimed that no project could go ahead without consensus: no individual would be brave enough to go it alone. Community consensus has to be guarded, it is the 'the mother of *adat*' (Zainal Kling 1997: 48). It is necessary due to 'the density and intimacy of social life' (Just, 2001: 110). Successful individual entrepreneurial activity can result in an observable difference in the community, leading to envy, resentment and lack of community cohesion. One villager brought groups of tourists to Wogo. His personal gains caused such rifts in the village that he has moved to Labuhan Bajo where he works successfully in tourism.

The villagers of Ngadha have experienced strong outside authority from both the Church and state (see Chapter 9). They have become used to acting on instruction and do not feel empowered to act without being directed. In Bena, representatives of the state reside both in the village headman's office, a mile uphill, and in the regency town of Bajawa, some 15km uphill. *Atas* (upper/above) was used both as a geographical term and metaphorical term from where the direction had to come. Such external power was resented but, without it, the villagers felt unable to act.

Further inaction resulted from 'the need to be asked'. The sale of ikats in Bena began when tourists requested to purchase ikat cloths hanging on washing lines. The request came from the tourists. Most long knives (*parang*) are still sold in this way although a few are now hung on terraces in Bena in a deliberate attempt to sell them. The villagers make and use rice baskets (*wati*), gourd bowls (*ngeme*), wooden and coconut ladles and draining spoons but these are not offered to tourists. As these are kept in the inner sacred rooms of Houses which tourists rarely enter, tourists do not see them or ask to purchase them. When villagers were asked why they did not sell these items to tourists, I was told: 'Tourists have not asked to buy them'.[14] The tourists I took to Wogo did enter the inner rooms and requested to buy various items. The villagers were happy to give them away: 'Have it, we can easily make another one.' It did not occur to them to sell these objects. Later, when recounting their strange experiences with tourists, they would giggle and say: 'They wanted our old spoons.'

The Tourism Department endorsed the view of waiting for requests to come from tourists by saying 'villagers shouldn't force their wares on tourists but should provide them if requested'. This view from the government may be an over-reaction to problems that have occurred in Bali, where over-zealous hawkers on Kuta beach annoyed tourists by forcing their wares on them. Tourists' dislike of being pressured into purchasing souvenirs and services may have been communicated through the Department of Tourism. However, there is a broad area of compromise between forcing items on tourists and waiting for requests from tourists.

The availability of villagers as Indonesian-speaking guides is not advertised. Several men in both Bena and Wogo are available and would like to act as village guides but they are waiting to be asked. On several occasions, I met tourists who, because they could speak Indonesian, were travelling without guides but did not know who to approach in the community (or how to do it). On a number of occasions members of the Tourism Department (also referred to as *atas*), said: 'Villagers know nothing; they are not educated enough to act as guides.' 'Guides know better (about the culture) than the villagers' and 'Villagers cannot work as guides because they are not licensed.' Villagers were aware of these views and felt angered and belittled by them.

The villagers' lack of tourism understanding is linked to the unfilled potential for further tourism development. The villagers did not have the confidence, knowledge or skills to put ideas into practice. In Bena, the state was blamed for not providing the necessary training. In Wogo, the emphasis was placed on the lack of community consensus and ill-feeling around political control at the village level (see below).

Problems with Tourists and Tourism

Although the villagers expressed overwhelming positive views of tourism, they also recognise a number of problems. The most frequently mentioned is tourists' disrespect, mainly through dress but also in their behaviour. Of the tourists that visited Bena in one month (October to November 1998), the villagers described two-fifths of them as impolite, and a tenth were considered rude. Views about indecency regarding dress were raised frequently by many of the villagers. It would be easy to assume the basic problem lay in the lack of clothes worn by tourists, that shorts and vests – common attire for tourists in hot weather – was the cause of the bad feeling. In fact, the issues surrounding tourists' clothing are far more complex than merely the lack of it. Aspects of clothing considered impolite fall into a number of categories, which, for the sake of clarity, I have separated below. It should be recognised that the separation is heuristic and in fact the different factors inter-play and are bound up with behaviour, for example how a tourist sits and how some positions are more revealing than others. Key areas of offensive behaviour are also examined.

The villagers had told me that one aspect of modernisation, brought by the Church, was the wearing of clothes by children. Indeed, one of the most conspicuous changes in Wogo in the years I have been visiting is the decreasing number of half-dressed children. While in the early 1990s many children in the *nua* wore few clothes, ten years later only the smallest of toddlers could be seen half dressed.

As villagers pointed out, in the gardens (*kebon*) children still run around free of clothing but they always wear clothes to go to market or to church. Entering public spaces requires the wearing of clothes. The *nua* is in an ambiguous position: at once people's homes – and therefore private – and at the same time the centre of village sacred space – and therefore public. With the advent of tourism, the presence of tourists would be used as an excuse to pressurise children to put clothes on. 'Look, there's a tourist, you should be shy not to have clothes on'; ' I feel ashamed (*malu*) that tourists can see your vagina/penis' relatives would retort to their half-dressed children. Parents always apologised to me if their child was not fully dressed.

Unclean clothes

Although, due to the nature of their environment and work, being dusty or muddy is normal for the villagers at home, they would not leave the village to go visiting without washing and changing into clean clothes. As tourists are visitors, they should be in their best clothes and these should be clean. It is offensive to your hosts to arrive in unclean clothes and it would be better not to come than arrive in dirty clothes. Tourists wearing dirty and/or torn clothing were considered disrespectful.

Sleeveless clothes

Men working in the village may take their shirts off but not when they go visiting. Male visitors, including tourists, should not take their shirts off. Vests are considered undergarments and therefore should not be the top layer of clothing for male or female tourists. Women in sleeveless tops are considered impolite. Body sizes and shape affect a villager's perspectives of what tops are acceptable. The fatter a woman, the more important it is for a top to be loose fitting. A tight-fitting vest is indecent and without a bra is considered rude.

Types of shorts

Shorts are worn by villagers on occasions and are therefore not a problem per se but the length and breadth of the shorts worn by tourists was criticised. They were considered indecent if too short or too tight, i.e. if they were revealing. Shorts were considered offensive if the tourists sat impolitely in such a way that undergarments could be seen. On one occasion, when a tourist was sitting in shorts that were short and wide enough for the villagers to see a lack of underclothes, utter disgust was expressed. As with tops, villagers' views were affected by the size and shape of the body under the shorts and by the amount and type of underclothes (which should not be seen).

Displaying navels

A navel is a person's centre, sacred and revered, and it is considered rude to put it on show. Pierced and adorned navels were met with horrified astonishment. As women said, 'We just have to look away', and another added, 'How could they do that?' On one occasion, a woman turned away as a young female tourist approached. The tourist wanted to examine the ikats on display. As she came nearer, the villager went inside to escape viewing the tourist. The tourist started asking me the prices. From inside, I was told, 'Don't bother' (*'tidak usah, jangan'*[15]). I knew how much the villager was looking forward to a sale as her son needed money for school, and was coming from Bajawa. The imperative to make a sale was, however, over-ridden by not wanting such a rude tourist to have one of her ikats. Cropped tops,[16] the most serious transgression of acceptable attire, were particularly popular in the summer of 1998 and provoked numerous debates about how to tackle the problem of 'such rude tourists' coming to the village. The fashion signalled a new type of tourist for many villagers, a particularly rude type.

Exhibiting amorous relations

The behaviour of tourists that upset the villagers extended from hand-holding to all other outward signs of physical relations between men and women. By 1998 kissing was rare because guides warned tourists that it is unacceptable. However, on a number of occasions one tourist would carry another, pick each other up, give 'piggy-backs', swing one another around or hug one another. Such behaviour was considered inappropriate and rude.

Ignoring greetings

Tourists that refused to return greetings were considered arrogant, conceited and impolite. When adults try either a 'hello' or another greeting, they are offended when it is not returned. There are two words in Ngadha language that translate to the Indonesian *sombong* (arrogant or conceited). *Melo* refers to someone who lacks respect for others or is over-confident and *sobo* refers to an unsmiling face. Both these terms are muttered about tourists. A tourist may also be considered *hunga hanga* someone who shows little interest, little curiosity or care. *Hunga hanga* tourists are the opposite of tourists that 'want to understand' (see above).

Tourists become frustrated by the constant 'hello mister' that rings from every passer-by on Flores (and other Indonesian islands). A lot of the time, children will incessantly call to tourists, and to respond to all of them is virtually impossible. When children shout out to tourists they may be playing a game of 'bothering them',[17] trying to get a reaction to break their boredom. Adults' greetings are different but tourists do not always differentiate. If an adult's greeting or smile is ignored villagers think that tourists are arrogant. On the contrary, when a tourist tries an Indonesian greeting, villagers are pleased and will enter into friendly communication.

Friendly communication always begins with a standard pattern of questions where the villagers attempt to locate the tourists socially. In order to place a tourist both geographically and socially, the following questions are asked before further communication can take place: 'What is your name?[18]', 'Where are you from?', 'What is your religion?', 'Are you married?', 'How many children do you have?' For a tourist, this question-firing feels rather like 'the Spanish inquisition', especially as most Indonesians who attempt communication with tourists ask the same series of questions. Only when these questions have been answered, and the tourist is socially located, can further communication take place. Tourists, frequently bored by the same line of questioning, try variations in their answers. For example, to the question 'Where are you from?' They will reply 'Bajawa' (from where they have just come) and not their country of origin. In such cases, further communication is unlikely to flow.

Sometimes villagers will ask tourists questions to which the answer is blatantly obvious, e.g. 'Are you looking at my ikat cloths?' (When a tourist is looking at one). As Just points out, asking 'banal questions' such as asking a woman who is weaving if she is weaving, are 'behavitives' 'that constitute part of the constant aural and oral backdrop to social life that establish the status of relationships [and] expectations of behaviour' (2001: 96). The villagers are attempting to establish a friendly relationship with tourists in a way that communication between villagers takes place. Tourists are usually perplexed and frequently miss this opportunity to enter dialogue.

Taking photographs without permission

On a few occasions, villagers in Bena complained that tourists had taken photographs without permission. On each occasion, the villagers in question were in ritual clothes and the offence was partly caused by the tourist intruding into sacred space. At profane times, villagers are happy to have their photographs taken. In Bena, some of the villagers are aware that this can be used for economic gain. Requesting money for photographs is very badly thought of by the management team, the Department of Tourism, guides and most villagers. Requesting money to view the new *ngadhu* (see below) was the cause of heated debates in the village. I witnessed payment for a photograph on only one occasion. An elderly man, failing to sell a long knife, took payment for being photographed holding it.

On one occasion, tourists wanted to make a video of a ritual in Wogo (see below). Although it is relatively common for tourists to use micro-recording equipment, the use of a large (professional looking) video camera led the villagers to conclude that the video might be used for commercial purposes. Both the fact that no permission was sought, and that a video of a sacred ceremony could bring the tourist financial gain,[19] were raised by villagers when I discussed the issue with them.

Refusing food

To refuse food offered is impolite and to refuse ritual food causes even greater offence. On a number of occasions at rituals, I would be required to eat five meals before midday and to refuse any of them would have been unacceptable. Eating a token amount or not finishing all that is provided does not cause bad feeling. Villagers expressed considerable upset at tourists that attended rituals but would not partake in the ritual meals. When tourists departed before a meal was ready, villagers would begrudgingly accept the situation.

Although there is a range of behaviour that upsets or is considered impolite by the villagers, they are unwilling to take action to prevent it. They were frightened of being assertive and did not feel able to raise issues with tourists directly. Two reasons were cited. Firstly, there is a fear that potential conflict can escalate and that tempers could be raised and fights would result. This has already happened once in Bena. Secondly, tourists are 'state guests' (*tamu negara*): this means that they are given a position of esteem and authority and cannot be confronted or rebuffed. The villagers felt: 'We should only serve them.' And that 'they might report us to the authorities'. The villagers brought matters to the attention of guides but generally only after the tourists had departed.

Tourists at Rituals

As I suggested in Chapter 2, an analytical division between tourists attending rituals (events for the community and ancestors) and staged performances (for tourists) is required. This section examines tourists at ritual events for the community. I will begin by recounting the events at rituals in three villages.

Clan-stone moving ritual

The *Robo Keri* is a clan-stone moving ritual, which formed part of a series of rituals, over a number of years, to rebuild a *nua*[20] in a village neighbouring Wogo. The ritual was of considerable significance, it took four days and involved the slaughter of five buffalo and 60 pigs. Participants travelled great distances, from Jakarta and Kupang for example, to attend. At the end of the first day, I sat with members of the hosting clan and they asked me to bring some friends to attend the following days of ceremony. When it was understood that I didn't know any other westerners, I asked if they wanted me to find some tourists to attend. This brought smiles of anticipation as the greater the number of guests and the further they travel brings status to the host. I spent the next day going to town to find and invite tourists. Although initially suspicious of my intentions, five Europeans and a Chilean agreed to come.

An entry step installation ritual

The Kaba Pere (entry step) installation ritual is one in a long series of house building rituals. Many Houses now omit it, so it is rarely performed. When it is conducted, the heavy wooden entry step is kept outside the village where it is tied to a bamboo frame. While men, shrieking with merriment, carry, shake and dance with it, a chosen male 'rides' it into the village with female members of the house dancing alongside (see Plate 12). On an occasion in Wogo, the villagers were preparing for a Kaba Pere installation ritual when, unannounced, a group of 16 Austrians arrived. The group's intention was to stop to view Wogo before continuing to Bena, but they were keen to stay for the duration of the ceremony, a two-day event, and so changed their plans. After the afternoon's events and arranging accommodation in the village, the tourists departed to buy packaged food in the local town before returning to sleep in a House. Some of them slept outside on the terrace. The villagers thought this was strange, especially as room had been made to accommodate them inside. The next morning the group stayed for the spectacle but not for the ritual meal. The tourists videoed the ritual and took photographs. At times, cameras were within a metre of the dancers' faces and at one point a villager was (gently) pushed aside to get a better photograph.

A new *ngadhu* ritual

For the major ritual of carrying the new *ngadhu* into Bena (*Bhei Ngadhu*), local guides were encouraged to bring tourists. When a local guide arrived with 14 tourists just after 10 a.m., a young bamboo shoot and an Indonesian flag[21] were evident next to the hole that the replacement *ngadhu* would be

Plate 12 A villager in Wogo rides a *kaba pere* into the village

planted in. Bundles of thatch lay next to them ready for thatching the *ngadhu*. Behind the houses enormous pans of rice were being cooked on open fires. Although these factors were evidence of the pending ritual, the clan was not yet in ceremonial costume, so the major events were not about to happen.

The guide entered the clan's central House and made a donation. In impatient tones, he said, 'You asked me to invite tourists. You said it would start early morning. Now its mid-morning so why is nothing happening yet, I told them by 10 a.m. it would have started ...' (The guide was agitated, as it had been hard to get such a large group together and get them to the village for 10 am. Some tourists had to be picked up earlier than they had wanted to allow the guide to pick tourists up from the various guesthouses. The guide was empathising with his tourists who had been awoken early, unnecessarily.) The elder that received the guide and his donation had just had a meeting with his clan about the shortfall in funds for the ceremony and was especially put out by the diminutive offer from the guide. The elder assumed (correctly) that one guide, charging higher than normal fees (because of the ritual) for a large group of tourists could afford to donate more generously towards the ritual. The guide was not prepared to give more of his takings or ask the tourists for any more money.

The elder then requested a dollar a photo (but was prepared to bargain). When the guide refused, the elder told the guide that none of his tourists were welcome and that none could take any photos without paying. The guide told the tourists he was a 'fucking bastard'. When the elder understood that the guide was swearing about him in English, the confrontation became heated. Other villagers moved in to bring peace and calm. Such a confrontation would upset the ancestors and was detracting from the ceremony. Furthermore, as the clan was split over raising money from tourists for the ritual, this conflict threatened to spill over and re-ignite clan divisions. Clan disharmony is certain to disturb ancestors. As the ceremony was being held to remember and thereby appease the clan's ancestors[22] any potential for overt disharmony had to be swiftly prevented.

While the guide took the tourists to the viewing post at the top of the village, the clan continued with their preparations. An hour or so later, after a preliminary dance, the clan in full ritual costume departed to the site where the new *ngadhu* trunk was resting. Preparations at the site were elaborate (See Plate 13). Some tourists felt uncomfortable taking photographs and refrained. Other tourists arrived with other guides and took photographs. Some took photographs of women in ceremonial dress without first asking their permission. This action upset the women (see above).

Villagers were also upset because female tourists got too close to the *ngadhu*. All the village women were keeping well back and observing the preparations from a distance. It is considered dangerous for a woman to get close to a *ngadhu*, personified as a male, until it is planted in the *nua*. During the time the trunk was resting outside the *nua*, girls were constantly reminded that, 'he can get you pregnant' or 'you might not have any children if you see him'. Although the trunk was to be brought into the village and would be seen by all women, it was still considered inauspicious to get too close to him, until he was in the *nua*. Tourists, keen to see the considerable commotion surrounding the preparations, wanted to be close up to the action, to observe what was going on. In doing so, they were not observing *adat* and were causing offence.

When the preparations for the new *ngadhu*'s journey into the village were complete, a meal, served on leaves, was eaten adjacent to the resting place. Many tourists refused what was offered to them. This also broke customary rules, as one woman put it, 'If you are here you have to eat; this is *adat* food' or as another said, 'It is not ordinary food; if you refuse it, the ancestors will be angry.' Their anger in part seemed to be about tourists getting in the way, taking up space, and not appreciating the importance of the event. They articulated their annoyance by referring to an obvious contravention of *adat*.

Plate 13 Villagers in Bena make preparations before a new *ngadhu* enters the village

Villagers' perceptions of tourists' attendance at rituals

These three cases reveal a number of perceptions about tourists' attendance at rituals.

Villagers are not only happy for tourists to attend rituals, tourists are actively sought to take part in them. It is common for guides to be pre-warned of rituals so that they can bring tourists. As has already been discussed, 'the more the merrier' (*ramai*) is a strong cultural value and the further people travel to attend a ritual the more importance is attached to it. For this reason, the Chilean tourist attracted the most interest from the villagers at the *Robo Keri* ritual, introduced throughout the day as 'all the way from Chile'.

As I have suggested, contact with the outside world increases status. The news and stories of the festivities would be spread further afield, abroad in the case of tourists, and thus fame would be bestowed on the hosts. When tourists behave according to local protocol, dress up in cere-monial clothes, dance and take part in ritual meals they are fondly remem-bered (see Plate 14). Rituals are identified and remembered as, for example, the one where 'that German danced so well'.

Tourists often promise and sometimes do send photographs of rituals to villagers. This used to be the only source of photographs of special events

Plate 14 A tourist learns to dance

that the villagers had and they appreciated this. This is, however, becoming less important as relatives from metropolitan centres often have cameras.

Tourists' attendance at rituals does, however, bring stress and incipient annoyance of tourism to the surface. During rituals, villagers have a heightened regard for custom and the wishes of the ancestors. They are less tolerant of the cultural insensitivity that tourists demonstrate. They complained about tourists not partaking in ritual food, about the inconsiderate taking of photographs and about tourists getting too close to the action.

With the exception of some members of the clan in Bena attempting to raise funds for the new *ngadhu*, Ngadha villagers do not expect tourists to pay cash to attend rituals. However, when tourists make donations in compliance with customary rules, for example a donation of rice, they are immediately regarded as a person who understands.

Villagers were happy for tourists to attend rituals spontaneously and are sometimes prepared to put on displays of music and dance for tourists, but disagreed with the idea of staging rituals for tourists. '*Adat* is sacred; it takes blood; it can't be done just like that; the ancestors would be angry', as one woman explained. Some villagers considered the staging of the customary marriage ceremony possible. However, as this is largely a discursive event between the bride and groom's kin and lacks any outwardly observable ceremony (costume, dance or merriment), it seems unlikely that this ritual would be attractive to tourists.

Performances for Tourists

In contrast to rituals, performances can be shortened, much of the ritual preparation would not be required and punctuality ordered to suit tourists' needs. The villagers did not show concern about taking dances out of their original context. Nearly all Ngadha dances involve groups of 20 or so individuals (Saju & Sawega, 1994). A group from Wogo performed at the MSPI[23] (Indonesian Performing Arts) festival in Maumere in 1994 and at the International Bamboo Music Festival held in Bali in 1995. Enjoying the benefits, as Sanger (1988) points out, of social cohesion and travel, the group established a *sanggar budaya* (cultural studio) hoping to perform for tourists. Erb (2000) claims these cultural studios have proliferated in Manggarai with state recognition and small amounts of financial help. However, in Wogo, as the group was large, remuneration for performances needed to be sufficient to share. Most tour groups are not willing to pay enough. In other regions, dances can be provided by smaller groups and therefore are less expensive. Further, as villagers pointed out, they received no deposit when they were requested to perform and no-shows were not infrequent. The group practised and some of them had to hire costumes. The income was considered insufficient to cover costs. For these reasons, the villagers are not enthusiastic about providing performances for tourists.

In Bena, the villagers were also unenthusiastic about performances for tourists. During my fieldwork, the caretaker and the chair of the tourism management group turned down a request. 'It would work out at a few thousand[24] each: it is not worth it', he told me. Putting on a performance meant having meetings to decide which dances to perform, checking dancers had complete costumes, organising practices. All these would eat into time that could be used for productive purposes such as weaving. As one woman pointed out: 'We don't enjoy the dancing as much (as for rituals). It's a job but the money is not worth it.' The woman said that performances were not *ramai*, expressing the lack of merriment and sociability she associated with performance dancing compared to ritual dancing. At rituals, there are the added benefits of eating meat, usually in large amounts, and substantial drinking. When they gave performances, all they got was a small amount of money and no associated benefits.

Perceptions of Tourists and Tourism in the Political Context

We have seen that, while residents in both Wogo and Bena express the desire for more tourists, there are aspects of tourist dress and behaviour of which they disapprove. At the same time, they are also unhappy at the ways in which tourists' expenditures are distributed, an unhappiness which relates more to the socio-political context in which tourism occurs than to the individual or group behaviour of tourists themselves.

In discussions with villagers about their experience of tourism over the last decade of the 20th century, the villagers' deep disillusionment with the village political system became central. In 1998, the second president of Indonesia, Suharto, had just resigned in response to mass demonstrations by students and opposition groups. Across the archipelago, corrupt officials were being rooted out. Against this backdrop, it is not surprising that the villagers' narratives so frequently referred to corruption. However, the narratives also reveal important perceptions about ten years of tourism development in the villages. In 2005 many of the same issues were still current. The two villages have had different experiences; they are thus dealt with separately.

In Wogo, tourism has not developed. I first took tourists there in 1989. Two years later, funds from our visits had brought water to two points in the *nua* and the village name had entered the Lonely Planet guidebook. The village was famous and I was sure that, given ten years, it would be 'touristic'.[25] A year later, our clients encountered other tourists in 'their village'. When independent tourists showed up to watch cultural shows that our company had sponsored, I realised that our competitive advantage depended on finding a remoter village. The villagers were extremely grateful that we had put Wogo on the tourist map and I was sure their tourist numbers would continue to grow.

As I visited Flores over the years, I saw tourism development continue apace. New guesthouses and restaurants opened nearly every year in both Moni and Labuhan Bajo as tourist numbers increased. The same increase in tourists has not been felt in Wogo.

As has been described, Wogo moved from its old site (Wogo Lama – see Plate 3) to its present site in 1932. The site of the present village is built on land owned by two clans, the upper third of the village by one clan and the lower two-thirds by another. The only direct male descendant (Stephen[26]) of the larger land-owning clan believes himself to be the landlord and 'ruler' of the *nua*. All the other clans and the many members of his own clan maintain that his ancestors gave over the land for the good of the village and approximately 100 buffaloes were slaughtered in their honour for the village to be united on its present site.

This man's mother's brother was democratically chosen to be head of the village and happily served one term. When he wished to step down (he was old, tired and in bad health), no one made any nominations. There was no will to instate a member of the 'land-owning clan' and no one from any other clan dared to come forward.

When the Department of Education and Culture chose a caretaker (*juru kunci*) from the village, he was not from the 'ruling clan'. Unable to carry out his job, he resigned and Stephen slipped into his shoes. The Department of Education and Culture did not realise the potential problems that this would lead to. As the caretaker, he collects the donations made by the tourists. The money then goes no further, unlike in Bena (see below) or other places [27] that use tickets. Hence the bad feelings that tourism brings up. All the funds are going into one man's pocket and are not being further distributed.

A number of reasons were given that such resentment exists without coming out into the open: 'The wounds run deep' and 'the conflict would spill over'. Already one clan has been forced to leave the village and set up a separate *nua*, another clan remains divided with their *ngadhu* but no *bhaga* in the *nua*. Secondly, 'God will deal with people like that', 'we believe that this will be sorted out in the next life'. 'We cannot do anything about it. It is better to ignore it.' Pretending that they do not care, the villagers were happier to leave the problem to fate or the next life. Belief in divine retribution is common in Eastern Indonesian societies. Just (2001) describes how bad deaths are attributed to improper moral conduct in life. Further views were expressed about why the villagers are prepared to ignore the man's behaviour: 'If we try to do anything it would escalate', 'Why should we fight over money we have not worked to earn.' 'If he wants to keep the money, he will live with a bad conscience. It is better we don't get involved.' Finally the villagers think 'it can only be sorted from above: we are powerless'. 'Above' here refers to government levels higher than the village.

Although the above quotes from villagers were obtained during discussions about tourism, on many other occasions similar disquiet was revealed. In the late 1990s the peace in the village was often disturbed by loud western music played on large (50 watts per channel) amplifiers and speakers. Not only was the volume considered inappropriate but so were the times of day, including late at night and early in the morning. Villagers were keen to point out that the perpetrators of the noise pollution were beyond reconciliation: they were Stephen's nephews. Following a serious road accident and illness in the family in 2004, many of those responsible had 'learned to understand'. Divine retribution was apparently beginning to work.

Adults in Wogo do not consider tourism development necessary or possible in this generation, a view that contrasts with discussions in the early 1990s when great excitement and enthusiasm was expressed. 'There's no point; there's no unity in the village; we are powerless for as long as that man is here' is a view that summarised the feelings. Younger people in Wogo readily expressed their anger and frustration.

The same man was keen to point out that tourism was dependent on the village remaining traditional. He used rank, a traditional form of social organisation, to serve his own interests. Many of the villagers believe that rank is important in choice of spouse, but did not believe that Stephen was due high rank or that it entitled him to the other power he assumes. As I have described elsewhere (Cole, 1998), tourism is being used to articulate a position of power based on antiquated 'traditional' structures.

Bena was the first Ngadha village to be 'on the tourist map' and has had more external input in tourism development than any other village. In Bena, disillusionment about tourism development centred on state power structures. The democratically elected village headman (*Kepala Desa*) was serving the last year of his first seven-year post in 1998-1999. Most of Bena's tourism development has taken place during this time and progress has been slow in comparison with other places on Flores.

Backpackers started to visit Bena in the 1980s. The Department of Education and Culture appointed a caretaker in 1982. The voluntary donations made by tourists when they filled in the visitors' book were kept in the *nua* and by 1991 there was enough to bring piped water to two points close to the *nua*. When, in 1993, the provincial-level Tourism Department became involved with tourism, a ticket system was introduced.

The division of receipts from tickets was the subject of controversy and bad feeling. The villagers in the *nua* are those dealing with tourists on a day-to-day basis, and incurring costs of village repairs, but received only a small proportion of the receipts. The money that goes into the village was not accounted for and villagers are keen to point out the headman's new motorcycle and shop. The villagers also felt that they received little support from the Department of Tourism and did not see value for money from the proportion the Department received.

The problem became worse because the money went first to the village, after which the *nua*'s 20% was returned. For the year to April 1998, none of the receipts had been returned to the *nua* and the village headman could not explain their loss. With agreement from the Department of Tourism, the *nua* kept all income until the debt had been paid. In 2004 Bena stopped selling tickets.[28] Instead they asked for 'voluntary contributions' of at least Rp5000, and were not sharing any of the revenue. This led to problems. Firstly, the Department of Tourism and Culture wanted a share of revenue to pay for marketing and promotion. Secondly, tourists were confused about a supposed 'voluntary' donation with a specified minimum amount and most tourists just donated the minimum, as if it was a charge. Thirdly, some villagers claimed that the voluntary donations system lacked transparency.

The decisions by the provincial Tourism Department to build three homestays in Bena, a souvenir shop and a viewing post were also subject to controversy. Firstly because the decisions were not taken at a public meeting, and secondly because the homestays were built but no interior facilities were provided in terms of mattresses, bedding, cooking pots, crockery or cutlery. As the villagers explained, no individual could afford to provide such essentials but, without them, the dwellings could not be used for guests. The provincial Tourism Department had organised the building of homestays without educating the people as to their purpose. Further, none of the villagers had any experience of managing a homestay and many of them did not even understand what a homestay was. The terminology is clearly confusing. These were not anyone's homes for guests to stay in; they are dwellings built in traditional style for use by tourists. No one was made responsible for hospitality to the tourists and, as one woman pointed out, she could not be preparing meals in them and in her own home. It is easier, she explained, to have tourists in her own house, although she could not provide the comfort or privacy that tourists may want. In 1999, members of the headman's extended family were living in the homestay buildings.

Many villagers also expressed discontent about the viewing post. Not only, like the homestays, was it built without labour from the *nua*, but it was also built too close to the villagers' Catholic shrine.

The provincial Tourism Department also set up the tourism management group (*kelompok pengolah*). Although the impetus for inception came from the government, its success in part came from the fact that the villagers were left to organise the group, as they felt fit. The group, made up of one representative from each clan, elected the various officials to be responsible for various tasks, such as chair, secretary, accountant etc. The members expressed discontent that their roles were unpaid and resentment that some members did not carry out their tasks thoroughly. However, they thought that such a group was a good way to manage tourism in the village. The group was responsible for the allocation of the *nua*'s share of tourism revenue. I was told, for example, that revenue in 1997 was used to help with the restoration.[29]

Only one woman is a member of the tourism management group. As women are responsible for finances in Ngadha, the villagers considered it essential that the treasurer's position was held by a woman. As one man said: 'It is difficult for men to hold money; women are more responsible for money, we trust women with money matters.' Men or women that I talked to did not consider the lack of other female representation on the group to be a problem. However, when discussing issues about the homestays, it was clear that the women had opinions that men did not express.

Underpinning the desire to air issues of corruption in narratives about tourism development are a number of important perceptions the villages have about tourism development that need to be considered. Firstly, village unity is required for successful tourism development. Secondly, tourism income in Wogo is considered to be unearned income because no effort is required on the part of the villagers in order to reap the financial reward. Although, through their experiences of their music and dance group, they are prepared to make effort for financial and other gains, hosting tourists has so far not been equated with work. The tourism management group in Bena would disagree; they consider their efforts essential. They were becoming disillusioned with voluntary work with minimal benefits and were frustrated that they did not understand tourism well enough to make more out of it. This is linked to the third clear perception in their narratives – that they are keen to have more tourism education. Fourthly, the ticket system was initially well thought of. Many villagers in Wogo and Nage (another 'cultural village' that has a caretaker and guest book) wanted to introduce the system. In Bena, the villagers supported tickets because they ensured transparency. However, the ticket price was unrealistically low, and the revenue shares unacceptable. Realising that without tickets the *nua* could gain more income, tickets were abandoned. However, members of the management team concurred that tickets would be reintroduced as long as the *nua* received an acceptable share. Although the introduction of tickets was a provincial Tourism Department initiative, their other initiatives have not been well received. Edifices without fittings were considered a waste of the Department's budget. Finally, decision-making about tourism development should be made at an open meeting (see further discussion in Chapter 9). With representatives across the clans, the tourism management group is considered a successful way to manage tourism in Bena. Potentially, this model could be exported to other villages.

Changing Views

This chapter has examined the villagers' opinions of tourists and tourism. Some views have remained constant while others have changed. In Ngadha, tourists are respected, they bring pride, excitement, knowledge and status to the villagers. While villagers most frequently expressed positive views of tourists and tourism, nearly all villagers complained about the clothes of many tourists and the behaviour of some. Tourists who wore dirty, torn or minimal clothing were considered impolite, while tourists who displayed their navels were deemed rude. Tourists that ignored adults' attempts to enter communication were considered arrogant and impolite, while those who refused villagers' food, especially ritual meals, were thought offensive. Although villagers were generally happy to be photographed, when, at rituals, tourists failed to seek permission first, they were badly thought of. These views of tourists have changed very little over the years. The villagers are no longer surprised but remain unhappy by what they consider to be the impolite behaviour of some tourists. In 2003 I convened a seminar with local stakeholders to share the results of my research. During the seminar we agreed a code of conduct – a list of 12 points that tourists should know before visiting a Ngadha village. The code of conduct was introduced in an attempt to persuade tourists to dress and behave in ways that were more suited to the local culture. An evaluation (see Cole, 2007) of the effectiveness of the code suggests that the situation has improved in relation to the dress of the tourists. However, despite the code many still refuse ritual meals.

Tourists were sought out to attend rituals as this brings pride to the host. However, villagers were less tolerant of tourists' cultural insensitivity during rituals as they have an increased concern for *adat* and the wishes of the ancestors at such times. Initially villagers hoped that tourists would provide an audience for their proud music and dance traditions. However, the villagers have become unenthusiastic about performances for tourists. The income was too small and benefits too few. The hope of deriving economic benefits from an activity they enjoy have been dashed and optimism has turned to disappointment.

Tourism has brought money, facilities, cultural preservation and revitalisation, and the potential for further development. However the development has been limited for a number of reasons. The importance of the community over the individual has restricted individual entrepreneurial spirit, and, in Wogo, a lack of community consensus has limited community efforts. The villagers have become so accustomed to only acting on instruction from higher authority that they are apprehensive about following internal initiatives. The villagers lack confidence and wait for tourists to make requests rather than proactively marketing their crafts. In both villages, village unity was considered essential for successful tourism development. In the early days tourism brought great anticipation of new opportunities. While many villagers remain enthusiastic, expectations have been reduced and optimism deflated.

Bena has seen considerably more state intervention than Wogo. The villagers welcomed some initiatives, for example the use of tickets and the tourism management group. Other initiatives have caused controversy. In both Bena and Wogo, the villagers bemoaned their lack of knowledge and expressed a desire for more tourism education. In Bena, there is resentment that the state has not provided this. As tourism has increased and villagers have become used to tourism, they have become proud to be associated with an activity representative of westerners and modernity. Tourism is imbued with power, a resource the villagers are learning to manipulate. As we shall see tourism has become the locus for contestation as different groups make use of the power tourism can bring.

Notes

1. When tourists were asked if they would like to stay in villages, nearly half said they would.
2. As Sanger reports, villagers in Bali 'miss meeting their friends' in the low season (1988: 95).
3. Similarly the Balinese hospitality offered to tourists is an extension of their tradition of accepting strangers (Sanger, 1988).
4. Others note respite from boredom as a reason for appreciating tourists (for example, Hitchcock, 1996).
5. *'Mungkin orang Bena sudah bosan sama turis, mereka kurang semangat'.*
6. The local expression *kakangai otaola* would translate as ventilation holes on the universe.
7. Literally to relate lips and bridge tongues.
8. Crick (1994), who carried out much more thorough research with high school students in Sri Lanka, found similar responses.
9. To leave one's home area. See for example Mochtar Naim (1985), also Blackwood (2000).
10. A standpipe was provided every four houses. The villagers used 3 million rupiah from tourism revenue while the agency funded the remaining 33 million.
11. Low/high spenders were identified in Bena but not in Wogo.
12. Some *Donngo Sao* are quite elderly and it is a physical struggle for them to live from agricultural production alone. While the extended family should provide for the dongo sa'o in some cases it appeared that they were not well provided for.

13. Indonesian family planning is divided into two types: natural (*alami*) and non-natural (*buatan*). The former refers to a complex version of the rhythm method. The latter refers to interventions such as hormonal pills, injections, patches and IUD. Natural family planning is backed by all sections of the Catholic Church on Flores. Non-natural methods are considered un-Catholic but many priests do not oppose their use. Although natural methods do reduce family size, they are not as successful as non-natural methods.

14. *Belum ada turis yang minta* (Ind)

15. Literally 'not necessary, don't'.

16. T-shirts or vests that are hemmed some centimetres below the breast and above the navel.

17. *menggangu*.

18. The verb to be is nearly always omitted i.e. Where you from? What your name? etc.

19. De Burlo notes that steep charges are set for entrance to the *gol* ritual in Vanuatu because the locals believe that photographs and videos will be sold for personal profits (1996: 268).

20. The old *nua* had been abandoned when the villages had moved into 'healthy homes' in the 1970s.

21. Cf. Visser (1997) for the use of the same symbols used in rituals in Halmahera.

22. The clan had wanted to replace the *ngadhu* since it had been damaged in a fire at the beginning of the century but serious planning had started when illness and death had struck the clan in recent years. Many thought the ancestors felt neglected and replacing the *ngadhu* would improve the clan's fortunes.

23. Masyrakat Pertunjuk Seni Indonesia.

24. Less than US$1.

25. In the sense Picard (1997) uses it.

26. Not his real name

27. For example in Singapadu (see Sanger, 1988).

28. This may have been in response to my research that showed that tourists donated more than the ticket price in villages that did not use tickets. Furthermore, the tickets were issued by the Department, by not using them, the villagers were not under obligation to share their revenue.

29. The figures I was provided with: two Houses @ Rp125,000), their *bhaga* (2 x Rp50,000) and *ngadhu* (2 x Rp50,000). Rp450,000 for sand and cement, food and cigarettes for working parties, to re-lay stones and the remainder (Rp650,000) was put towards the village's New Year celebrations do not tally with 20% of the revenue from 5959 tourists.

Part 3

The Influence of Tourism

Chapter 8
'Conflicts of Tourism'

Chapters 5, 6 and 7 examined the different actors' – tourists, villagers and mediators – perspectives on tourism, and how they relate to their cultural norms, values and positions. This chapter highlights how the differences in values, perceptions, attitudes and priorities, on a number of different levels, between the villagers and the other actors, reveal the 'conflicts of tourism'. The villagers not only experience value clashes and conflicts with other stakeholders but also as a result of the processes of tourism development, as the demands of modernisation conflict with the demands to maintain tradition. These 'conflicts of acculturation' are also discussed. Before an examination of the 'conflicts of tourism' between actors, the differences between Bena and Wogo, established in earlier chapters, are brought together and summarised, as a background to why their conflicts differ. At the end of the chapter I summarise how these conflicts have changed both as a consequence of evolutionary processes and as reactions to particular initiatives.

Bena and Wogo Compared

The villages differ in topography and resultant agricultural production. Wogo has largely flat, fertile fields sustaining at least two harvests a year. Coffee is the most important cash crop, followed by vanilla, which has recently been introduced. By comparison, Bena has steep to very steep fields, which are highly denuded in places: most only give rise to one crop and much land is left fallow. Candlenuts, coffee, cocoa, cloves, pepper and vanilla are increasingly grown for cash. Bena's poorer agricultural endowment has lead to a greater dependence on tourism.

Wogo supports a much denser population than Bena, and has a higher rate of population growth. The villagers in Wogo are aware that agriculture alone will not support the next generation and view tourism as an important economic development option.

The two *nua* are very similar in size. Bena is an 'original village' while Wogo has been on the present site only since 1932. Bena is considered the first Ngadha village to be settled, and is referred to as the 'eldest sibling' village. As Molnar (2000) and Smedal (1998) discuss, originality and precedence are central concepts in Ngadha. They are considered an important aspect of Bena's attractiveness in tourism and were articulated in various aspects of conflict, including the date of *Reba* (see Chapter 9).

External influences, prior to tourism, have been greater in Wogo than in Bena. As a result of proximity to the parish church and mission at Mataloko, villagers have had more contact with European priests, and more village members have become priests and nuns, who have worked elsewhere and then returned. Some villagers have also transmigrated (initially to Kalimantan and then to Malaysia), many of whom have also returned. Villagers in Bena have had less contact with European priests, fewer have taken up church professions, and transmigration has been less popular.

Educational opportunities in Wogo are far greater and easier than in Bena. As a result, more Wogo children go on to high school and beyond, and many have taken the opportunity to study in Java and other Indonesian islands. By contrast, far fewer children in Bena take up educational opportunities.

Wogo lies only 2km from the Trans-Flores highway, a main road with frequent and varied transport. Bena is approximately 12km from this main artery and transport is limited to two or three truck-buses a day.

Despite the more difficult access, Bena has received far more tourists. Backpackers began to visit Bena in the early 1980s in tiny numbers, less than ten a year. This had reached over 2000 by the end of the decade and nearly 9000 a decade later.[1] Fewer than a dozen independent tourists had walked through Wogo when I began taking groups, of a dozen tourists at a time, in 1989. Small groups and independent tourists increased to 2000 per year during the 1990s.

The organisation of tourism in the two villages is different. In Wogo, tourists sign a visitors' book provided by the Department of Culture and make voluntary donations. Considerable controversy surrounds the use of tourism funds, exacerbating bad feeling that exists between villagers. The Department of Culture was aware of the corrupt use of the tourists' donations but was without authority to do anything about it. The Department of Tourism tried to encourage the use of tickets without success. In Bena, ticket sales were introduced in 1993. Ticket proceeds were split between the village, the Department of Tourism and the *nua*. Controversy surrounded how the money was split and corruption of the funds, the sale of tickets ended in 2004 and all funds were being retained by the *nua*.[2] Tourism is organised by a management group, set up by the provincial Department of Tourism but run on a voluntary basis by members of the village. Although either unused by tourists or disliked by the villagers, the provincial-level Tourism Department has built tourism infrastructure in Bena, including homestays, toilets and a seating area.

Neither the provincial- nor regency-level Department of Tourism has had any such direct initiatives in Wogo.

The tourists' experiences in the two villages are different. In Bena, following the purchase of a ticket, tourists' visits are easy. Their gaze is directed by the production and sale of ikat fabric and by the viewing post. In Wogo, as the villagers are usually in their fields, the village appears empty and, beyond the physical props: houses, *ngadhu*, *bhaga* and megaliths, there is little to engage the tourists' gaze.

Villagers' attitudes to tourists and tourism development share similarities but also reveal differences. In Bena, tourists were more normally referred to as *turis* (tourists) whereas in Wogo they were frequently referred to as guests (*tamu*). In Bena, tourists were seen to provide the villagers with entertainment but in Wogo they were seen as opportunities to provide glimpses of the wider world. While in Bena the villagers claimed they would keep their traditional culture with or without tourism, in Wogo tourism was considered to reinforce traditional culture. In both villages, it was widely believed that tourism could not erode traditional cultural values but that it had the potential to cause conflict between villagers.

In both villages, community unity was considered essential for economic development. In Bena, where tourism is considered an essential aspect of economic life, lack of village unity was considered to impede further tourism development. In Wogo, lack of community consensus meant, for many villagers, dampened hopes of future economic development through tourism. In both villages, the villagers complained of a lack of understanding about tourism and the need for both general and specialist education in order to develop and manage tourism more effectively.

'Conflicts of Tourism' between Tourists and Villagers

Guests of honour?

Tourists are valued as 'guests from afar'. Contact with the outside world increases status, and status increases with the distance guests travel (Volkman, 1987). Travel is considered an important way to get wisdom, and entertaining guests is a paramount objective of Ngadha feasting (Daeng, 1988). For these reasons, tourists are welcomed to Ngadha villages and are invited to rituals. However, there are a number of reasons why tourists as guests are in an ambivalent position in Ngadha. When tourists are considered as guests, the villager–tourist relationship reveals conflict on a number of levels.

Tourists that travel to Flores are of a 'hardy' type (Erb, 2000). Flores is very dusty in the dry season, which results in clothing getting dirty quickly. Many tourists stay only one or two nights at each destination, which means it is difficult to wash and dry clothes before moving on. Many tourists arriving in Ngadha will have been travelling for several days with little opportunity to wash their clothes properly. After travelling for a number of weeks many tourists give up on trying to keep their clothes clean. Although dress codes varied according to the type of tourists, by and large – with the exception of specialist interest tourists and some incipient mass tourists – villagers considered tourist clothing disrespectful.

Some tourists would like to 'fit in' in villages and therefore feel at ease being 'dirty' like the villagers. In discussions I had with them, tourists said they thought that they were like the villagers wearing old, sometimes torn, and not very clean clothes. The difference in values results from the villagers' classification of tourists as guests, reinforced by the state view that tourists are guests of the state (*tamu negara*). According to the villagers, a guest should show respect to their hosts by wearing clean and smart clothes.

The classification of tourists as guests also reveals conflicting values in relation to tourists giving children sweets and pens. In Ngadha, guests normally bring gifts when they make visits. However, the presentation of gifts by tourists, as will be explained below, does not fit in with the cultural norms of Ngadha society.

Tourists often give sweets to children as an icebreaker. Not knowing how to communicate with adults, but wishing to proceed from unfocused to focused interaction with villagers, tourists see children as easier targets. By giving sweets, it is possible to enter into focused interaction. Some tourists gave sweets or other gifts as a way of sharing their wealth when faced with the economic poverty of the villagers.

Some guides felt tourists had a right to give gifts and should not be denied those rights. This view differed from the view of the tour operator, who said: 'We do not allow our tourists to give out sweets.' Indeed, when I led tours, I would not allow my clients to give out sweets. My view was that to give sweets and not toothbrushes would cause dental problems, which would be acute as no dental service was available to the villagers.

The villagers' view on sweet-giving has changed over the years of my research. Initially, these gifts were appreciated, as a gift from any guest would be. In Wogo, when older women are left to look after children, while the more able-bodied are in the fields, they approved of sweet giving. It entertained the children, kept them out of their hair and stopped the children nagging their grandparents for sweets. However, as more tourists have visited and children have become used to this source of sugar, the children have begun asking tourists for sweets.

When tourists enter the *nua* children may approach them. Most children will remain a few metres away and some will put out a hand and say 'pen' or *'bon bon'*.[3] If the tourist responds, by crouching to the child's level, searching in their bag or presenting a sweet, other kids will run across the *nua*. Some will snatch the gift, others will join the chorus of requests or join the queue in the hope of a hand-out. Some children that run across the *nua* will remain at a distance, hoping to share an older sibling's or friend's bounty.

My daughter joined the other children in running after tourists to see if she could get sweets. For her, and I suspect the village children, 'chasing sweets' was a game, which like any game had winners and losers, those that got sweets and those that didn't. My daughter usually didn't like the sweets she got and passed them on. She still took part in the game, as something to do, as fun, as play. 'Chasing sweets' was also a game of bravado. Figuring who would dare get close enough, who would dare to ask first, were ways the children assessed each other's courage. Children asking for sweets were trying to initiate a game that some tourists played and others didn't, but it was frequently viewed as begging by tourists and has been transmitted as such to the children's parents via guides.

Both villagers and tourists dislike what they see as 'begging'. As village children do not ask Indonesian visitors for sweets, begging behaviour is clearly linked to tourism.[4] The reason that the villagers gave for their dislike of sweet-giving was different in the two villages. In Wogo, villagers said 'we spend more time consoling the children that don't get sweets and more money buying them sweets to make it fair. When it was a novelty to get sweets from tourists, there was less fighting: now it always causes fights between the children.' In Bena, the reason was 'tourists don't like begging children'. Indeed, according to tourists, children begging is a symbol of a spoilt or commercialised village. Begging children is a sign that many tourists have passed through the village before, and a visited village is less authentic precisely because earlier tourists have spoiled it.

Some tourists give sweets as a gift in the way that a guest would bring a gift. The sweets (or pens or biscuits) are presented to an adult on the terrace of a house, for further distribution by that adult. These gifts are appreciated as such as they fit into the cultural norms of gift-giving. Hosts, upon receipt of gifts, are entrusted with their distribution. However, the majority of sweet- (and pen-) giving was by tourists to individual children. The tourist remained in control of the distribution. As Erb (2000) discusses, with reference to the Manggarai, the hosts' relationship with a guest is one of power and control. As the tourist guest maintains control, they are, inadvertently, transgressing the norms of guest behaviour.

Tourists' attempts to get focused interaction through distributing sweets were not necessarily successful. When a child gets a sweet, others will try and snatch it, so frequently children who got sweets ran off leaving the tourist without the counter-gift, i.e. focused social interaction. On other occasions, sweets were used to reward children who took part in social interaction. This, however, can be seen as buying the interaction with payment in sweets. On a number of occasions, non-local guides were observed handing out sweets from a bag large enough to give any children that approached. The rational for this sweet-giving was to stop children from hassling their clients, i.e. a payment for non-disturbance.

A Ngadha guest should return hospitality. Just as guests in Ngadha society bring gifts and receive counter-gifts, a guest should also return hospitality. A smile should be returned with a smile, a greeting with a greeting, conversation with further conversation. Villagers often initiated encounters, but, although tourists were keen to have focused interaction, engagement did not occur because villagers' overtures were missed. Tourists failed to understand the need for questions of social location and missed the opportunity to enter dialogue through banal questions. Tourists who ignored greetings and the villagers' efforts to communicate failed as guests.

In summary, although, according to the government, tourists are guests of the state (*tamu negara*), tourists do not behave according to the cultural norms of guests. Tourists do not value clean clothes as a mark of respect for their hosts. Tourists value sweet-giving as icebreakers in social interaction, but by controlling their distribution transgress the norms of gift-giving. The villagers no longer value sweet-giving as gift-giving, but consider it as a nuisance. In failing to respond to smiles, greetings and villagers' questions, the tourists fail to return hospitality and be true guests.

'Tourists' *adat*'

In the neighbouring district of Manggarai, Erb heard villagers refer to the clothing of tourists as 'western *adat*' (2000: 725). In Ngadha, guides suggested that the tourists' minimal clothing was their *adat*, and this was given as the reason, by some, not to address the issue with tourists. 'I cannot ask a tourist to change their clothes for a village visit: that would be asking them to go against their own *adat*.' 'Tourists want to be free, they are on holiday, that's their way, … villagers wear *kain*, tourists wear what they want …Westerners like their freedom.'

The most upsetting aspect of tourists' way of dressing was the revealing of navels. Navels are revered as centres of vitality and power in many Indonesian societies (cf. Waterson, 1990) and many consider displaying them pornographic.[5] Not wearing bras, wearing thongs as undergarments and generally wearing tight or revealing clothing were all considered indecent by the villagers. Villagers' uneasiness about tourists' clothing is also related to body posture, for example how they sit, or how they bend over rather than crouch down or squat. The conflict of values occurs when tourists adhere to their own norms in the villagers' sacred space. The *nua* is the ritual centre of Ngadha villages and, even when no rituals are taking place, behaviour is subject to more restrictions than in other parts of the village. The tourists are transgressing village norms in the sacred centre of village space.

The conflict that is expressed in relation to tourists' clothes and behaviour is about individualistic values versus the values of community. As I have suggested, following Zainal Kling (1997), *adat* regulates individual behaviour to ensure peace and order in the social domain. Community consensus and unity of the community are guarded by the restriction of individual freedom. The wearing of inappropriate clothing causes disquiet not only for an individual who observes the skimpily dressed tourist but upsets the state of equilibrium in the village. The equilibrium is an ideal state rather than a reality, and community consensus 'the mother of *adat*' (Zainal Kling, 1997: 48) is constantly being negotiated. Any overt challenge brings the threat of conflict.

For an individual villager, observing too much foreign flesh makes them feel *malu*.[6] As discussed, avoiding feelings of *malu* is an important value in Ngadha and other parts of Indonesia. In the next section I will examine other ways in which tourists cause villagers to feel *malu*.

Proud or ashamed

Tourism promotes pride, self-confidence and solidarity among those being visited, pride in being associated with outsiders, pride in their customs and villages, which tourists come so far to see. However, these feelings need to be juxtaposed against the very opposite feeling that tourism also brings, namely *malu*.

The front-stage/back-stage analogy works well in relation to village visits in Ngadha, as the sacred area of Ngadha homes lies at the back of their Houses. Tourists normally wander around the public space in the centre of the *nua*. Sometimes, they will be invited into the outer terrace area, still in public view and thus still front-stage. Occasionally, a tourist will be invited into the non-sacred family space and very rarely they will enter back-stage into the inner sacred space of a house. Thus, the further back-stage is rarely accessed. The inner parts of Ngadha home are dark. Even so, I observed tourists trying to spy through cracks in walls or to peep through partly-open doors to see what lies behind the front-stage. In reference to mass tourism in Europe, Boissevain (1996) relates increasing back-stage penetration to a resultant loss of privacy. In Ngadha, the reasons to avoid tourists penetrating back-stage are different: they are bound up with feelings of *malu*.

Villagers feel uncomfortable revealing how little they have to tourists. Due to their humility, villagers do not feel good enough for tourists. A tourist, on the other hand, may appreciate a back-stage visit precisely because it reveals the real, poor life of the villagers. As discussed, tourists equate authenticity with poverty. Although outwardly proud to be hosting a 'guest from afar', inwardly the villager will be dealing with feelings of *malu*. This internal contradiction meant that tourists are rarely offered the opportunity to see inside the inner sacred rooms or stay overnight in the villagers' homes. Generally speaking, tourists are only put up in villagers homes if they are known through a third party (who should have apologised in advance for anything that is lacking, so, at least, the tourist is not shocked) or if they were desperate, for example if the tourist had no way to return to accommodation in town.

One of my categorical nephews worked in a guesthouse in Bajawa and as an occasional guide. I asked him why he did not invite guests to stay at his House in Wogo. He replied that it would cause anxiety for his aunt. 'She would be *malu*; she would worry that our food is not good enough to offer a tourist. She would be embarrassed to offer her only mattress to a tourist: it is too old.'[7]

Guides take tourists back to their homes or the homes of their relatives. Guides often provide lunch for tourists in their family's homes. The lunch, however, is not typical of what others in Ngadha eat: it is a meal appropriate for tourists, and frequently pan-Indonesian dishes such as fried noodles, *gado-gado* and stir-fry vegetables or *tempeh* are served. The guides are aware that their tourists would not enjoy a truly authentic Ngadha lunch. Few tourists would appreciate a shared bowl of highly spiced maize, yam and pumpkin stew, or rice and maize with a slither of salt fish, for lunch. The tourists I took to stay in Wogo for 48 hours ate with the villagers. However, we were provided with two days of meals that the villagers would normally eat only on special occasions. We had meat twice a day, whereas when I lived in Wogo we could go several weeks without eating any meat.

Crowds

As discussed, villagers like crowds. Crowded and noisy (*ramai*) are positive attributes of Indonesian places in the eyes of Indonesians. Lacking an

Plate 15 Tourists attend a re-thatching ritual

understanding of tourists' values of not wanting too many other tourists, villagers want to encourage more and more tourists. The tourists, on the other hand, expressed disappointment at meeting other tourists. To be the only tourist or only tour group in a village was positive. Tour operators deliberately seek villages that do not receive backpackers in order to enhance their clients' experience. Villagers enjoy the presence of many tourists at once, precisely because it makes their village *ramai*. This is especially the case for wedding and first communion parties. 'If there are lots of tourists it makes it more *ramai*, more enjoyable.' For tourists, the reverse is true: the fewer other tourists the better. Plate 15 shows tourists at a re-thatching ritual.

Tourists sought the opportunity to attend villagers' rituals when villages were most crowded with other local people. Crowds of 'the Other' are sought by tourists but not crowds of themselves. The villagers were less discriminating about the make-up of crowds.

Time, process or event

The final conflict of values between tourists and villagers are values surrounding time. This conflict is most apparent during rituals and more obvious between some types of tourists than others. The structured nature of tours of 'incipient mass tourists' meant that, even if their arrival coincided with a ritual, they would still stick to the schedule provided by the tour operator, although more time for photography might be allowed. Special interest tourists who chanced upon a ritual were more likely to adapt travel plans to incorporate attending part of it. The story of the Austrian group that arrived in Wogo demonstrates how travel plans can be altered at the last minute. Most groups, however, will not be able to make such alterations at the last moment due to their having accommodation booked. In the mid-1990s there was a lack of accommodation at both Labuhan Bajo (Erb, 2000) and in Moni (the village at the base of Keli Mutu, the three coloured lakes). If a group arrived late, they would find their accommodation occupied by other tourists.

According to the villagers of Wogo, only my own tour company arranged tours to coincide with rituals. This involved negotiating a year in advance before brochures went to print. In Bena, no tour company had made arrangements to make visits coincide with rituals.

Eastbound 'shoestring tourists' and 'Bali-Lombok strays' were the tourists whose values clashed most overtly in the villages. These tourists had little time. The two-month tourist visa or connections with international flights were the main reasons offered for being in a hurry. Flores is nearly the end of the trail for the 'eastbound shoestring tourists' and the limits of 'Bali-Lombok strays' journeys. Many of the latter do not get further than Labuhan Bajo. If they do, they are hurrying to Keli Mutu and back. Further, having formed temporary groups, members were frequently adapting their wishes to others in the group whose time was more or less restricted.

Lacking time, but accepting invitations to attend rituals, results in value conflicts between tourists and villagers for two reasons. Firstly, tourists expect the ritual to occur at a particular time, usually suggested by their local guide, who will have informed them of the event. They become annoyed when their plans do not work out. If they postpone their departure to Keli Mutu for half a day, to attend a ritual that their guides says will take place in the morning, and by noon they have been unable to observe significant events, they will become anxious.[8] They will question if they should stay another hour to see if 'it' happens or they should cut their losses and get going. Disagreements among group members or between members and their driver can result in bad feeling, which will have a bearing on how they evaluate their experience.

Secondly, tourists expect a particular event, which, in their eyes, requires an recognisable beginning and end. Ngadha rituals begin with a chant or shriek (*sangazar* Ng) and end with a 'cooling' (*kelanio* Ng). These events may be separated by days.[9] A repetitive rhythm played on gongs and drums, used as a calling to the surrounding area, may be heard for some hours before a ritual begins. In rituals involving dance, one or two dancers begin. The number of dancers increases to a peak and then falls again, sometimes with prolonged breaks. Although these are performances (for the ancestors and community), the rituals do not conform to tourists' expectations of performances, as the beginning and end are not clear to them.

Some aspects of the ritual process are not performances. Attention to the detail of the ritual process (Hoskins, 1987) and clothing is regarded as important. In Ngadha, no woman will go out in ceremonial costume until her hem is perfectly straight at the right height just below the knee. A male headdress is tied and re-tied before it is considered perfect. Gold earrings are heirlooms worn by women at rituals. They are kept in a special three-layered purse (*kepe* Ng) and each layer must have 'blood'[10] spilt on it before it can be opened. Some tourists appreciate the authenticity of attending rituals over performances but they are frequently not prepared for the length of time they take. The preparation phase, which goes on inside Houses, can take too long for tourists keen to see action of some kind. However, this phase cannot be omitted or the ancestors will be angered.

Tourists who attended the slaughter day of rituals could witness a slaughter and know they had witnessed *the* event. However, these tourists then frequently caused offence by not sharing in the ritual meal or, worse, watched others eating but did not partake. For the villagers, the ritual is processional and takes prolonged, uncounted[11] time to complete. Eating the meal is an essential aspect of partaking in a ritual, but tourists frequently missed this, due to insufficient time being allowed to attend the ritual. For the tourists, rituals are an attraction, objectified as a (special) thing, on their list of experiences to be 'seen and done'.

Guides exacerbate the situation. They attempt to persuade tourists to attend rituals, to get their guiding fee, but do not provide the tourists with full enough information regarding the amount of time it will take, or the behaviour required, to prevent them either becoming anxious and or causing offence to villagers. This conflict of tourism has become confrontational at times (see for example Chapter 7).

Observing or taking part

Tourists are invited to attend rituals. There is a conflict of values over what it means to attend. Tourists are sought in order for them to take part, not just observe. During rituals, villagers look their most exotic, are most photogenic (see Plate 4, used in marketing our tours) but are less tolerant to cultural insensitivity as they concentrate on the needs of the ancestors as well as their living guests. Tourists may attend a ritual to observe the 'real tradition' of a 'fascinating culture' but they are not invited as just observers but as participants.

Ngadha guests who attend rituals follow strict protocol: they dress appropriately, either in their best clothes or in ceremonial dress if they are dancing, bring gifts, dance or watch the dancing, and share in the ritual meal. As not all villagers dance, tourists are not expected to, but are appreciated if they do, for the entertainment they provide. In order to dance, a villager or tourists must be in ceremonial dress. If tourists borrow ceremonial clothes from the villagers, they may be denying a villager the chance to dance, unless, with extra foresight, they have hired the ceremonial dress in another village. Only once have I known a guide organise this. It was in Nage where tourists are not allowed to enter the arena where a village ritual takes place, if not in ceremonial dress. In that case, it is not possible to even observe much of the ritual without wearing ceremonial dress.

Few tourists bring gifts to present to their hosts when attending rituals, while all local guests do. Some guides may make donations on their behalf. Villagers rarely complained about this, but were disgruntled about the meagre offerings made by guides when they brought large groups.

Tourists also lacked cultural sensitivity and reverence of rituals in their observations. At rituals, slaughters are the highlight for villagers and tourists. In Ngadha society males crowd around the beast to be slaughtered; women do not. Many female tourists join their male companions close to the slaughter. Tourists compete with locals for 'front row' positions close to the action. Some tourists (usually women) have a dilemma whether to watch the slaughter or not. The majority observed chose to.

As described in Chapter 6 and depicted in Plate 11, some women tourists do not observe the gendered division of space and express shock and upset at an occasion intended to be proud and happy. By displaying the opposing emotions, and not restraining their body language, these tourists once again transgressed local norms.

Making villagers *malu*

Table 8.1 summarises the value conflicts between the tourists and villagers. It should be noted that tourist behaviour causes the villagers to feel ashamed as a result of holding different values. Many villagers used the word *malu*, when speaking Indonesian, to express their personal feelings at seeing a scantily clothed tourist. They felt ashamed that their children were becoming beggars. They were ashamed about ritual food that tourists would not eat. The villagers felt sad for the tourists who felt they had not seen 'the event', and on occasions used *malu* to express their inability to satisfy the tourists' desires.

Table 8.1 Summary of different values between tourists and villagers

Villagers	Tourists
Expect tourists, as guests, to be respectful and wear full, clean clothes	Some wear dirty minimal clothes as an attempt to 'fit in' or without thinking
Gifts should be given to hosts to distribute	Give gifts as icebreakers, and deny villagers the power of redistribution
Children want to play	Dislike 'begging' children
Community consensus is important	Individuality is expressed in dress and behaviour
Like crowds of tourists	Like crowded villages but not crowds of tourists
Time is unrestricted, especially during rituals	Time is constrained
Rituals are processional	Rituals are objectified events

'Conflicts of Tourism' between Guides and Villagers

Many villagers believe that guides' cultural knowledge is insufficient to provide the correct narratives and that they are more interested in making money than providing the 'right' information.[12] Local guides would claim that they knew Ngadha culture because they lived it. The villagers claimed that certain aspects of culture were specific to their village, and that these variations were important. The local expression used to emphasise that each *nua* has different rules or different *adat* is *go'o Wogo, pesa Bena*.[13]

The local guides, they said, did not understand the differences because they came from a different village or they came from Bajawa, the local town, where important cultural details have been lost, by and large. While some guides acknowledge that their cultural knowledge is inadequate, they employ a variety of strategies so that tourists are unaware of this.

The villagers also think that guides should take responsibility for managing tourist behaviour. As discussed, attempted management of tourists' clothing could result in the guides feeling shame (*malu*) and is therefore avoided. Several tourists were critical of their guides who did not tell them what to wear and a few of them felt embarrassed when they realised that their clothing was inappropriate. 'We asked our guide about clothing: he said it doesn't matter – you're a tourist.' 'We took our sarongs expecting our guide to tell us to put them on before we went into the village but he didn't say anything. I wish I hadn't left it in the car. I would feel much more comfortable with it on.'

The guides act between tourists and villagers: they are dependent on both. However, there are many villages in Ngadha that tourists can be taken to. The guides, then, are more dependent on the tourists, who provide their living. Bena is in all the guidebooks, is more commercialised and more visited, and tourists increasingly regard it as 'more of a museum for tourists than a real village'. Cultural tourists seeking authenticity want to see less spoilt villages. They opt for tours that take in 'more authentic' villages as well as the famous Bena. As transport improvements have made the journey time to Bena quicker, changes to the standard itinerary have been made. The tourists stop and look at two *nua* before arriving in Bena, and some tourists continue down the road to others. As the opportunity to spend more time in other villages increases, tourists spend less time in Bena, resulting in fewer sales.

The villagers in Bena were aware that they are largely dependent on guides to bring tourists to the village. Weavers would stop to chat to guides, hoping that their tourists would wait around and take a closer look at their wares and perhaps buy some. Although critical of guides, villagers generally maintained friendly relations with them. This was a strategy to encourage them to return with more tourists.

In Wogo, villagers were more critical of guides. Fewer Ngadha guides visited Wogo, and proportionately more 'driver guides' did. Few Wogo villagers had much social interaction with guides, apart from the woman who sold her bags. Some Ngadha guides have been made to feel unwelcome in Wogo. They have been pressured by the caretaker to extract larger donations from their clients when they fill in the guest book or have been asked for donations themselves. Some have had to put up with verbal abuse when the caretaker has been drunk. The guides therefore choose to take tourists to other villages.

A guide's position in Ngadha society is to some extent marginal. Their choice of hairstyle (for example, a long pony tail), clothing (for example jeans, a shirt and an ikat waistcoat) and their behaviour (for example drinking beer alone with a female tour leader or greeting her with a hug) are indicative of this. However, hair and clothing styles were strategies to appeal to tourists, and familiar relations with tour leaders is a necessary strategy to maintain friendship and trust through which they get continuing work. Tour leaders are crucial contacts to get regular work leading tours and making arrangements for the groups while in Ngadha.

By arranging tours that visit more places rather than fewer in a limited time frame, the guides are aligning themselves with the values of the majority of tourists rather than those of the villagers. In doing so, they make themselves marginal within local society. Guides are aware that they transgress local values with some of their behaviour but see it as part of their work. For the villagers, this can mean that guides are not trustworthy. This lack of trust has the potential to lead to conflict.

As the boycott of Sade (Bras, 2000) demonstrates, tour operators and guides are able to choose alternative cultural villages. If a village becomes too modern, too commercial or the villagers too economically minded or unfriendly, the guides and operators can move on to a new village. The guides' role to prevent misunderstandings and conflict caused by cultural differences is overshadowed by economic imperatives that lead them to play to the wishes of the tourists rather than those of the villagers. Guides, in their role as bridge-actors place more emphasis on one side of the bridge than the other side. Allowing the tourists freedom in behaviour and dress is a strategy to ensure satisfied customers on the tourist side of the bridge. The village side of the bridge is given less support as it can be more easily replaced.

Differing Values between the State and Villagers

The state has been instrumental in the objectification of culture and the reduction of it to the 'cultural arts': dance, music, costumes, handicrafts and architecture (King & Wilder, 2003; Picard, 1997). Once objectified, culture can be sold. This view is epitomised by the Department's statement that 'ceremonies could be sold to tourists'.[14] This view conflicts with the villagers' views. Although the villagers point to the material manifestations of their culture as tourist attractions and welcome tourists to view them, they do not think it is appropriate to stage rituals for tourists.

Fixing dates for rituals can be regarded as part of the process of the commodification of ceremonies. The Indonesian tourism departments are fond of their calendar of events (cf. Yamashita, 1994). The provincial calendar of events is available on the Internet (http://www.nusa-tenggara.com). The controversy about the annual ritual, *Reba*, in Bena is detailed in Chapter 9. Its date used to be fixed by a specialist according to the moon. If this system is maintained, the date cannot be fixed in advance. The villagers are under pressure from the state to fix the date so it can be put in the calendar and used to attract tourists.

The objectification and, I would argue, appropriation of the villagers' culture by the state for economic exploitation began, inadvertently, with the appointment of caretakers (*juru kunci*) in 1982. These officials were appointed by the Department of Education and Culture to facilitate the preservation of material culture in a number of villages. In doing so, the preservation of material culture was state-sanctioned while at the same time the associated beliefs were devalued. As the objects are documented as part of the national heritage under the 1992 Law No. 5 'Preservation of Cultural Sites and Objects' (*Pemeliharaan Benda Benda dan Situs Benda Cagar Budaya*), they have become possessions of the state. The material aspects of the villages were transformed from the property of the clans to the state, which became the custodian of their preservation.

Although villagers are proud that their heritage is considered a national asset, the appointment of the official is a cause of conflict in Ngadha villages. It is the caretaker who keeps the visitors' book and collects donations made by visitors. Where these donations are kept, and not redistributed, conflict arises. In Wogo, this is the major source of conflict associated with tourism, but the problem is not restricted to Wogo. In all villages with guest books and no tickets, villagers made accusations about the caretaker getting rich at the expense of the village.

Four of the Ngadha villages are *obyek wisata unggalan* (Ind, prime tourist attractions[15]) referred to as *kampung budaya* (Ind) or cultural villages by the provincial Department of Tourism (Dinas Parawisata Prop. Dati 1 NTT, 1998), and locally referred to as *kampung adat* (Ind). The entire villages are regarded as national assets and conflict has arisen as a result. As cultural villages must be kept 'traditional', conflict arises over *how* traditional and the villagers are limited in what they can do to their own homes.

Two houses are completely refurbished in both Bena and Wogo each year. Conflict arose in Bena over methods of thatching. Although many reasons were given in discussions about a household's autonomy to decide how to thatch their home, the consensus was that it should be done the traditional way (i.e. by the *wae* method rather than the *tusuk* method[16]). A House that was refurbished in 1998 was built without any opening wooden windows. The headman's rationale for this was: 'It is a traditional village. From now on, all houses must be traditional: traditional houses do not have opening windows.' Variation occurs across the four villages labelled as cultural/traditional villages. What is traditional is a matter of debate, but as I discuss below, competition between villages is now articulated as conflict resulting from tourism.

The state's direct involvement in tourism has been greatest in Bena. (Ticket sales and management group formation has taken place in Bela but State involvement is limited to this.) The villagers are not happy about the actions of the Tourism Department. Bad feeling resulted from the

Department of Tourism taking 30% of the income from ticket sales but the villagers felt that they do not get anything in return. The Department maintained that expenditure far outweighed income. Conflict at this level resulted from the perceived lack of reciprocity as the villagers questioned: 'The Department gets money because tourists visit our village, but what do we get in return?'

One further area of conflict between the state and the villagers is centred on perceptions of ignorance. An issue raised on numerous occasions by villagers was the Department of Tourism's assertion that 'guides know better' and that the villagers lack the education to work as guides. The villagers are clear that their lack of foreign language skills prevent them from becoming guides, but they object to the idea that they know less, especially about their own culture. Villagers could act as guides for groups who are accompanied by out-of-area guides who could then translate. Villagers could also act as guides for Indonesian-speaking tourists.

A dominant view held across the Indonesian archipelago is that peasants are ignorant. The villagers themselves frequently referred to their ignorance as the cause of unfulfilled tourism potential in their villages. However, the values attached to the type of education the villagers are lacking differ between the state and the villagers. When the state claims that the villagers are not educated enough to act as guides, they are referring to formal education. When the villagers bemoan the lack of education provided by the state, with reference to tourism, they are referring as much to specific types of training. The educational needs for furthering the villagers' tourism development are discussed at length in Cole (2005).

As Robinson (1999b) says, the 'conflictual arenas'[17] between the villagers and state relate to rights, ownership and consent over cultural property and cultural capital. The appropriation and manipulation of the villagers' culture for the state's economic benefit has been eased through the devaluing of local knowledge and 'ignorant peasantry' values. Empowering the villagers is therefore central to successful tourism development in the future.

Inter-*nua* and Inter-clan Conflict

Inter-*nua* conflict already exists and there is potential for further conflicts. The best example to illustrate this is the acrimony that exists between Bena and Luba. Luba is a *nua* about 500m from Bena in the same administrative village. Many local guides take tourists to Luba first, to explain about Ngadha culture there, and then walk down to Bena. Ticket sales take place in Bena, where, at present, the money stays. The villagers of

Luba are unhappy not to be participating in any of the financial benefits from ticket sales. The administrative head of the village has so far refused to allow the people of Luba to raise money of their own account.

The villagers of Bena say that their village is famous: people only stop at Luba because they are coming to Bena anyway. Further, they claim Bena is original i.e. has always been on its present site but that Luba was formerly located in the mountains and that the present site is not original. They are unhappy that guides spend more time in the quieter village because it means tourists spend less time looking around Bena. Less time translates into fewer sales upon which the villagers are dependent for part of their income. This example of inter-*nua* conflict is the most transparent: others potentially lie in wait. For example, the villagers of Wogo were very upset that a tourist brochure produced by the province had a photo of Wogo that was labelled as Bena. There is further potential for similar conflicts in the administrative village of Dariwali where there are five *nua* but of them, so far, only Nage has got into the guidebooks, has a caretaker and is marketed as a cultural village.

As Bena is the only *nua* to have received direct state involvement, including funds for tourism development, others are envious and rivalry between *nua* is evident. Villagers in Nage and Bela were resentful that Bena had received state help that they also needed. Rivalry between *nua* is not new. However, as Wood says, tourism becomes 'an important new resource for inter-group rivalry and status competition' (1997: 16).

At a lower level of analysis this inter-group rivalry is expressed at the clan level. This is most obvious in Wogo, where inter-clan conflict lies at the root of non-development and animosity. As explained earlier, the caretaker is the grandson of the original landlord and has assumed a 'feudal' landlord position. He openly admitted to me on more than one occasion: 'This is my village: no-one can do anything without my agreement.' Many of his clan distance themselves from him and some are openly critical of his behaviour. However, other members of the village believe that control must come from within the clan before anyone else can interfere. The lack of community consensus was the most common reason the villagers gave for the lack of tourism development. Many felt that tourism would not develop in this generation.

The structure of the tourism management group in Bena was important in preventing inter-clan rivalry. The group comprises one member of each clan: the original land-owning clan has no more say than the others do.

Gendered Conflict

Overt conflict of values between genders was not conspicuous. Men and women's views differed in terms of development priorities, but perceptions about tourism were very similar. However, it would appear that tourism has the potential to cause gendered conflict.

Ngadha women have experienced more balanced gender relations than other groups in Eastern Indonesia. This I would argue is reflected in Ngadha symbolism. 'The complementary or creative fusion of male and female pairs' (Waterston, 1990: 171) reflects less about opposition (as many male anthropologists have suggested, e.g. Needham, 1984; Van Wouden, 1935) and more about mutual dependence. As men normally marry out, the tie of women to property has resulted in greater economic independence for women. However, 80 years of the Catholic Church and 50 years of incorporation in the Indonesian state have affected gender relations. The patriarchy of Catholicism has favoured male dominance, likewise the patrimony of the Indonesian state. Several older women talked about the more divided roles between men and women in Ngadha now in contrast to when they were young. As Nene Yuli told me '... before, men and women hunted together as a big group (*ramai ramai* Ind): now men go alone'.[18] In discussions about the next village headman in Wogo, several people said the best candidate was a woman. However, many thought that she would not get through the vetting procedure[19] just because she was a woman. 'We have heard of women becoming village-heads, but it is very unusual ... it is still normal for men to do those kind of things, ... mama Yani[20] might not be strong enough at all those male meetings ... I still wish she would stand ...'

There are a number of ways in which tourism affects gender relations in Ngadha. For example, the male symbol of clan identity is used more in tourism marketing than the corresponding female symbol. Focusing on a male symbol over a female may give this symbol, and corresponding maleness, prominence in the future.

Echoing state views, villagers consider that males should deal with outsiders, i.e. tourists, and women should deal with internal, family and home matters.[21] However, in my observations I saw more women dealing with tourists on a day-to-day basis than men. Furthermore, women from Bena travel to Bajawa to sell their ikat cloth, again dealing with outsiders. This mismatch between theory and practice could easily lead to men receiving training in tourism when the women equally need it. Since women deal with tourists as much or more than men, they need equal access to discussions, decisions and training relating to tourism.

Cloth production is largely a female domain. Men produce plying and weaving equipment. Recently, since sales to tourists started, men have begun to help with plying. This is generally undertaken inside the house and not on the terrace. The husband of one of Bena's most successful weavers plies on the terrace. In response to questions about undertaking 'women's work' in public and he replied: 'Why should I be ashamed to help my wife: we are dependent on her income from weaving.' However, he would not help with threading up a loom or actual weaving. It is much easier for two people to thread a loom[22] and women often seek help from friends, kin and children to carry out this task. The nine-year-old son of the same women would, under protest, still help although his 14-year-old brother would not. The nine-year-old protested that he was a young man and should not be expected to undertake this female task.

As discussed earlier, tying the warp threads, to resist the dye and produce patterns, is dependent on both age and blood-lines. In Sumba, a neighbouring island famed for its ikat textiles, tourist demand for the cloth has resulted in men weaving, and the tying of threads is 'practised by almost any young woman' (Smedjebacka, 2000: 287). Further, according to the same author, '… women have lost artistic control, … men create the desired designs, and women are left to the less creative stages' (2000: 288). If education about tourists remains largely the domain of men and they better understand tourist desires, it is possible that this loss of female control could occur in Ngadha. Under such circumstances, there is potential for conflict between the genders.

The final potential arena for conflict between men and women in Ngadha villages in 1998 as a result of tourism was gambling. I observed both men and women gambling but far more men take part in this pastime, especially on Sundays. In Bena, little attempt is made to hide this activity: in Wogo, it is less easy to estimate the extent of gambling because it is less readily observable. The results of Bena's Sunday volleyball match and a local version of rummy are the usual forums for gambling. Women expressed annoyance at the amount of time men wasted gambling on card games but said that, at present, this was limited by the small amounts of money that men had. All earnings are usually passed to women so men had minimal amounts of money 'stolen from shopping change' to gamble with. I observed ten-hour stints of gambling on several occasions, apparently the same small amounts of money circulating around the village men. The village shopkeeper and his (non-Ngadha) wife frequently gambled and his terrace was the most used space for gambling. Sales to tourists were a significant part of this household's income. From this one example it is not possible to generalise about the potential impact of further revenue from tourism. However, some women shared my view that if men received unknown amounts of money from tourists then the amount of time 'wasted' on gambling could increase. This problem may be averted, as gambling has since been made illegal. However, since the law was passed I have seen men in Bena gamble. They told me 'with our little stakes, no one is going to bother with us'.

It appears that, as Sinclair (1997) suggests, gender definitions and the division of labour are being renegotiated, at least in some households, as a result of tourism. Long and Kindon concluded, in reference to Bali, 'tourism development is interacting with systems of gender ideology to strengthen and reinforce the status quo' (1997: 114). In Bena, where tourism income is from weaving, a women's domain, women's economic independence is reinforced. However, state and Church gender ideology, i.e. that men should deal with outsiders, is likely to result in more male involvement in tourism education and decision-making. Women need equal access if they are to have a voice in decision-making for future developments in tourism.

At present the make-up of the tourism management group reflects the state view. Of nine members, only one is a woman. If tourism liaison and education is enacted through this group, it is unlikely that views of women would be equally represented. However, according to the villagers, both men and women, the men would adequately represent the women's voices. 'Their sisters tell them and their wives; they know what we think; they are better at meetings ...', one woman told me.

Conflicts of Acculturation

As discussed in the introduction, cultural tourism involves fulfilling the desires of tourists 'to access primitive societies ... to taste traditional ways of life ... to see ... exotic practices' (Sofield & Birtles, 1996). Tourism, as an important form of globalisation, results in greater socio-economic integration with the wider world. The processes of socio-economic integration result in modernisation, a loss of the 'primitive' and result in the tourist product being, from the tourists' viewpoint, 'spoilt'. On the one hand, tourism brings (or has the potential to bring) wealth and modernisation while, on the other hand, for the product to remain attractive, the villages must remain 'primitive, traditional and exotic'. These conflicts between modernising and remaining traditional I refer to as 'conflicts of acculturation'. In this section, I will examine how these conflicts are manifested.

From discussions with the villagers in Bena and Wogo, the only conflict between modernisation and tradition that was articulated was over the competing demands on their economic resources. *Adat*, conceptualised as the way of the ancestors, manifest in House, clan and *nua* relations and the rituals to maintain them, did not – in the eyes of the villagers – conflict with modernisation. Modernisation is understood to refer to electricity, education and health care, all of which compete with rituals for available funds. None of the villagers believed that modernising forces would diminish the value of *adat*. Slaughtering fewer animals at rituals was considered an essential compromise in order to finance modernity.

However, earning an income did involve conflicts with tradition. Villagers in Wogo criticised the use of Bena Houses for sales. According to several women in Wogo, hanging out goods for sale devalued the sacred status of a House. The woman who made bags for tourists in Wogo did not display her wares for tourists. She said, 'this is a House: it cannot be a market stall'.

On days when House building was being undertaken, women in Bena did not weave. If they were not helping in ritual preparations, they felt uncomfortable to be undertaking private income generation in the *nua*. When House building or other rituals in the *nua* became protracted, several women expressed frustration at not being able to weave. Behind closed doors they used their time in plying.

Villagers' views conflicted over raising money from tourists to pay for the new *ngadhu* in Bena. In 1998, one of the *ngadhu* in Bena was replaced. Between the planning and the execution of the replacement, the Indonesian economic crisis unfolded and funds were insufficient to complete the rituals. Some members of the clan wanted to raise money from tourists to cover the shortfall. Many members were reluctant to allow for this aspect of their culture to be commodified. *Adat* should not be bought and sold, they claimed. Although proponents agreed 'it wasn't really right', the economic imperative to go against tradition forced a pragmatic solution. The compromise position, after long and occasionally heated discussions, was to charge tourists to view the carving of the *ngadhu*. Some members of the clan wanted to charge tourists to attend the largest ritual. However, other members of the village and guides prevented this. Although the total funds raised from tourists that viewed the carving was insignificant, just $5, this case and those above illustrate how acquiring income can clash with tradition.

The government's perspective on the conflicts of acculturation is reflected in their reversal of policy. Tradition was seen as a barrier to development and traditional houses as unhealthy. Now, the state, recognising the value of tradition for tourism, wants traditional villages preserved. As discussed further in Chapter 9, questions about the power of the state to dictate the use of villagers' space in their own homes needs to be addressed.

Shortly after I began taking tourists to Wogo, electricity was installed. The electricity poles were run, by the shortest route, diagonally across the nua. All tourists we took to the village on subsequent trips commented negatively about this highly visible sign of modernisation as it 'spoilt' their village photographs (see Plate 15). Further, in discussions with one of the members of the Tourist Department, the electricity poles were given as a reason Wogo was less visited than Bena. Could Bena then be denied electricity as it would detract from its attractiveness as a prime tourist attraction? The villagers of Bena saw electricity as a high priority for development. Electricity was highest on the priority list for young people, second (after road improvements) for men and third (after water supplies to individual houses and road improvements) for women.

The provincial Tourism Department built a souvenir shop in Bena in an attempt to stop the villagers turning traditional houses into market stalls. Their rationale was that such sales reduced the attractiveness of a traditional village because it became too commercialised. The interviewees made no mention of the sacred nature of Houses as a rationale. Keeping the village *appearing* traditional was the fundamental underlying value. This value corresponds with the tourists' values, as explained below.

Tourists hold two predominate views: firstly, that the villages should keep their traditions and, secondly, that villages that receive fewer tourists and appear poorer are considered more authentic and less 'spoilt'. Although Bena was liked, due to its stunning scenic position, many tourists thought it was 'spoilt'. Some even thought it was not a living village but preserved just for tourism. The sale of tickets, Coca-Cola, ikat fabrics and a few other souvenirs were given as examples of why Bena is considered commercialised and thus spoilt. The tourist dissatisfaction resulted from the villagers not living up to the tourists' image and expectations.

As Bena attempts to increase income from tourism, tourists like it less. Guides already take tourists to other villages and therefore spend less time in Bena. As transportation improves, more villages will be accessible and it is likely that tourists will visit other 'less spoilt' villages. Being less developed gives a village competitive advantage. As new (to tourism) villages are visited, it is likely that they will attempt to raise income from tourism and attain the trappings of modernity. Tourism will then have a levelling effect on the villages. As poorer, more peripheral villages become more accessible, they will receive more tourists and if they, like Bena, 'become commercialised', by attempting to make sales to tourists, tourists will in turn seek other 'less spoilt' villages.

However the tourists do not visit other villages *instead of* Bena, they still want to visit Bena, but only in passing. As I have suggested, less time spent in the village results in fewer sales, so that Bena deals with the negative effects of crowding without increased sales.

Having examined the 'conflicts of acculturation' from the perspectives of our three major stakeholder groups, tourist, villagers, and mediators (in this case the government), it is clear that income generation from tourism conflicts with the tourist and state views of the tourist product to be sold. Initial attempts by the villagers to derive economic benefits from tourism have resulted in the product being commercialised and the resource being 'spoilt'. Balancing the 'conflicts of acculturation' needs to be considered, together with the stakeholder conflicts, in the policy and planning of further tourism development in Ngadha villages.

Changing Conflicts

The conflicts of tourism have changed over time. Sometimes as a result of evolutionary change i.e. that which has occurred as a slow process over the past 15 years, and sometimes change that has resulted from particular actions as a result of external initiatives.

As more tourists have visited Ngadha the villages have become accustomed to the different ways of strangers. They are no longer horrified or shocked to see the naked white flesh of tourists. However, they are still unhappy that tourists wear inappropriate clothes in their villages. They are no longer surprised when tourists attend rituals but do not accept ritual food but they are still concerned that it will upset the ancestors. In 2005 a villager said: 'Tourists feel pain and fear at seeing a buffalo slaughtered.' He had come to understand their emotions but wanted to point out that they opposed their own: 'We feel happiness and pride,' The villagers have become accustomed to tourists, and their ways, but they still wished tourists would adopt their behaviour while in the villages.

In 2003, local stakeholders and I produced a code of conduct in an attempt to educate the tourists about how to behave. As discussed fully in Cole (2007), research in 2005 suggests that it was successful in persuading tourists to dress more appropriately. That as a result of the code fewer tourists gave gifts directly to individual children and more of them presented gifts to hosts when they attended rituals. However, there were limits to tourists' compliance with the code, for example, many continued to refuse ritual food.

As we have seen, as tourist numbers have increased, villagers have attempted to derive some financial gain from them. Villagers in Bena have displayed ikats and other souvenirs for sale, the local shop has stocked items for sale to tourists and due to an initiative from the provincial government entry tickets were sold to tourists. According to the tourists, these attempts to derive economic benefits from tourism represent a loss of authenticity, the commercialisation of culture and the village has therefore been 'spoilt'. As a result guides, who are more dependent on tourists than villagers, take tourists further off the beaten track to poorer 'less spoilt' villages. Tourists then spend less time in Bena and the villagers make fewer sales. These conflicts result in greater envy and inter-nua conflict. Furthermore, only Bena has received financial help for tourism development from the state, causing resentment in other villages. Tourism development has brought hope and some economic benefits but this has, in some cases, turned to apathy when villagers lose out in the battle for the limited resource of tourists.

'Conflicts of tourism' exist between villagers and the state departments empowered with tourism organisation. The nature of the conflict has changed over the years. Initially the villagers rituals were considered wasteful and their homes unhealthy. When their potential to attract tourists was recognised, the state changed its views. Aspects of the villagers' material culture were given state protection and the villages were to be kept looking traditional. The state echoed tourists' views that the resource is 'spoilt' by any overt signs of modernity. In order to remain traditional, villagers were denied the rights to have windows in their homes. No mains electricity has been installed in Bena as electricity in Wogo is considered to have spoilt the village.

The promotion of traditional culture does not match the government's urge to pursue modernisation, but does serve a role to satisfy the tourists' thirst for authenticity. If the culture in cultural villages continues to be based on markers related to the past, on tradition as unchanging or on fixed material elements, it will work to preserve the villagers' underdevelopment rather than being a tool for development.

Notes

1. Local Department of Tourism statistics.
2. But there were plans for the ticket system to be re-introduced.
3. The use of French might indicate that French tourists began giving sweets to children.
4. Other authors have made a clear link between begging and tourism, e.g. Van den Berghe (1992).
5. In 2004 the president referred to the revealing of navel as pornographic. Cf. *Jakarta Post* December 22 2004.
6. Multiple Ngadha expressions are incorporated in this Indonesian term. However, to translate it as merely shy or ashamed misses the subtle nuance in meaning that lies between shyness, shame, embarrassment and loss of face

(cf. Draine & Hall, 1991). Another related Indonesian term the villagers used was *segan*, the feeling that one is dealing with someone that has a higher position.

7. *Nanti Nene Yuli malu, segan-kan, mungkin makanan tidak cocok untuk turis, casur kan terlalu tua, tidak baik, bikin Nene malu.*
8. This anxiety will compound anxiety created from the culture shock suffered from entering an alien environment (Pearce *et al.*, 1998).
9. Or even weeks and months where a disagreement arises.
10. Often betel juice replaces actual blood (cf. Molnar, 2000).
11. The only time I heard villagers make negative comments about the length of time a ritual took to complete was the new *ngadhu* ritual in Bena, which took three and a half weeks!
12. The right information refers to the villagers' view of what tourists should be told.
13. *Go'o* means different so does *pesa*. The use of the two *nua* names is coincidental, but they rhyme. Often the Indonesian expression *lain ladang lain berlalang* is used, which means different field, different grasshopper.
14. Statement made by provincial head of tourism (see Chapter 5).
15. Literally prime tourist objects.
16. The *wae* (Ng) method of thatching involves bundles of thatching grass being folded over roof struts by a party of villagers. The *tusuk* (Ng and Ind) method involves small bundles of thatching grass being attached to a stake to create sections of thatch. These are then lifted and tied on to the roof during the thatching ceremony. The *wae* method lasts longer, is less labour-intensive and means repairs are easier. However the thatching party is hard to control, takes longer and the resulting roof is less neat. The *tusuk* method is more labour-intensive in preparation but much quicker on thatching day and is a newer innovation that looks neater.
17. Expression borrowed from Greenwood (1989).
18. Hunting used to be common but is now rare.
19. All village head-person candidates have to be vetted by higher levels in the Indonesian bureaucracy, before they can stand for village election.
20. Not her real name.
21. As King suggests, Indonesian development policies locate women within the home and family (1999: 63).
22. I used the strategy of helping women thread looms as a means of carrying out interviews with them.

Chapter 9

Tourism, Power and Socio-cultural Change

This chapter examines tourism and socio-cultural change in Ngadha. As I suggested in Chapter 1 it is not possible to disaggregate change brought about by tourism from other influences. Instead tourism is seen as one of the many factors affecting change in the lives of the villagers. The chapter begins with an examination of the dangers and ambiguities of equating globalisation with westerisation and the importance of tourism as a localising force in identity affirmation and the commodification of the villagers' otherness.

The chapter then unwraps the onion skins around the Ngadha cultural core and illustrates how tourism is incorporated within a complex nexus of forces that shape Ngadha society. The story of the ordination of a village priest is used to illustrate how nationalism, Catholicism and *adat* are intertwined: how the beliefs are at once syncretised while also competing for legitimacy and authority in the villagers' lives. The layers are then stripped away for closer examination. A detailed account of *Reba* in Bena, in 1998, is provided to illustrate how tourism is utilised, accommodated and appropriated within the competition for legitimacy and authority in the lives of the Ngadha villagers. The chapter examines how tourism is affecting the balance of power between the competing forces in the villagers' lives.

Tourism and Gobalisation in Ngadha

Visual signs of globalisation do exist in Ngadha villages. Coca-Cola bottles are on sale in the village shops. Sales are largely to tourists but also occasionally to locals. Tourists and locals buy biscuits. This, originally, western import has little to do with tourism. The Catholic Church introduced the baking of cakes, biscuits and bread into Ngadha. Sponge cakes are prized as they are considered essential at church weddings (but not at traditional marriage ceremonies). One of the most frequently purchased items in the village shops is instant noodles. Although now widely available in western supermarkets, instant noodles are a Chinese not a western product. The danger of assuming that globalisation equals westernisation needs to be heeded. As Howell (1995a) argues, the flow is not unidirectional.

Young people of Ngadha strive for clothing they deem 'fashionable', but linking this with tourism would be inaccurate. Images of a variety of clothing styles reach the villagers from tourists but also from magazines brought home by family members who return from the metropolitan centres of the Indonesian archipelago. As detailed in Chapter 7 villagers frequently comment on tourists' clothes. Occasionally a pretty blouse or smart shirt will be commented on in a complimentary manner. However, by and large, the clothes worn by tourists were not admired or considered appropriate to be copied.

Dress in Ngadha has changed in the years I have been visiting. Children in particular increasingly wear more clothes. Young and old wear t-shirts but to attribute this change in dress style to copying tourists i.e. 'the demonstration effect' would be false. Tourists do occasionally donate t-shirts to villagers, but they do not constitute a status symbol as a clothing style. As gifts they signify the closeness of a relationship with a tourist and are prized as such. Further the hard-wearing nature of t-shirts over locally available clothing is the significance of their value. Villagers acquire clothes from the *lulos* (second-hand stall) in Bajawa. Charity shop and jumble sale remainders, exported from the west, provide this cheap source of second-hand western clothing. They were purchased for their quality and value for money rather than as signifiers of fashion. Occasionally labelled products such as Benetton or Gap clothes were obtained but the fashion status value of these labels was unknown to the villagers. Jeans are valued but I would argue that this has little to do with copying tourists. Tourists visit the villages during the day and jeans are generally considered too warm to be worn. It is more likely that awareness of jeans comes from Indonesia's jeans industry. There are two shops that sell jeans in Bajawa. Other prized clothing in Wogo includes jackets, jumpers and sweatshirts. These clothes are sought for their warmth, but, like jeans, are infrequently seen on tourists.

Western commodities, at least our cast-offs, are exported to Ngadha. However to suggest that the values attached to western clothing are exported must be questioned. The most highly valued clothing in Ngadha are the ceremonial clothes. These black and white, hand-woven *ikat kains*, long tubular cloths, are worn for the ancestors and more recently at some church services. For women the second most highly prized clothing was other *ikat kains*. When I wore a Bena *kain* to Wogo, admiration was shown from women of all ages. All my close friends and relatives wanted to borrow it to go to church, an opportunity used to show off best clothes.

The value of western clothing is in its durability and warmth. Local hand-woven cloth is warm and durable but it is expensive. Villagers who opt for jeans, T-shirts and sweatshirts are frequently purchasing what they can afford, and what is hard-wearing. This contrasts with the western consumer value of clothes that are replaced every season. Western clothing does not signify fashion status but durability and warmth. The commodity is exported but the value placed on it is changed. As Hannerz (1990) suggests, the goods are transferred but not their meanings.

Not only are western cultural values in relation to dress only superficially incorporated into Ngadha, a flow of Eastern Indonesian dress values, travels west. The majority of souvenir purchases in Ngadha are ikat cloth. Although rarely sewn to create ready to wear clothing, the appreciation of Ngadha cloth, if not clothing, is clear. The fact that the word 'sarong' has become part of international clothing language attests to the flow of clothing values from the east as well as the west. As discussed by Forshee (1998) ikat has fashion value and is exported worldwide.

Exposure to western cultural values can also be examined in relation to music. Ngadha villagers enjoy a variety of genres of European music. Again this cannot be attributed to tourism, as tourists will rarely be playing or listening to music during village visits. Tourists used to carry cassettes, and more recently iPods, and play them in the vehicles that transported them to the villages, so drivers and guides would hear tourists' musical tastes on occasions. This however is minimal in comparison to the influence of the radio. Dance styles have however been affected by tourism. At Ngadha weddings and first communion parties western music is played. Most is 'old time' ballroom music locally referred to as *dansa*. This music was brought by Catholic priests and is extremely popular. More old and young people know the ballroom dance steps than the majority in the west from where the music originated. In recent years there is a trend to also play 'pop' music at these celebrations. Tourists are invited. Their attendance is not so important as 'guests from a far', for which they are valued at *adat* ceremonies, although this factor may have some significance. They are invited as part of the entertainment. Observing tourists dance is enjoyed and copied by young people in Ngadha.

Older members of Ngadha society considered tourist dance movements too liberated and in some cases erotic. In contrast to the strict movements of *adat* dance and the formal movements of ballroom dance, uninhibited free-style dancing worried village elders. On more than one occasion village elders attributed teenage pregnancy to young males getting 'carried away' and losing their inhibitions 'like tourists'. The liberated dance of tourists (combined with their minimal clothing), when copied, was considered to arouse local young men who became 'unable to control their natural desires'.

'To speak of individualisation and of modernity is to speak of the same condition' (Bauman, 2001: 124). In as much as individualism is a consequence and value of globalisation, the change in dance styles can be seen as part of globalisation. Ritual dances are always performed in groups and follow strict protocol. Ballroom dancing, although performed in pairs, is stylised also to a formal set of rules. However the modern dance of many tourists is individualistic and hedonistic. The young people of Ngadha enjoy copying tourists' individualistic dance styles, but whether or not this involves incorporating individualistic values is debatable, the effect maybe superficial. Tourism has clearly exposed local people to behaviour from different cultural backgrounds and in the case of dance, the youngsters of Ngadha clearly challenge the norms and boundaries of locally accepted styles. However, the individualistic values underlining tourist dance styles may be incorporated superficially both in aspect and time. Individualism may only be incorporated as part of dance and not into other aspects of their lives, or it may just be while they are 'teenagers'. It would be dangerous to base any observations on changed values on this group within society; an age group known to push at society's boundaries.

Localisation and Tourism in Ngadha

The other side of the globalisation coin is localisation. An examination of this demonstrates that tourism is an important part of the localisation processes in Ngadha. Having been given an identity, the Ngadha are making use of their cultural distinctiveness, as a resource.

In Indonesia, the treatment of populations as homogeneous and bounded units began with the Dutch (Hitchcock & King, 1997). The number of 'ethnic groups' on Flores has always been open to interpretation. As I have suggested in the introduction, based on linguistic and ethnographic evidence, there would appear to be a continuum of people occupying the west and central parts of the island, rather than a number of distinct bounded groups. The Dutch created colonial districts across the island and named them after the largest local group. A *'raja'* (king Ind) was installed in Bajawa in the 1910s (Smedal, 1993). Some groups were subsumed into the regions of others, which according to Forth (1998) has relegated certain populations to subordinate status. The Indonesian state kept the five districts on Flores that the Dutch had delineated. The Ngada district includes three, four or five groups (depending on how such groups are defined) within its boundaries, of which the Ngadha are one.

The anthropological endeavour that began during colonial times has contributed to the creation of ethnic groups with the erection of cultural distinctions and borders (Hannerz, 1996). The Indonesian state has continued the process but has favoured region and religion over ethnicity (Wood, 1997). From the government's viewpoint, Ngadha is part of Eastern Indonesia and Catholic. Ngadha is part of East Nusa Tenggara. The reductionist and diluting effect of this regionalisation is clear (cf. Picard, 1993). The idea of ethnic groups is also forged in primary schools. The state schoolbooks provide images of traditional costume and dwellings and assign them to particular groups across the archipelago. Certain groups are more prominent than others; certain aspects of the culture of these 'famous' ethnic groups are known to schoolchildren throughout Indonesia, e.g. Bali's dancers, Minang Kabau's matrilinity, Torajan funerals, and Asmat penis gourds.

Tourism is about selling places and cultural tourism is about selling the culture attached to those places. Marketing tourism is simplified where cultures begin and end, and where they are specific to places. Just as anthropological maturity is leading to the growing recognition that place is a social construction, many groups desire to construct cultural identities attached to place (cf. Hastrup & Olwig, 1997). The use of cultural identity, of ethnicity, and of 'being an ethnic group' is in part a response to, and consequence of, tourism.

The ethnic pride resulting from tourists' visits that is widely reported elsewhere (e.g. Adams, 1997; Crystal, 1978; Van den Berghe, 1992) is apparent in Ngadha, and this is a clear reason why tourists are appreciated. Further, I would argue that a Ngadha ethnicity is being created largely through the presence of tourists. Guides create the image of a fixed bounded group of people who share a specific culture. They tell the tourists the classical, the historical, traditional elements of the culture as if unchanging, supplanting the contemporary, dynamic, aspects of the villagers' lives.

The Ngadha appear to have come into being, in the sense of a discrete bounded group with an identifiable shared culture, as an ethnic option. There is a notion of shared descent among the Ngadha. In the different villages very similar stories of their origins are told.[1] The villagers claim a number of other criteria that make them Ngadha. Language, frequently an essential aspect of ethnic identity, varies across the region, there are dialects within Ngadha (cf. Grimes *et al.*, 1997) and the neighbouring languages of Nage, Riung and the languages of Eastern Manggarai are mutually comprehensible.

Other criteria are based on what villagers' claim are the fundamental aspects of their customs. The marriage rule 'that men marry out' applies in the majority of villages, but not all. The rule has always been, and remains, subject for negotiation (cf. Barnes, 1972). In some villages, for example Were, a village neighbouring Wogo, it is the women that marry out, as bridewealth is always paid for them. My adoptive mother was from Were and had moved to Wogo to join her husband.[2] My brother-in-law was also from Were and his parents had wanted to pay for my sister. My father had said that he wanted her to remain in Wogo[3]. By asking for a bridewealth beyond the means of any villager, his statement that 'his daughter was priceless' was clear. Although 'marrying out' is a rule that many people claimed as part of their ethnic identity, in fact the rule varies according to village and family circumstances.

Whenever a guide talks to tourists about marriage in Ngadha they are always contrasted with other ethnic groups on Flores. 'In Ngadha, men marry out' is always one of the first cultural elements recounted about Ngadha culture. This feature combined with children following the rank of their mothers has, with embellishment and translation led to narratives that the Ngadha are matrilineal, and even matriarchal. When I first visited Wogo I felt a strong sense that women had more value and power than in other parts of Indonesia I had visited. I wrote in my notes that every house had a female head of household (in fact the *donggo sa'o* see Chapter 4). The women were more outspoken in comparison to other village women I had met in Indonesia. The women of Bena all told me how important it was to have a daughter 'to stay at home and look after us', because 'our sons will leave us'. A local priest told me that the Ngadha are unproductive compared to other groups on Flores because the men marry out and therefore it is not in their interests to clear land or work hard on their own family farms. If 'men marrying out' becomes a defining term of Ngadha ethnicity, will the rule become more fixed and less dependent on circumstance and will this feed into gender values?

The clearest criteria of Ngadha identity are their houses, cloth, *ngadhu* and *bhaga*, megaliths and annual *Reba* gatherings. These criteria are not only identified by the locals but are also the symbols that are taken and used in tourism. They are tangible markers that can be photographed and marketed. These markers have become objectified and externalised and this in itself 'tends to make people self-conscious and reflexive about the "cultural stuff" which, before, they may have taken for granted' (Wood, 1997: 19).

Traditional houses are used throughout the Indonesian archipelago as ethnic markers. It is hard for tourists to Indonesia to avoid images of traditional dwellings representing ethnic groups. Erb suggests Indonesian houses have become 'badges of identity' because they can so readily accessible as tourist attractions (1998: 187). Adams (1984) discusses how houses in Toraja have become markers of ethnic identity and Allerton (2001) discusses how the Manggarai tried to transform a house into a tourist site.

The majestic, high thatched, wooden houses of Ngadha are no exception. But they are houses like the others, and very similar in shape to the houses of central Flores and Sumba. The Ngadha, however, have additional obvious symbols: the *bhaga* and *ngadhu*. A *bhaga* is a house in miniature; in a photograph a *bhaga* would look little different from a house (just smaller and unfinished). It is for this reason that the *ngadhu* has become the archetypal symbol of Ngadha society.

The carved pole with its conical thatch represents the first male ancestor of the clan to which it belongs, together with a *bhaga* and *peo* these symbols represent clan unity. The *ngadhu*'s carving i.e. art, and thatch i.e. traditional (roofing), provide the tourist with the quintessential symbols of an 'ethnic culture'. The *ngadhu* is a 'primitive' object that is specific to the Ngadha (the neighbouring Nage have a forked pole but it is not thatched). Used in tourism marketing literature they are divorced from *bhaga*, separated from their context and their unity.

By representing *ngadhu* individually their essential symbolic meaning of unity is obscured. Furthermore, I am concerned that the male symbol is given dominance over the female. Will this make the Ngadha self-conscious and reflective in an unconscious or sublime way, and lead to a prominence or importance of males? As the male symbol is more photographed, more used in marketing, and if it is used on postcards first, will this feed back into society and give males a new power from tourism?

The Ngadha have never formed a unified political group. Tourism, however, is creating the internal recognition of a defined group based on the above set of markers. Their ethnicity is being reconstructed, as MacCannell (1984) would have it. Differences are re-invented and commodified, to be consumed by the tourist, in their search of otherness (Schelling, 1998). The creation or affirmation of an ethnic identity and the importance centred on a local identity – localisation – is a consequence of tourism.

Localisation – the emphasis on the local – in Ngadha, raises two issues that require further discussion in relation to tourism development: firstly to examine what is local; secondly, to consider the impact of the 1999 regional autonomy laws.

What is local?

Recognising that tourism is a localising force, the question of what or where is local or at what level of abstraction it is best understood and interpreted needs to be raised. The symbols of Ngadha that are used for and by Ngadha people would suggest a bounded and united group with shared traditions. As an inter-marrying group with a shared history, culture, political and economic structure, one definition of community could cover the whole region. However to do so would be to lose the important details that are pertinent. Important differences exist between villages, and, as discussed, villagers are adamant that they do not like generalisations about cultural rules. In both Wogo and Bena I was frequently told 'different village, different cultural rules'.[4] Interpreting local at the micro-level i.e. that of the *nua* makes planning and policy difficult. Further it fuels real and potential conflict between *nua* and villages. Tourist numbers to Ngadha are limited, and for the reasons discussed tourists are wanted. Competition between villages therefore exists to attract tourists. Inter-*nua* and inter-village conflict already exists. There is clear evidence of villages laying claim to certain traditions. This exercising of ethnic options, as Wood puts it, 'is inherently political and contentious' (1997: 19). Defining community at the most local level will increase the likelihood of tourism development being a divisive force.

The Ngadha consider the annual *Reba* gathering as an essential aspect of their identity. The order that different villages celebrate *Reba* is vital to village identity. For example Wogo must have *Reba* after Bena, Sadha, Doka and Dada Wea (in that order). The ordering of the villages is related to when the villages were originally settled and this is reaffirmed each year. It is important to Bena that their *Reba* is first, as they consider their village the first to have been settled. Bena is referred to as 'the eldest child of Ngadha'. This primacy is reaffirmed every time the villagers claim it was the first village to be visited by tourists. In Ngadha culture, this first position is important.[5]

The Church attempted to appropriate *Reba*, a House unity ritual and make it a parish unity ritual. The clergy took the central symbolism, the cutting of yams, and claimed they had become the body and blood of Christ, the bread and wine in Holy Communion. The meaning of cutting the yam could change over time, if changed in this way by the priests. However, the root of the major controversy over the date of Bena's *Reba* celebrations (see below) was not about changing the meaning central to the ritual, or changing the ritual from House to parish. At the heart of the controversy was Bena loosing the primacy of their village to the parish as a whole, or even worse to the village of Jerebuu where the parish church is located. In considering which village is to hold *Reba* first, the specificity of what is local is important in the Ngadha context.

Regional autonomy

Otonomi Dareah (or regional autonomy) was the Indonesian government's answer to a long period of growing distrust and antagonism consisting of a number of laws drafted to appease separatists (Seymour & Turner, 2002). As

Erb (2001b) suggests in reference to the Manggarai, the regional autonomy laws compound the process of identity creation and reaffirmation. The new laws invite intense competition over local resources and political power. With autonomy bestowed at the regency level the leader who can claim 'local' voice will have potentially far-reaching powers.

The Benda-Beckmanns' findings in West Sumatra suggest that the new laws are resulting in 'a process of localism and ethnisation' (2001: 5) with heightened emphasis on ethnicity. Since the laws came into force there have been calls for Flores to become a separate province.[6] In 2005 the Ngada regency, which is occupied by a number of ethnic groups, decided to split into two along broadly ethnic grounds with the Nage and Keo in the east with Mbay as their capital; and the Ngadha and Riung in the west around the present capital of Bajawa.

As Usman (2001), Benda-Beckmann and Benda-Beckmann (2001), and Antlov (2001) comment, with new democracy and autonomy for the regions, comes the power, obligation and responsibility to raise local revenue. This may be especially important in reference to tourism in Ngadha, as it is the regency's second most important industry, after agriculture. The issues discussed regarding the splitting of tourist ticket revenue in the villages are likely to become more heated. The regency will see tourist payments as an important mechanism to raise revenue. On the other hand, the village has also been given autonomy in legal terms (Antlov, 2001) and may also need to generate its own financial resources (Benda-Beckmann & Benda-Beckmann, 2001).

The notion of a bounded, localised, cultural whole of Ngadha is a creation of outsiders. The villagers in this study, in their daily lives identify local at the *nua* level. Awareness of a delimitable, bounded area of Ngadha is being created, in part at least, by tourism. Tourism is providing the villagers with the pride of an identity. Minor ambitions, for example to be included in provincial-level tourism marketing material, will be an initial step in being recognised.

The cultural commodification of their otherness has led to a recognisable 'ethnic group' identity. This commodification is frequently regarded negatively, as the 'west's' objectification of a cultural other. However this masks the social empowerment that comes with the pride brought by tourism, and the political resource that their new definable identity offers.

State, Church and *Adat*

Ebu po, nusi pera or *uku adha*[7] are the rules of respect, teaching and advice from the ancestors (*adat* in Indonesian). This worldview provides a fundamental underpinning in the villagers' culture to the present day. This cultural core is not static but has changed, and continues to be changed, by more recent influences. The Catholic Church, increasingly influential from the 1920s onwards, has provided the villagers with different rules of behaviour and way of life, rules that frequently conflict with their pre-existing norms and practices. The Indonesian state is a third force shaping the lives of the villagers. These forces compete for authority in the villagers' lives. The three forces are a triangle of power, which, like a three-legged stool, can be strong and level. However, when more weight is put on two legs an imbalance will result. Tourism, an essential aspect of globalisation, is now being added as a fourth dimension to the complex picture. It is affecting the articulation of power and the balance between the influences. Before examining each of the forces, the story of a priest's first service will be used to illustrate how the forces are intertwined in the villagers' daily lives.

A priest's first service

When a priest is ordained he gives his first service in his own village (see Plate 16). On one such occasion during my fieldwork a priest returned to give his first service. A temporary church was constructed in the centre of the *nua*. Work on the structure was organised according to prayer

Plate 16 The ancestors are invoked and a newly ordained priest is blessed before he gives his inaugaral mass

groups while a ritual meal was prepared in the priests' House. As custom dictates the cooking of the meat was carried out by the men whilst women cooked the rice. In this *adat* ritual, male and female work was divided along gender lines, whilst outside men and women shared construction jobs. The sanctuary of the makeshift church was constructed with a carved wooden entry step (*kaba pere*). Usually reserved for entry into the inner sacred room of a House, the sacred portal was transformed as the entry step into the sanctified area of the makeshift church.

Before the service the priest was led around the village in a decorated car. Driving slowly, the car followed a procession of dancers in full costume that took the same form as in house building ceremonies, and my first group's arrival, with the men at the front waving swords and the women dancing behind. The only difference was that, on this occasion, many more villagers danced. As the villagers explained: 'We love to dance and on this occasion we do not have to be pig donors, anyone can dance.' Before the priest gave his service, a pig was slaughtered and, as always, the ancestors were invoked. Even at this Catholic ceremony the ancestors' blessing was essential. During the sermon, generations of House members were remembered, and, after Holy Communion, blessings were given to both living and dead relatives.[8]

For village members the lunch that followed the service was pork and rice served in customary style: men used their bare hands to serve meat and rice into individual baskets, to be eaten with the hands. The villagers sat in their prayer groups. However, for outside, invited guests, the lunch resembled that of a wedding in Java. A buffet was served consisting of dishes such as beef in soya sauce, stir-fried green beans and carrots, fried noodles and fried chicken. These dishes are served across the Indonesian archipelago on formal occasions when guests from a variety of backgrounds are expected. Having served ourselves (in strict order, according to status) we ate the meal with a spoon and fork off a china plate.

Dancing and eating continued into the evening. A family planning van arrived, and parked at the edge of the *nua*, offering advice and information on modern methods of contraception.[9] Its presence on this particular occasion shocked me more than the villagers. Although ordaining a village priest is one of the most important of Catholic rituals the family planning team overlooked Catholic opposition to family planning and saw a gathering of villagers, who are frequently inaccessible in their gardens, as an opportunity to market their services.

The above story not only illustrates syncretism, but demonstrates how the villagers participate in, and their lives are shaped by nationalism, Catholicism and *adat*. The different influences, in this case, apparently blended harmoniously. Men and women flowed between gendered *adat* roles in the kitchen, where a customary meal was prepared for groups of people divided along church lines. While outside women and men shared construction work to create a 'church' fashioned on a traditional House. The priest entered and left the sanctuary through a *kaba pere*, entry step or vagina (see Chapter 4). Traditional dress at church events and singing hymns in the local language is not unusual in Ngadha and were often quoted as examples of 'enculturation',[10] the Church's attempts to incorporate custom. Invoking the ancestors and requesting their blessing for the ordination of a priest demonstrates just how far the Catholic Church on Flores has moved to accommodate traditional beliefs.

The Indonesian buffet served to indicate the influence of the Javanese *selamatan*[11] (cf. Geertz, 1960) and how the presence of state dignitaries is required in legitimising a Catholic/*adat* celebration. The family planning van stuck out to me as symbolising the dominance of state ideology, but for my friends it symbolised no more than the thick-skinned attitude of the family planning team desperate to increase its clientele.

The state

In its peripheral position, with limited resources, Ngadha has, in the main, been bypassed by central government development initiatives. There have however been important impacts of the highly bureaucratic, hierarchical structure of the Indonesian state system, with state administration extending to very local levels. The Javanese patrimonial system, based on a patron–client relationship in which the patron is the father (*bapak*), the client deferential and obedient, and confrontation avoided, has reached every village in the Indonesian archipelago. In dealings with state officials the villagers' fear of authority could easily be sensed.

The legitimacy of the New Order government was based on stability and development. In order to achieve development, stability had to be maintained and individual interest had to submit to collectivity, in the interests of harmony (Maurer, 1997). Confrontation is avoided at all costs. In Ngadha villages avoiding confrontation was a recurring theme. Whether it was teenagers making too much noise at night, youngsters firing homemade bamboo cannons during Advent, or the misappropriation of income gained from tourists, villagers always claimed that it was not worth a confrontation. 'Our ancestors would have fought; murder would have resulted. But that is not the way now', I was told.

The pervasive development ideology of the Indonesian state has meant that all villagers are able to articulate concepts of development and progress (*maju* Ind). In discussions about the meaning of development people said that development involved being like city people, having money, electricity and health care and children wearing clothes. They also said that in order to be developed one must get an education. State doctrine attributes 'underdevelopment in large part to a lack of education' (Dove, 1988: 7). Both state and Church sponsor the hegemonic view that formal education is a precursor to development. As a consequence the value of traditional knowledge has been undermined leaving the villagers belittled.

Village people in general and peasants in particular say: 'We are only peasants.'[12] They do not feel 'developed' (*maju*) and have a low opinion of themselves. When in discussions I asked why they had not tried a number of initiatives to raise money they always said: 'No-one has told us to' (*tunggu diseruh* Ind). The patrimonial hierarchy of the New Order appears to have smothered personal initiative. The paternalism of the state system meant that the villagers thought that mechanisms to achieve development came from outside instructions and they lacked the confidence to act on their own initiatives.

The establishment and prominence of Indonesian as the national language has had great impacts. Indonesian is the language of authority. It derives its power in part from mystification. The nuances of formally structured Indonesian can make it barely intelligible to people mostly familiar with colloquial forms. It was used to set an educated opinion above the opinion of the uneducated masses (Cole, 1999). The national language has primacy over local languages. Some villagers, who could speak Indonesian well, did so at meetings. Others, who were able to communicate well in Indonesian, did not feel comfortable using the language publicly. As they have learnt Indonesian informally and not at school they lack the confidence to challenge educated users of the language.

A good command of Indonesian is an indicator of a person's education and the accompanying status. Education beyond the first two years of primary school is in Indonesian. As it is younger people who gain the ability to speak in Indonesian, authority is challenged. In Ngadha *adat* authority resides with elders. The influences of *adat* and the state come into conflict in relation to language use and authority. As Lutz discusses in relation to Adonara, an island off the east coast of Flores, 'bilingualism has political ramifications' (1998: 93). As tourism is a localising force and as a local language is an essential aspect of local identity, tourism may be a force to protect the Ngadha language. Maintaining the use of their local language may become a strategy to remain traditional, and therefore retain touristic appeal.

Contrary to the villagers' views, one of the contradictions between development and *adat* is education. The requirement for education has meant youngsters in Bena have to spend three to six years out of the village, where they are exposed to a wider media, develop greater expectations and find it hard to return and settle in the village. An Australian priest working in Flores wrote 'because of the many schools and irrelevant education, our most intelligent and able young people flee the village and do not wish to become farmers' (quoted in Webb, 1986: 179). Youngsters also find it hard to return to their village with ideas and initiatives. Out of respect for their seniors they do not like to appear to have ideas above and beyond them.

Government plans for the development of Wogo and Bena include developing tourism. In furtherance of this objective the villagers were provided with direct education in the form of a tourism awareness programme (*sadar wisata*). This programme was an attempt by the government to gain villagers' support for tourism development. It represents the bottom rung of Pretty's (1995) participation ladder. It was not designed to empower the villagers to develop indigenous plans. The essence of the programme was that tourists are the nation's guests, so the villagers should be good hosts to them.[13] As I have reported the villagers were dissatisfied with the type of tourism education that they received.

The Church

Although the Portuguese began the conversion of islanders in East Flores in the 16th century, the Catholic Church was not brought to Ngadha until the 1920s. Conversion of the villagers in Wogo and Bena began in the late 1920s and early 1930s. The influence of the Church has been great.

The administrative structure of the Church, as described in Chapter 4, closely follows the pattern of the Indonesian state hierarchy in the number and approximate size of sub-divisions. However, the boundaries of the units do not coincide. The Church then has a hierarchy that both affirms the state hierarchy but also competes with it. The smallest sub-groups of both cut across the *adat* organisation of clans.

The provision of grass for thatching serves as an example of these competing forms of organisation. Grass for thatching used to be provided by the House. Due to the difficulties of collecting grass and the cheap availability of corrugated iron, more and more people started using corrugated iron for roofing material. In order to encourage the use of thatch again, it was agreed that grass collecting would be shared. In Bena, instead of increasing the unit of *adat* organisation from House to clan, each member of the RT[14] (state structure) contributes; in Wogo organisation is under the auspices of the prayer group (church structure).

The impact of the Church varies from one village to another, and this is largely a result of the attitude of the local priest. For example Molnar reports, with reference to the Sara Sedu, on how little change there has been in 'the traditional belief system ... [as] the local priest's approach has been very tolerant of local traditions' (1998: 53). The influence of the Church also depends on the distance of a village from the parish church. As discussed the Church's influence has been greater in Wogo than in Bena due to its proximity to the parish church and mission at Mataloko. More villagers attend church services and other activities organised at the parish church more frequently. Furthermore, the mission is also the biggest employer in Wogo.

The Church has been influential in education development all over the province, building schools long before the Indonesian government did. In 1958 there were 525 mission primary schools and only 75 government schools on Flores (Webb, 1986). The Church continues to be an important provider of schools in Flores, offering not only primary but also secondary- and tertiary-level education. The tertiary level is a seminary for the educa-tion of priests, and teacher training. Although Catholic schools are more expensive than state schools they are favoured as they offer a more disci-plined learning environment.

The Church has also been influential in funding development projects. According to Webb (1986), the economic development of Flores has almost entirely been paid for with Catholic Church (especially German) funds. The Flores–Timor Plan (FTP) was an ambitious socio-economic development project worked out by missionaries and the Catholic Churches Social Institute in The Hague. It began in 1957 with funding from Germany and support from the Indonesian government (Webb, 1986). Agricultural devel-opment was at the centre of the plans that concentrated initially on water supply and then on increased agricultural production. The agricultural experts that came from Germany were quick to denounce traditional feasts as a waste of beasts and man-hours. In some areas there was a ban on slaughtering (Erb, 2001a; Molnar, 1998). In spite of the assault on *adat*, the FTP brought many benefits to Flores, including the introduction of credit union schemes that were still flourishing at the time of writing.

By the end of the 1970s recognising that *adat* still had a part to play in the life of the villages, attitudes in the Church softened. This was in part due to the ordination of Flores priests who recognised that *adat* had too often been ignored. It became apparent, for development projects to be successful, that open consultation is required with all elders and that co-operation will only come from a consensus at such meetings. It is customary in Ngadha to hold public meetings (*utu bhou* Ng) on the *lenggi* (flat stones used as village court). The discussions (*soro mazi* Ng) are to resolve conflict between Houses or clans and to discuss matters of concern to the whole village. Although this is recognised by the Church, the state (or members representing it) appear not to have learnt this, as the Bena *Reba* story below illustrates.

As Webb (1986) notes the Church supports the government and had little to say in criticism against the Suharto government. As a minority religion in Indonesia the Catholic Church is keen to maintain the support of the state. However as Fr. Burt (1971 quoted in Webb, 1986) suggests 'in Flores there are two governments. The official one and the richer, possibly more influential one is the Church.' The villagers of Ngadha are fearful of the authority of both, as they compete for legitimacy in their lives.

The Church acts as a tax collector on Flores. In 1998 parish taxes were substantial, each month an adult had to pay $0.70,[15] school leavers for the first two years after leaving $0.35, and those still at school $0.08. These were regular payments that all individuals had to pay to the Church. The church in Wogo also raised further money, for example for a new roof on the Church, using the collective savings (*arisan*) system. This was $1.75 per individual, including babies, per month. Religious ceremonies conducted by the church such as baptism, confirmation, and marriage also have to be paid for. The villagers were more worried about not paying Church taxes than state ones. If, for example, you had not paid the Church taxes, the Church would not marry you or baptise your child. The Church keeps records of debtors. My niece was unable to get married in church until her mother's debt of $40 had been paid. Her (single) mother had an income of $5 or $6 dollars a month. Whenever villagers bemoaned the need to be involved in the market economy the first three factors to be mentioned were school fees, health care and Church taxes (*Yuran* Ng). In some cases, where children were attending a Catholic school, and health services were provided by a mission clinic, virtually all disposable income was going to the Church. The state and the Church compete for the villager's meagre disposable income and in the services they provide.

When I first visited Wogo, I was not introduced to a priest. Church personnel seemed conspicuous by their absence. On the first evening of our second visit villagers told us that Church reactions to the water project were problematic. The Church had said that to bring water to one *nua* was unfair on people living in other areas. They considered clean water for some but not all members of the parish an unworthy plan. The villagers also informed us that they should attend a practice ceremony in the church the next morning (a Saturday). Obligations to their guests–tourists – and the Church clashed.

Some informants said the practice at the church was entirely unnecessary and that organising a clash with our events was deliberate. The Church had been the provider and controller of all forms of aid, they were worried about the threat of competition we posed, perhaps especially as the instigators were a Muslim from Java and an English woman. Bringing tourists interested in the villagers' traditional culture, the Church may have feared that we were sponsoring a revival of paganism.

By the end of the 1970s *adat* and religion began to be 'enculturated'. The words of a priest wearing *adat* clothes, giving a new year mass clearly demonstrates how the Church deliberately attempts to incorporate *adat*: 'Christ came among us not to push out *adat* but to complete and perfect what our ancestors taught us. The yam is the original food of Ngadha, now it is the symbol of our ancestors and of Christ.' It would appear that having failed to obliterate *adat* the Church is trying to appropriate it. The yam was taken from being a symbol of agricultural fertility to a symbol of Christ. In a similar vein, Erb (2001a) recounts how, in neighbouring Manggarai, the diocese attempted to appropriate a village-based ritual.

Adat: The way of the ancestors (*Uku adha Ebu po, nusi pera*)

The Indonesian word *adat* is usually used to refer to non-Muslim customs. For the villagers *adat* is 'the way of the ancestors'. In tourism *adat* is often used to mean tradition, for example, the villages in this study are frequently referred to as *kampung adat* (in this case *adat* can be translated as traditional). The multiple meanings and uses of this single word is representative of the strategic use and appropriation of culture in tourism.

Although in theory fixed and unchanging, in practice *adat* is constantly negotiated. According to the villagers *adat* is so strong it will endure regardless of external pressure. However *adat* has been changed both by the state and the Church. Historically both the Church and the state have undermined the power of *adat*.

As discussed, the government has devalued traditional beliefs, associating them with being primitive, without religion, and an obstacle to development (Dove, 1998: 1; Koentjaraningrat, 1971: 202–203). Some government actions in Ngadha have been more concrete in the social dislocation of people from their *adat*, than others. In order to be able to reach villagers,[16] the government has pressurised them to move from their hilltop settlements to more accessible locations.[17] This has resulted in villagers being physically and psychologically removed from their ancestors. Bena claims to be a superior tourist attraction on the basis of its being in its original location and therefore more intact. The conflict between Bena and Luba, a neighbouring *nua* in the same administrative village, results from claims that Luba is not 'original'.

The Department of Health was instrumental in moving people out of traditional Houses into 'healthy homes' (*rumah sehat* Ind). In the 1970s many of the Ngadha abandoned their Houses and built new homes. Some people placed the inner sacred rooms at the back of their new 'healthy homes', a strategy to enable communication with the ancestors to continue. The villages that now receive the largest numbers of tourists are those that kept their Houses. The government has changed its policy and is now instrumental in keeping Houses traditional. In Bena considerable controversy resulted from a villager thatching a house by a method not considered traditional. All villagers agree that the houses in the *nua* must be thatched i.e. traditional, however, some would like to specify the method of thatching. Further, according to the village headman, all new houses in Bena must be built without opening windows because these are not in line with tradition. His wife's family's House, the most recent House to be renovated in 1998, was indeed built to this specification.

What is traditional is now seen by the government to be attractive to tourists and therefore to be safeguarded. However from an analysis of the views of tourists many felt that Bena was too perfect. Some even believed it to be a living museum rather than a normal functioning village. Tourists who made the extra journey to Nage, a *nua* with both traditional Houses and some concrete houses, generally preferred this village: 'It was more real.'

The government and the Church have also tried to limit the number of animals that can be slaughtered, justified on the grounds that these rituals were impoverishing the villagers. This creates a barrier to communication between past and present generations given that it is based upon ritual sacrifice (Howell, 1995b). Feasting is an essential part of maintaining social ties between villagers. Rituals are also important for attracting tourists. Observing sacrifice is especially prestigious for the traveller seeking the authentic exotic that travelling to Ngadha potentially offers. If sufficient tourists are attracted to rituals involving slaughter it is likely that the government's line will change: rather than being regarded as impoverishing, animal sacrifices may be fundamental to the development of villages as traditional villages (*kampung adat*) and tourist attractions.

The Church in Toraja, Sulawesi, has been one of the more vocal critics of rituals that cater to tourist audiences, claiming that funerals, fundamentally religious events, are being turned into spectacles (Volkman, 1987). In Ngadha, while tourists are actively sought to attend house building and other *adat* rituals, weddings and first communion parties, I have not yet encountered tourists being invited to funerals. While it seems unlikely, owing to the costs involved, that animal sacrifices will be staged in Ngadha for tourists, it does seem likely that the events will be pre-planned and publicised in advance in order to attract tourists, if there are sufficient numbers and/or economic incentives. Should this come about it is possible that villagers could compete for tourists through the marketing of rituals. If, however, significant numbers of tourists were to start to attend funerals, which involve both animal sacrifice and Catholic religious elements, a reaction from the Church, similar to that in Toraja, could be expected.

Children having to leave Bena to attend school beyond primary level also compromises *adat*. The state and the Church have both emphasised the importance of education and some villagers who are able have followed this option. However, in doing so they are removed from their village and their *adat*. All Bena youngsters claim *adat* is very important part of their lives. However schooling competes with the less formal education that learning *adat* offers.

Bena's *Reba* festival

Reba is the most important of Ngadha rituals. The annual harvest and thanksgiving festival, lasting three days, is held in all Ngadha villages. Attendance is compulsory for all House members, who share food and make decisions for the following year. All heirlooms held in the House are brought out of their 'hiding places' shown to members (proving they haven't been pawned or sold) and ritually cleaned. It is at this time that all engagements are arranged and traditionally all marriages took place. Preparations begin some days beforehand. All *ngadhu* and *bhaga* are attended to; thatch is repaired and stones realigned. The ancestors are thus at their best to attend the ritual. Family members then gather, and male kin brings animals into the *nua* for brides-to-be (*tua mano* Ng). On the first night, in each House, a ritual meal is prepared, where yams are peeled and cut.

The date of *Reba* was traditionally determined according to the moon and in Bena it usually fell in the middle of December. Because of its primary position, as eldest sibling, it is essential according to *adat* that Bena is the first village to celebrate *Reba*. Other villagers hold their celebrations later over New Year and in early January. Announcing the date of *Reba* is the prerogative of the calendar holder (*pemengang sobe* Ng), a hereditary position passed down through the clan's second House.

However, *Reba* in mid-December meant that it fell during Advent, when it is inappropriate to drink, dance and be merry. Under the influence of the Church, in the late1960s, the date of *Reba* was moved and fixed to 27 December. This arrangement ran satisfactorily for 30 years. Although the date of *Reba* was no longer determined by the moon, Bena maintained its primacy, being first to celebrate *Reba*.

The fixing of the date of *Reba* is also important for tourism, so it can be advertised in advance and used to attract tourists. This is particularly important because *Reba* falls out of the peak Tourist Season and can therefore attract tourists out of season. The provincial Tourism Department makes comparisons with *Pasola* on Sumba. This annual ceremony has been successful in bringing tourists to an island that otherwise receives very few tourists.

In 1996, the Church decided it would hold a parish *Reba*, on 26 December. The parish church is 8km away in a village called Jerebuu. The parish *Reba* then usurped Bena's primacy. In 1997, in order to restore Bena's primary position the village headman, a state official, using *adat* as the justification, argued that 'the village should return to tradition' and decreed that Bena would celebrate *Reba* on 15 December. That year *Reba* neither followed *adat*: the date determined by the moon, nor religion: refraining from merriment during Advent.

In 1998, the date of *Reba* became a contentious issue. Although *Reba* was three months away, I was first alerted to the issue in September. 'Have you decided on a date for *Reba* yet?' an official from the Department of Education and Culture asked the caretaker. 'Kupang [the provincial capital] want to know to put it on the calendar of events, Nage and Wogo have their dates fixed ... they say it is important to attract tourists out of season.' 'It's difficult, following *adat* means it could be in Advent, the Church want it after Christmas, now there is tourism to consider…', the caretaker replied.

While the Church attempted to appeal to the parishioners to return to the previous status quo of *Reba* on 27 December. The headman tried to retain authority by announcing that *Reba* would begin on 15 December. Many villagers expressed their confusion: 'If we follow religion we must not celebrate in Advent, if we do *Reba* will not be as it should be.' In an attempt to use tourism as a reason for the latter date a villager asked me, in front of several people 'Would the 27th be a better date? Between Christmas and New Year tourists are more likely to be on holiday aren't they?' Finally the village headman agreed to allow *Reba* on 27 December but said that there could be no dancing on 28 December because there was to be a working party.

On 27 December the sound of bamboo cannons could be heard 3km away. The road was crowded with people making their way to Bena. In the *nua*, extended families were gathered in the *sa'o* having family meals. The sense of build-up for a great ritual hung in the air.

The next day drinking, dancing and merry making were expected to go ahead as usual. The working party seemed forgotten. The calendar holder then went around the *nua* carrying the old and new calendars and invited the villagers to dance. Many of the villagers began, only to be brought to an abrupt end by the headman, who said that it had been agreed there could be no dancing on 28 December.

A spontaneous village meeting began on the *lenggi* (stone meeting place*)*. As the meeting continued it became more and more heated and threatened to get violent at times. I was standing on the periphery with other women, listening. Mama Mia squeezed my hand and tugged me back. She sensed emotions could boil over at any minute. During the meeting the village headman claimed to be the regional head (*Kepala Wilaya* Ind), and therefore had the authority to make decisions. He was the father who should give direction and lead. He likened the villagers to naughty children who had disobeyed their father and made him very angry; he claimed that he was customary head (*Ketua adat* Ind) and that the villagers were not following *adat* if they did not follow his decisions.

After a couple of hours villagers began to return to their homes both sad and angry. They had left the village headman to appear victor. Conflict was avoided. 'It is better to walk away than let it go any further', I was told. People had travelled some distance at considerable expense. *Reba* dancing only takes place once a year. As one old man said almost in tears: ' I will pray to god that I will be healthy enough to stamp the ground and sing *O uvi*[18] [i.e. to sing and dance *Reba* style] again.'

On the third day of *Reba* there was little joy and celebration but a lot of anger and bitterness and talk. There was, as custom dictates, plenty of drinking of locally distilled spirit. Late that night some youngsters began to dance and sing the refrain of the *Reba* song. They stamped around the *nua* to the trance-like rhythms, getting louder and more threatening as they went. Relatives inside their houses were frightened, some took to praying, some women cried, others directed husbands and elder brothers to stop them; they were sure their youngsters would provoke violence. Using the rhythm and chorus of the traditional Reba song they accused the local headman of corruption. The village headman did not rise to the threats but remained behind closed doors and the youngsters eventually gave up. The 1998 *Reba* thus came to an end in an atmosphere of frustration, sadness and anger.

The youngsters and their reaction probably had a lot to do with the political climate at the time in Indonesia. As students were demonstrating all over the archipelago to rid the country of corrupt officials, the youngsters in Bena vented their own frustrations and directed them at the most local level of the political web. However, the discussions and issues raised during the many *Reba* discussions and meetings in Bena serve to underline the competing power factions articulated at the village level, and a number of salient issues are illustrated by the story of Bena's 1998 *Reba* festival. In part they reflect the historical process of change of a remote society's incorporation into the world system. The Christian calendar has become dominant: both as part of Catholicism, and as part of international time, including tourism. The appeal to return to moon date fixing was a call to limit the power of the state representative. Moon time has been supplanted by ubiquitous global time in Ngadha. The calendar holder did however want to retain his ritual role, his moment of glory, to parade old and new calendars around the village.

At the same time the events reflected the contemporary political turbulence in Indonesia in 1998, played out on a local stage. The local youth, aided by Dutch courage, also challenged state authority. The youngsters also used *adat* as their vehicle to vent their frustrations. Between the 'Oh Yam' choruses of the *Reba* song, elders would normally use parallel poetic phrases to remember the ancestors and their stories. Many of the lines are used only during *Reba* songs. By stopping the dancing, and therefore the singing that goes with it, the headman caused the youngsters to miss out on an opportunity to hear and learn 'the songs of the ancestors'.

Both the young and old appeal to *adat* to express frustration and dissatisfaction with the present political structures. While accepting and inviting modernising forces including global time and tourists into their lives, the villagers cling to their central core framework to give them the power to resist unwelcome modern authority. The villagers strategically use *adat* to support their causes. *Adat* has become, and is increasingly a powerful force that is manipulated by the state, for example in tourism, and articulated by the villagers, who, as the custodians, want to claim the power of ancestral force.

Tourism, although the most modern force to be affecting the villagers lives, is inextricably linked with *adat*. Although driven by the state, tourism in Ngadha relies on selling images of local culture and customs. Without *adat*: the *nua*, Houses, rituals, weaving and lifestyles there would be no attraction for tourists. As *adat* lies at the heart of Ngadha's tourism, decisions pertaining to tourism development will need to be made within the *adat* framework if they are to be regarded by the villagers as legitimate and binding.

Power Balance, Tourism and Change

The state, *adat* and the Church compete for authority in the lives of Ngadha villagers. They can, as the example of the priest's first service illustrates, act simultaneously in relative harmony. However when two of the forces combine, an imbalance results. When the combined forces of state and Church undermined *adat*, traditional villages were abandoned and conflicts over land ownership developed, but the villagers felt no more prosperous. Now that the value of *adat* is recognised, both the Church and state are appropriating it. The central symbols of *adat* now have a new value: tourism. Tourism is thus affecting the balance of the competing forces.

Tourism is a state-sponsored activity. If the government did not issue tourist visas there would be no tourists in Ngadha. Indeed, as discussed in Chapter 3 the change in the VoA in 2003 and 2004 had a tremendous negative impact on tourist arrivals. Tourists come to Ngadha for its exotic culture i.e. to gaze upon the central symbols of *adat*. In this way, the state is bolstering the *adat* leg of the stool. However by assigning cultural village (*kampung budaya*) status to the villages and heritage status to the symbols, the state may be working to preserve the symbols of *adat* for the tourists, but not the values of *adat* for the villagers. As I have suggested elsewhere (Cole, 2003), transforming contemporary symbols into heritage assigns them to the past (cf. Bruce (1998) on the roots of the word 'heritage' and how it is related to the past). This may be a powerful and indirect way to further sever villager–ancestor relations.

The ownership of heritage is also a complex issue (cf. Turnbridge & Ashworth, 1996) especially where it refers to a village, its occupants and their customs. Both Bena and Wogo, as sites, have been objectified by the state as cultural villages, and the villagers' material ritual assets have become objects the state preserves. The state already dictates activities in the villages, for example all houses must be thatched. How far will the state be able to control *adat* resources? The balance may well lie with the Church. Although all new houses built in Bena should not have opening wooden windows because this is not traditional, they will all have a separate adults' room. Such rooms are not traditional and some houses in other villages do not have them but the parish church insists that consenting adults must have their own room and that all houses in Bena have these additional rooms.

As tourism shores up the leg of *adat*, it is used as an excuse to return to past power structures, by those whose interest this serves, for example Stephan's claims in Wogo (cf. Cole, 1998). The villagers of Ngadha have suffered from the hierarchical power structures of both the Church and the state and they have been disempowered from acting on their own initiatives and have been made fearful by the authoritarian rule of both. These two external influences have been responsible for belittling the villagers, and devaluing traditional knowledge by placing emphasis on formal education.

As outlined in Chapter 2 missionaries separated *adat* from religion. *Adat* has also been separated from administration. The 1979 Law No. 5 makes the distinction explicit (Soemardjan & Breazeale, 1993). Tourism continues the process of the separation of *adat*. Tourism objectifies *adat*, it takes symbols and separates them from their meanings, as we have seen in relation to the *ngadhu*. Tourism creates pride in *adat* and shores up the *adat* leg of the stool. Furthermore, the 1999 autonomy laws are renewing the importance of *adat* (Benda-Beckmann and Benda-Beckmann, 2001).

Adat itself becomes contested. It is essential for attracting tourists, essential to the villagers' pride; it lies at the heart of their new power in identity. How far the state and Church will use their power to appropriate the villagers' resource and manipulate its meanings remains to be seen. Will the new force of tourism continue the separation of symbols from their meaning? Will the villagers internalise the West's false image of them? Or can the villagers use tourism as an empowering force, a force for socio-economic development, a force to retain the power of the ancestors? The answers must be subject to inter-village variation. Certainly, if the use of disposable income to fund *adat* rituals can be used as a measure, *adat* still retains considerable and potent power in many villages. The answers must also be dependent on the way that tourism is developed.

This chapter has unpeeled the onion skins around the Ngadha cultural core. Tourism is the outer global skin. While the Ngahda have been superficially incorporated into the world system there is little evidence of homogenisation or the demonstration effect resulting from this external global force. Tourism has however been an important force in localisation and a defined Ngadha ethnicity has been created in response to their otherness becoming a consumerable commodity. The self-conscious awareness of their culture as a resource has given the Ngadha people pride and political capital to manipulate. Local differences have been asserted and, as discussed, the local regency has now chosen to split, along ethnic grounds.

There is evidence of the active and creative roles of local people who have used the power that tourism has brought. Tourism was used to support the Church's preferred date of *Reba* in Bena and tourism has been articulated to restrict the power of local state officials. Knowing westerners brings pride and having relations with westerners, usually tourists, can have far reaching effects. Knowing how to relate to westerners can bring political and economic advantage and there is evidence that certain local community members, such as the guides, have been able to make use of their contacts.

The Catholic Church and Indonesian state compete for legitimacy and authority in the villagers' lives. They compete in the provision of services and the collection of taxes. Both have attempted to undermine the power of *adat* and sever relations between the villagers and their ancestors. Having failed to debase the resilient cultural core, both attempt to appropriate it. Enculturation is the outward sign of how the Church now incorporates *adat* elements into church services. The state has taken the material cultural assets of *adat* and redefined them as national heritage. Property of the clans has become property to be preserved by the state. On the one hand, tourism has continued the separation of *adat* from religion and administration. It has separated the symbols of *adat* from their meanings and has linked *adat* with the past. On the other hand, tourism, the most recent external force, is inextricably linked with *adat*, it therefore works to bolster the *adat* leg of the stool, and works to counterbalance the powers of Church and state.

Notes

1. The O Luka ceremony and song retold at Nage's *Reba* every year is considered to recount the ancestors journey from Java via Sumba to Ngadha.
2. My grandparents had only three children, the eldest son married out into a neighbouring *nua*. My aunt is disabled and thought unlikely to attract a husband. My grandparents therefore insisted that my father pay bridewealth so he and his wife could stay with them.
3. Although my father had eight children, he had a job at the Department of Education and Culture so my mother carried out the agricultural work. My sister was needed to run the house.
4. Sometimes the claim was different clan, different rules and even different house, different rules. This underscores the house as the fundamental level of social organisation
5. The expression *Du Wungu, Ngalu Wunga* conveys the first is the eminent.
6. See for example, Kompas, *9 Mei 2001* Flores Siap Jadi Provinsi Otonom Denpasar, http://www.kompas.com/kompas-cetak/0105/09/ daerah/flor21.htm.
7. *Ebu* = grandparent; *Po* = advice; *Nusi* = great-grandparents; *Pera* = teachings; *Uku* = restriction/rule; *Adha* = showing respect.
8. The priest laid his hand on the imaginary heads of the dead kneeling next to his live relatives.
9. Family planning has been a national policy promoted with considerable success and international acclaim. Indonesia's annual population growth rate has fallen from 2.3% in 1972 to around 1.6% in 1996. http://w3.whosea.org/ LinkFiles/Family_Planning_Fact_Sheets_indonesia.pdf.
10. Enculturation is used as the Anglo-American translation of *inculturisasi* by Molnar (2000) and Erb (2001a). It describes the deliberate blending of customary and Catholic traditions.
11. A communal feast symbolising the social unity of those participating in it.
12. They would use the expression '*Kami hanya petani saja*' which uses two words for only, before and after the noun for emphasis.

13. This remains the government line, for example see Megawati's comments (*Guardian*, October 2001)
14. Neighbourhood organisation consisting of approximately 12 houses (see Chapter 4).
15. Using an exchange rate of Rp10,000 to the $1. All figures US dollars.
16. To facilitate the governments wish to count, tax and school them.
17. A local law still prevents the construction of permanent dwellings in gardens. All must be built at roadside locations. Although weakly enforced, this law continues to cause problems. The price of roadside land fetches premiums many times other land and houses are built on precarious slopes and unsuitable sites in order to conform with the law.
18. 'Oh yam', the staple food in the past.

Chapter 10

Conclusions: Tourism, Culture and Development – The First 20 Years

The Development of Tourism

This book has provided a longitudinal study of emergent cultural tourism. In order to understand the interaction between culture and tourism the study has examined tourism development internally. It has, following King's suggestion, examined their 'cultural values and ideologies and the ways these are constructed, used, debated, sustained and transformed' (1999: 77). By providing a detailed study at the micro-level it has revealed weaknesses in some of the broad macro-level tourism theories. Before drawing together the concluding thoughts about tourism, cultural change and development I will review how tourism itself has changed in Ngadha.

Tourists started to visit Ngadha villages in the 1980s. Only the most intrepid of travellers attempted to make the journey, they had to have time and be prepared to adapt significantly. There were no services aimed at tourists and no telephones in town. By 1989 arrivals per month could still be counted on one hand. A few local high school students would take tourists to the villages as a way to hone their English language skills. Villagers, while slightly fearful of the new visitors, would welcome them as guests of the 'guides' and extend hospitality to them. The children would initially run away but the braver ones, while always maintaining a safe distance, would gradually creep closer.

Statistics are very unreliable but by the mid-1990s approximately 7000 foreign tourists visited Bena a year while less than 2000 visited Wogo, despite easier access to the latter. The majority were Europeans with increasing numbers of Australasians. The number of guesthouses in Bajawa increased and restaurants opened to cater for the tourists serving dishes such as fried potatoes, guacamole, and egg on toast. It was possible to make international telephone calls, although with difficulty via an operator. As roads improved the intrepid travellers were joined by long-term shoestring tourists and then by Bali-Lombok strays and incipient mass tourists. The children in frequently visited villages began to see tourists as a source of sweets, pens, balloons and chasing games; instead of running away they would run up to tourists or call to them.

In the years I have been studying tourism in Ngadha the travel patterns of the tourists have changed. This largely relates to improved infrastructure and changes in transportation. The amount of time tourists spend on Flores has decreased while the amount of villages they visit has increased. At the same time there has been a wider variety in the types of guides that bring tourists to the villages. As discussed in Chapter 6 tourists are now taken to the villages by a number of different intermediaries. Local guides face competition not only from international tour leaders, provincial guides, and wild guides but also drivers and more recently motorcycle taxis that deliver tourists to the villages without guides. While the local guides have worked hard to maintain good relations with most of the villagers and facilitate communication between tourists and villagers, many of the new intermediaries do not. Villagers therefore have less interaction with the tourists and miss out on one of the perceived benefits: 'tourists are a window on the world'.

As tourism was increasingly incorporated into the lives of villagers, they, like other villagers in other parts of the world, developed methods to protect their back-stage regions. MacCannell's (1976) back-stage/front-stage analogy, where the authenticity-seeking tourists attempt to get further and further back-stage, is commonly used in the tourism literature. The analogy works well in this case due to the spatial arrangements of a Ngadha *nua*. According to Ngadha cosmology Houses reflect life stages. The area of a Ngadha House open to tourists is considered the child. Only those tourists who can adapt, who respond to greetings, answer banal questioning, and put the villagers at ease by not transgressing *adat*, can ever penetrate further back-stage. Only when a tourist displays a more mature sensitivity can they progress from the childhood terrace to the adolescent central room of a Ngadha House. Very few tourists ever penetrate the fully mature adult, inner sacred space at the back of the House. As tourist numbers have increased, and the types of tourists and their intermediaries have changed, a far smaller proportion of tourists obtain access even to the central room of Houses.

While global tourist typologies (e.g. Cohen, 1974; Smith, 1978) attempt a macro analysis of a micro phenomenon, the ethnography reveals that these mask the reality of events in tourist destinations. These broad typologies are not subtle enough to identify the important details at a local level.[1] By developing a specific segmentation of the tourists that visit Ngadha villages I was able to highlight the differences between eastbound and westbound shoestring tourists. The former were more able to adapt their behaviour in the villages, but were often travel weary. The later were frequently still suffering from culture shock. As they lacked experience in

Indonesia they did not have the social capital to enable them to adapt to the cultural norms in the village.

One thing that has not changed is the tourists' desire for authenticity. From the tourists' perspective authenticity was frequently equated with poverty, i.e. signs of modernity and/or touristification in the villages decreased its authenticity. Any attempt by villagers to raise an income from tourism is considered to spoil the authentic nature of the traditional village. Tourists considered poorer, less touristy villages as more authentic, aestheticising poverty as Mowforth and Munt (1998) suggest. The villagers' marginality, underdevelopment and poverty, celebrated by tourists, is on the one hand an opportunity to shake off the shame of poverty, while on the other a powerful force keeping the Ngadha 'primitive'. This is particularly prominent in Bena where, for example, attempts are being made to enforce the building of Houses without windows 'to keep them traditional'. While the villagers in Bena want electricity, tourists, guidebooks and the government consider the electricity poles in Wogo to have spoilt the village.

Villagers in Ngadha have a positive view of tickets. *Nua* that could be 'sold' are considered superior, and superiority is linked to concepts of precedence and originality, thus tickets 'authenticate' the villages for villagers but tourists think they diminish the authenticity of the villages. Selling tickets to the villages is part of their commodification.

In order to satisfy the tourists' desire for authenticity, guides take the tourists to remoter less visited villages, to villages where all the children still rush out and shout 'Hello mister'. This means that tourists spend less time in Bena, and other villages that have become used to tourists. Some villagers had started to incorporate income from souvenir sales to tourists into family budgeting. With less time spent in the village, fewer sales are made and the villagers' enthusiasm for tourism is diminished.

By 2005 Bajawa boasted its first hotel with spring beds, hot water, western-style flush toilets, and even TVs in the two VIP rooms. At the telephone office[2] it was possible to make direct dial calls across the world but Bajawa did not have an Internet café. Due to national visa policies and international politics the type of tourists had changed and the season was significantly shorter.

Authenticity and Commodification

Authenticity and commodification are central in academic debates about social and cultural issues in tourism. As Taylor suggests, 'the moment culture is defined as an object of tourism ... its authenticity is reduced' (2001: 15). When tourists started visiting Ngadha villages they made requests to buy ikats they saw hanging on washing lines. When villagers hang ikats out in the hope to make sales to tourists, the authenticity of the village, according to the tourists, is reduced, it is spoilt, commercialised and they have commodified their culture.

The commodification process is at an early stage in Ngadha in comparison to other, more widely studied areas of Indonesia. The commodification of crafts has begun. Small scarf-sized ikats are woven, displaying the *ngadhu* symbol, for sale to tourists. However, at least half the ikats produced in Bena, the most visited village, are for local consumption. Long knives produced in Wogo, although purchased by tourists, have not yet been changed to appeal to the new market.

Likewise, there has been minimal commodification of the performing arts, as the villagers did not consider these cost-effective or festive (*ramai* Ind). No ceremonies are as yet staged for tourists, but the fixing of dates for village ceremonies can be considered as a first step in their commodification. As tourists confer pride on their hosts, as prestigious visitors, tourists are invited to attend rituals. However, unlike in Toraja as Adams (1993), Crystal (1989), Volkman (1985) and Yamashita (1994) have reported, there has not yet been a re-orientation of rituals towards outsiders.

The cultural studio set up in Wogo did result in positive benefits for the villagers initially, increasing social cohesion and offering the villagers a chance to travel as Sanger (1988) suggests. However, its impact on the revitalisation of traditional cultural has been minimal.

The raw materials of cultural tourism exist in Ngadha but their refinement for tourism consumption is at an early stage. The refinement process is critical, without it there is minimal economic benefit from tourism, too much and the resource is spoilt.

As identified in other areas of Indonesia (cf. Adams, 1997; Erb, 1998; Picard, 1996; Volkman, 1987), tourism is an important force in the creation of ethnicity and the affirmation of local identity. The commodification of the villagers' identity has begun in Ngadha. Tourism is creating a bounded, discrete, identity in this area where anthropologists suggest unbounded, fluid, fuzzy continuums between groups existed (cf. Molnar, 1998).

This process of commodification of the villagers' identity is bringing them pride and a self-conscious awareness of their traditional culture. Traditional culture has become a resource that they manipulate to economic and political ends. Tourism is used as a rhetorical weapon to underscore the power of *adat*. As discussed in Chapter 9, tourism reinforces *adat* and works to counterbalance the power of the state and church.

While tourism has in part been responsible for the creation of a Ngadha ethnicity, the unity under this ethnic label is far from clear. Outsiders (e.g. guidebooks and anthropologists) refer to the Ngadha, and new emerging elites, as manipulating ethnic sentiments, amplifying similarities and difference for political ends. However, the villagers still identify the community at the most local level. There has always been inter-nua competition over the limited tourism resources, a competition that has become worse since tourist numbers have fallen. Community participation may be a mantra for sustainable tourism but the issue of how the community is defined, who is in and who is not, and who has the right to take decisions are all being contested in Ngadha.

While western analysts have regarded the commodification of otherness 'as a kind of institutionalised racism that celebrates primitiveness' (Mowforth & Munt, 1998: 270) it needs also to be recognised as part of a process of empowerment. Analysts have criticised cultural tourism as leading to the reinterpretation of poverty, suffering and inequality as cultural diversity. This suggests that tourates are passive. While the state maybe responsible for 'museumising' the villages and creating a straightjacket for their visible cultural assets (e.g. architectural styles) tourists' visits per se bring pride, and a self-conscious awareness of their traditional culture, which is a step on the ladder to empowerment.

As Adams (1984) and Cohen (2001) have observed, the preservation of a group's cultural distinctiveness and the commodification of their identity, results in a group's representation tending towards essentialisation. The most immediately apparent symbols of a culture that carry the most exotic connotations become a group's ethnic markers. In the case of Ngadha the most obvious ethnic marker is the *ngadhu*. This symbol of a clan's founding male ancestor is objectified, externalised and stripped of its context. It occurs in marketing literature, alone, separated from its female co-symbol, the *bhaga*, together with which all *ngadhu* stand. As discussed in Chapter 8 this emphasis of a male symbol over a female symbol may have consequences for gender relations in Ngadha.

Complete *nua* and the Ngadha megaliths are secondary ethnic markers. The latter are a source of cultural confusion for tourists. Found alongside Catholic graves, these large stones are significant cultural symbols for the villagers. Preserved as heritage by the state, the villagers' megaliths are reified and consigned to the past by government and tourists (cf. Cole, 2003). This raises questions over ownership. As the property of the clans is appropriated as national heritage, it becomes the property of the state. The ownership of heritage is a complex issue (cf. Turnbridge & Ashworth, 1996) especially where it refers to a village, its occupants and customs. The difficulties experienced by villagers in Lombok reported by Fallon (2001) Cushman (1999) and Bras (2000) all suggest that ownership of the resource base is crucial to maintaining control over 'tourism development. If the state can appropriate the clans' property, it could lay claim to other aspects of the villages. In Lombok the provincial government made plans to move the villagers out of a cultural village (Bras, 2000). Furthermore, who benefits from the economic growth of tourism is directly related to its control and ownership (Gunn, 1994).

Picard (1996), in reference to Bali, has observed the process of objectifying, externalising and reifying cultural symbols. The touristification process, as he calls it, is at an early stage in Ngadha. Guides, guidebooks and the state, which all romanticise this marginal community and present their lives in a series of unchanging frozen, exotic images and narratives, drive the touristification process. The state has attempted to control what the villagers can do with their own homes. For example they must be thatched, and they should not have opening wooden windows. However, the villagers' blind obedience to the state is being challenged. The change in Indonesian politics, with the fall of Suharto and the regional autonomy laws, has added to the confidence and power that tourism has brought. As we saw, the youngsters in Bena challenged a local government official, and the tourism management group reported a corrupt local officer – either of these would have been unheard of 20 years ago. Many suspect that Bena has been denied electricity to keep the village 'traditional', the villagers have responded by installing generators. This is an uneconomic, unecological way for the villagers to produce electricity but it shows that the villagers refuse to be frozen as cultural relics and will, where possible, take development into their own hands. Meanwhile the villagers of Wogo have chosen to put street lamps on their electricity poles – further spoiling the village according to tourists.

Globalisation, Peripherality and Modernisation

Ngadha was and still is in the super-periphery of the world. It remains a backwater and tourism has done little to change this. The main town Bajawa has no ATM machines, no postcards for sale and no Internet café – facts bemoaned by the modern tourists who have come to depend on their existence everywhere. However, the town has changed. There are far more cars and, recently, vast numbers of motorcycles.[3] There are three mobile phone towers connecting those in town with friends, relatives and businesses across Indonesia. The town has become more cosmopolitan with immigrants from other Indonesian islands. In recent years Javanese immigrants have become increasing conspicuous with women wearing *jilbab* (Muslim female headgear) and there are an increasing number of cafés serving Javanese style food.

In the villages there has been change too – and much of it can be attributed directly to tourism. In the late 1980s and early 1990s funds from tourism brought piped water to both villages. Since then, in Wogo several houses have used electric pumps to run water to bathrooms (*kamar mundi*)[4] behind their houses. In Bena an aid agency match funded donations collected from tourism to provide one standpipe per four houses.

As I have suggested, the roads in Flores have been improved substantially in the last two decades of the 20th century. Although woefully inadequate, the road to Bena has been upgraded, in part due to the needs of tourists, and the villagers are aware of this fringe benefit from tourism. The improvements mean that villagers can travel to and from Bajawa more easily. This has meant better access to schools for teenagers in Bena[5] and the access has improved sales both of ikats and agricultural produce. Furthermore, it has facilitated the purchase of diesel for generators. However, as roads have improved, tourists are taken to more villages and spend less time in each village. This has had a negative impact on sales of souvenirs to tourists in Bena.

The change in clothes the villagers wear may, to some outside observers, be considered signs of modernisation. However, the evidence does not support the demonstration effect – a concept used by many tourism researchers to describe the process of local people emulating the behaviour of tourists. To suggest that local people will want to copy the clothing, language and habits of tourists merely through observing them masks the ability of the villagers to choose if and what they want to copy and why. The ethnography does not bear out a simple equation that what tourists have and do villagers aspire to. With regard to clothing, choice was made about its durability, price, and in Wogo, its warmth. The villagers sought jeans, jumpers, jackets and sweatshirts for their durability, warmth and relatively cheap price not because they wanted to copy tourists. Many of the clothes worn by tourists, the villagers thought were thoroughly unsuitable and impolite.

The only actors who seemed keen to 'copy' tourist clothing were some of the guides. Their motives were also practical. Some guides sought currently fashionable tourist clothing, so they could be recognised as guides by tourists. The guides, like the villagers, are cultural strategists, they may copy some clothing from people they meet, including tourists, and they make choices about the most practical attire from the range that is on offer.

Furthermore, the tourism development literature fails to mention tourists copying local people. A sarong has become a common, fashionable item of clothing across Europe. Sarongs are everyday clothing for many Indonesians and other people in South East Asia. Ikat fabric originating in Indonesia is now fashioned into numerous types of clothing for sale to tourists.

The ethnography also suggests that the idea that acculturation leads to cultural homogenisation is an oversimplification. While there is clear evidence that cultural contact has had a significant impact on the villagers' lives, the evidence for tourism leading to the homogenisation of culture is scant. Moreover, it would appear that as tourists have shown interest in the villagers' lives, the villagers have developed a self-conscious awareness of their traditions. While the villagers were classified as *masyrakat terasing* (most remote communities see p. 62) by the state, they were regarded as an *'primitif'*, indigenous and undeveloped people and a problem. This shame of isolated peasantry is being replaced with pride, as people come all the way from the other side of the world to see their villages. Tourism has thus increased the villagers' self-esteem; it has brought contacts in distant places, and links to the wider world. The pride and power of an ethnic identity is now articulated in local power struggles.

Globalisation is about interconnectedness and the people of Ngadha are being incorporated into the world system. This is not new – it pre-dates tourism. The Catholic Church brought a world religion, formal education and changed how the villagers determine time. The European priests introduced new dance styles and different foods. The emphasis on formal education has led to villagers leaving the village for high school and being influenced by events in the local town. A lucky few have been able to continue to further education in Kupang and Java. The villagers have become connected with communities and networks beyond the confines of the village, region and province. Students have returned bringing magazines, images and stories of lives elsewhere. The influence of the Ngadha extended community is especially prevalent at Reba and major House rituals when relatives gather from distance corners of the Indonesian archipelago and share stories into the night.

Tourism has added an important layer of interconnectedness – connections with westerners and their resources. In Ngadha cosmology both having many friends and travelling lead to knowledge, prestige and respect. Knowing foreigners brings social and potentially economic advantage. The two members of the villages that have studied to post-graduate level outside Indonesia both worked as 'guides' in the early days of tourism. Other guides have used their European friends to help with education for themselves and for their relatives. Other tourists have helped with medical care or sent regular donations to help families in the villages. Through tourists some villagers have become well interconnected with the wider world.

Globalisation is often conceptualised in terms of a global consumerism and in the past 15 years the villagers' desire for certain consumer goods (stereo systems, TVs and motorcycles) has emerged. Motorcycles driving through the *nua* are a recent phenomena (see Plate 17). However, consumerism is dependent on disposable income, a resource that remains rare and beyond the reach of the majority of villagers. The shift from a subsistence-orientated economy to one based on cash is still at an early stage, and the sale of ikats has played an important part in that shift. Meanwhile the Ngadha culture, products and images have been appropriated by world capitalism, and the villagers are increasingly aware that other people maybe be making money from what is theirs.

Another facet of globalisation is that events many miles away shape local happenings (Giddens, 1991). As we have seen, international, national, political and natural events many miles from Flores have had a significant impact on tourism development. Tourism has offered the villagers chinks of economic light, and even the brightness of opportunity, only to see them

Plate 17 Modernisation: a motorcycle is driven through the *nua*

fade and virtually disappear. It has offered hopes and dreams but for the vast majority it has changed the economics realities of their lives very little indeed.

Notes

1. Donald MacLeod (2004) found the same problem in his examination of tourists and their impacts on La Gomera.
2. A *Wartel* or *warung telecommunikasi* – in this case a state owned telecommunications office.
3. Two agents, one Suzuki, one Honda have opened. They offer motorcycles on credit with very low initial down payments. Many young men have been tempted and use the motorbikes as taxis (*ojegs* Ind).
4. An Indonesian bathroom consists of a large tank of water and a scoop. Water is splashed over oneself elephant style.
5. Although it is not feasible to commute each day so teenagers still have to board with relatives or in boarding houses during the week.

Glossary

Indonesian Terms

Adat	tradition, custom, the ways of the ancestors, a map of life
Agama	religion – monotheistic
Arisan	communal savings group
Atas	above, also used to refer to higher authorities
Desa	administrative village
Dusun	a subsection of the administrative village, a hamlet
Hiburan	entertainment
Inculturisasi	enculturation. The deliberate blending of tradition and religion
Juru kunci	caretaker
Kabupaten	regency area, headed by a Bupati
Kain	fabric – locally used to mean woven, tubular garment
Kebon	gardens, including cultivated fields
Kecamatan	district headed by a *camat*
Kelompok doa	prayer group
Kelompok industri	industry group
Kelompok pengolah	management group
Kepala Desa	elected head of administrative village
Malu	shy, ashamed or bashful
Musyawarah	public meeting
Obyek wisata	tourist attraction
Parawisata	tourism
Parang	long knife used for agriculture, domestic purposes and defence
Paroke	parish, an area approximately equal to a *kecamatan*
Penilik kebudayaan	cultural officer / supervisor
Propinsi	province
Ramai	crowded and noisy
Rumah	house
Sadar wisata	tourism awareness campaign
Sanggar budaya	cultural studio (music and dance group)
Sombong	arrogant, conceited

Tamu Negara	guest of the nation
Tua tua adat	elders respected for their knowledge of *adat*
Turis	tourist
Wisata budaya	cultural tourism

Ngadha Terms

Ana ye	super miniature house on roof apex that indicates *saka pu'u*
Bela	gold earrings
Bere eko	hanging basket
Bhaga	miniature house representing first female ancestor
Boku	male headdress
Dongo sa'o	female keeper of a traditional house
Ebu po, nusi pera	advice and teachings from grandparents and great-grandparents
Gae	nobles
Gae kisah	commoners
Go'o Wogo, pesa Bena	expression used to suggest each village has its own rules, literally different Wogo, different Bena
Ho'o	slave
Hunga Hanga	to show no interest, couldn't care less
Kabe pere	an entry step into the inner sacred room of a house
Kakangai otaola	windows on the world
Kelanio	cooling, to end a ceremony, also spelt *gelanio*.
Kepe	three-layered purse used to hold *bela*
Lavo	traditional dress for a woman
Lega	ceremonial bag for men
Lenggi	stone area to hold communal meetings and settle disputes
Lue	male traditional dress
Mata raga	centre of a houses sacredness. Place to hang sacred heirlooms
Melo	lack of respect, usually due to overconfidence
Moke	fermented sap from hairy palm (*Arenga saccrifera*)
Muvu	communal savings system (*arisan* in Indonesian)
Ngadhu	carved tree trunk with conical thatched roof associated with first male ancestor. Also spelt *madhu*
Ngeme	gourd bowls
Nua	the ancestral heart of a Ngadha village

Peo	a stone used to tie a buffalo to before it is slaughtered
Rante	gold chain
Reba	annual harvest festival and family gathering
Saka Pu'u	clan's central house. Literally root or trunk rider
Saka Lobo	clan's second house. Literally shoot or tip rider
Sangazar	shriek to begin a ceremony
Sa'o	named house
Sobo	unsmiling
Tureh	stone, laid with purpose (megalith)
Wado lima	pig exchange
Woe	a corporate descent group, referred to as a clan
Uku adha	rules to show respect
Utu bhou	public meeting
Uvi	yam
Wati	round, lidded rice basket

References

Abram, D. (2000) Guidebooks turn travellers into package tourists, a debate. *In Focus* 34, 5.

Abram, S. (1996) Reactions to tourism: A view from the deep green heart of France. In J. Boissevain (ed.) *Coping with Tourists. European Reactions to Mass Tourism* (pp. 174–203). Oxford: Berghahn Books.

Adams, K. (1984) Come to Tana Toraja "Land of the heavenly kings". Travel agents as brokers in ethnicity. *Annals of Tourism Research* 11, 469–485.

Adams, K. (1990) Cultural commoditization in Tana Toraja, Indonesia. *Cultural Survival Quarterly.* 14, (1), 31–33.

Adams, K. (1993) Club dead, not Club Med: Staging death in contemporary Tana Toraja (Indonesia). *South East Asian Journal of Social Science* 21 (2), 62–73.

Adams, K. (1995) Making-up the Toraja? The appropriation of tourism, anthropology and museums for politics in Upland Sulawesi, Indonesia. *Ethnology* 3 (2), 143–153.

Adams, K. (1997) Touting touristic 'primadonnas': Tourism, ethnicity and national integration in Sulawesi, Indonesia. In M. Picard and R. Wood (eds) *Tourism, Ethnicity and the State in Asian and Pacific Societies* (pp. 155–180). Honolulu: University of Hawaii Press.

ADB (Asian Development Bank) (2002) Indigenous peoples/ethnic minorities and poverty reduction Indonesia, http://www.adb.org/Documents/Reports/Indigenous_Peoples/INO/default.asp (accessed November 2005).

Allerton, C. (2001) Authentic housing, authentic culture? Transforming a village into a 'tourist site' in Manggarai, Eastern Indonesia. Conference paper, EUROSEAS, SOAS, London University.

Anderson, B. (1972) The idea of power in Javanese culture. In C. Holt (ed.) *Culture and Politics in Indonesia* (pp. 1–69). Ithaca, NY: Cornell University Press.

Anderson, S. (2000) What's in a guide book? *In Focus* 34, 6–7.

Antlov, H. (2001) Village governance and local politics in Indonesia. Conference paper EUROSEAS, SOAS, London University.

APEC (2003) Asia Pacific Economic Cooperation, www.apec.org./apec/news (accessed 8/10/2005).

Appadurai, A. (1986) Introduction: Commodities and the politics of value. In A. Appadurai (ed.) *The Social Life of Things. Commodities in Cultural Perspective* (pp. 3–63). Cambridge: Cambridge University Press.

Arnstein, S. (1971) Eight rungs in the ladder of citizen participation. In E. Cahn and A. Passett, (eds) *Citizen Participation: Effecting Community Change.* London: Preager Publishers.

Ashley, C., Roe, D. and Goodwin, H. (2001) *Pro-poor Tourism Strategies: Making Tourism Work for the Poor. A Review of Experience.* London: Overseas Development Institute.

Azarya, V. (2004) Globalization and international tourism in developing countries: Marginality as a commercial commodity. *Current Sociology* 52 (6), 949–967.

Barker, T., Putra, Darma and Wiranatha, Agung (2006) Authenticity and commodification of Balinese dance performances. In M. Smith and M. Robinson (eds) *Cultural Tourism in a Changing World* (pp. 215–224). Clevedon: Channel View Publications.

Barnes, R.H. (1972) Ngada. In F. Lebar (ed.) *Ethnic Groups in Insular South-East Asia. Vol. 1 Indonesia, Andaman Islands and Madagascar.* New Haven: Human Relations Area Files Press.

Barnes, R.H. (1974) *The Kedang: A Study of Collective Thought of an Eastern Indonesian people.* Oxford: Claredon Press.

Barnes, Ruth (1989) *The Ikat Textiles of Lamalera. A Study of an Indonesian Weaving Tradition.* Leiden: Brill.

Bauman, Z. (2001) Identity in a globalising world. *Social Anthropology* 9 (2), pp. 121–131.

Belau, D. (2003) Tourism employment in the Asia Pacific region 2003, http://www.ilo.org/public/english/dialogue/sector/techmeet/rtmhct03/asiapacific-emp2003.pdf. (accessed November 2005).

Benda-Beckmann, F. and Benda-Beckmann, K. (2001) Recreating the *nagari:* Decentralisationn in West Sumatra. Conference paper EUROSEAS, SOAS, London University.

Bhattacharyya, D.P. (1997) Mediating India, an analysis of a guidebook. *Annals of Tourism Research* 24 (2), 371–389.

Bhopal, M. and Hitchcock, M. (2001) The introduction: The cultural context of the ASEAN business crisis. *Asia Pacific Business Review* 8 (2) 1–18.

Blackshall, S., Leffmann, D., Reader, L. and Stedman, H. (1999) *The Rough Guide to Indonesia* (1st edn pbk). London: Rough Guides.

Blackwood, E. (2000) *Webs of Power. Women, Kin and Community in a Sumatran Village.* Lanham, MD: Rowman and Littlefield Publishers, Inc.

Blanton, D. (1992) Tourism education in developing countries. *Practicing Anthropology* 14 (2), 5–9.

Bleasdale, S. and Tapsell, S. (1999) Social and cultural impacts of tourism policy in Tunisia. In M. Robinson and P. Boniface (eds) *Tourism and Cultural Conflicts* (pp. 181– 204). Oxford: CABI Publishing.

Blust, R. (1984) Indonesia as a linguistic field of study. In P.E. De Josselin de Jong (ed.) *Unity in Diversity: Indonesia as a Field of Anthropological Study* (pp. 20–36). Dordrecht: Foris Publications.

Boissevain, J. (1996) Introduction. In J. Boissevain (ed.) *Coping with Tourists. European Reactions to Mass Tourism.* (pp. 1–26). Oxford: Berghahn Books.

Boniface, P. (1999) Tourism and cultures: Consensus in the making? In M. Robinson and P. Boniface (eds) *Tourism and Cultural Conflicts* (pp. 1–32). Oxford: CABI Publishing.

Boorstin, D. (1964) *The Image: A Guide to Pseudo-events in America.* New York: Harper and Row.

Booth, A. (1990) The tourism boom in Indonesia. *Bulletin of Indonesian Economic Studies* 26 (3), 45–73.

BPS (Indonesian Government Statistics) (2005) http://www.bps.go.id/index.shtml (accessed 10/10/05).

Braden, S. and Mayo, M. (1999) Culture, community development and representation. *Community Development Journal* 34 (3), 191–204.

Bradt, H. (1995) Better to travel cheaply? *Independent on Sunday Magazine* 12 February, pp. 49–50.

Bras, K. (2000) *Image Building and Guiding on Lombok: The Social Construction of a Tourist Destination*. Amsterdam: Cocktail Communications.

Bras, K. and Dahles, H. (1999) Pathfinder, gigolo, and friend: Diverging entrepreneurial strategies of tourist guides on two Indonesian islands. In H. Dahles and K. Bras (eds) *Tourism and Small Entrepreneurs* (pp. 128–145). New York: Cognizant Communication Corporation.

Britton, S. (1982) The political economy of tourism in the third world. *Annals of Tourism Research* 9, 331–358.

Brohman, J. (1996) New directions in tourism for third world development. *Annals of Tourism Research* 23 (1), 48–70.

Bruce, D. (1998) Tourism, history and local pride. In J. Swarbrooke (ed.) *Heritage, Culture and Community: Four International Case Studies* (pp. 3–20). Tilburg University: ATLAS.

Bryson, J. and Crosby, B. (1992) *Leadership for the Common Good: Tackling Public Problems in a Shared World*. San Francisco: Jossey-Bass.

Burns, P. (1999) *An Introduction to Tourism and Anthropology*. London: Routledge.

Burns, P. and Holden, A. (1995) *Tourism a New Perspective*. London: Prentice Hall.

Butcher, J. (2001) Cultural baggage and cultural tourism. in J. Butcher (ed.) *Innovations in Cultural Tourism*. Proceedings to 5th ATLAS International conference. Tilburg: ATLAS.

Butler, R.W. (1980) The concept of a tourist area cycle of evolution: Implications for management of resources. *Canadian Geographer* 24 (1), 5–12.

Carsten, J. and Hugh-Jones, S. (1995) Introduction. In J. Carsten and S. Hugh-Jones (eds) *About the House, Lévi-Strauss and Beyond* (pp. 1–46). Cambridge: Cambridge University Press.

Caslake, J. (1993) Tourism, culture and the Iban. In V. King (ed.) *Tourism in Borneo*. Borneo Research Council proceedings. Papers from the biennial international conference. Kota Kinabalu, Malaysia, July (1992) .

Causey, A. (1998) Ulos or Saham? Presentations of Toba Batak culture in tourism promotions. *Indonesia and the Malay World* 26 (75), 97–103.

Causey, A. (2003) *Hard Bargaining in Sumatra*. Honolulu: University of Hawaii Press.

Chambers, E. (1997) *Tourism and Culture. An Applied Perspective*. Albany: State University of New York Press.

Cochrane, J. (2005) The backpacker plus: Overlooked and underrated. Conference paper ATLAS SIG Meeting – Backpackers Research Group 2005: The global nomad – an expert meeting on backpacker tourism. Kasetsart University, Bangkok, Thailand, 1–3 September 2005.

Cohen, E. (1974) Who is a tourist? A conceptual classification. *Sociological Review* 22, 527–555.

Cohen, E. (1979) Rethinking the sociology of tourism. *Annals of Tourism Research* VI (1), 18–35.

Cohen E. (1985) The tourist guide, the origins, structure and dynamics of a role. *Annals of Tourism Research* 12, 5–29.

Cohen, E. (1988) Authenticity and commoditization in tourism. *Annals of Tourism Research* 15 (3), 371–386.

Cohen, E. (1989) Primitive and remote. Hill tribe trekking in Thailand. *Annals of Tourism Research* 16 (1), 30–61.

Cohen E. (2001) Ethnic tourism in Southeast Asia. In Tan Chee-Beng, C.H. Sidney, Yang Hui Cheung (eds) *Tourism, Anthropology and China* (pp. 27–53). Singapore: White Lotus Press.

Cohen, E., Niv, Y. and Almagor, U. (1992) Stranger–local interaction in photography. *Annals of Tourism Research* 19 (2), 212–233.

Cole, S. (1997a) Anthropologists, local communities and sustainable tourism development. In M. Stabler (ed.) *Tourism and Sustainability* (pp. 219–230). Oxford: CABI Publishing.

Cole, S. (1997b) Cultural heritage tourism: The villagers' perspective. A case study from Ngada, Flores. In W. Nuryanti (ed.) *Tourism and Heritage Management* (pp. 468–481). Yogyakarta: Gadjah Mada University Press.

Cole, S. (1998) Tradition and tourism: Dilemmas in sustainable tourism development: A case study from the Ngada region of Flores, Indonesia. *Anthropologi Indonesia* 56, 37–46.

Cole, S. (1999) Education for participation: The villagers' perspective. Case Study from Ngada, Flores, Indonesia. In K. Bras, H. Dahles, M. Gunawan and G. Richards (eds) *Entrepreneurship and Education in Tourism* (pp. 173–184). ATLAS Asia conference proceedings, Bandung, Indonesia.

Cole, S. (2003) Appropriated meanings: Megaliths and tourism in Eastern Indonesia. *Indonesia and the Malay World* 31 (89), 140–150.

Cole, S. (2004a) Beyond authenticity and commodification. Conference proceedings, *Tourism: State of the Art II* University of Strathclyde, Glasgow 27–30 June 2004.

Cole, S. (2004b) Shared benefits: Longitudinal research in eastern Indonesia. In J. Phillimore and L. Goodson (eds) *Qualitative Research in Tourism: Ontologies, Epistemologies and Methodologies* (pp. 292–310). London: Routledge.

Cole, S. (2005) Community tourism education: Case study from Ngadha, Flores, Indonesia. In D. Airey and J. Tribe (eds) *An International Handbook of Tourism Education* (pp. 395–410). Oxford: Elsevier.

Cole, S. (2006) Cultural tourism, community participation and empowerment. In M. Smith and M. Robinson (eds) *Cultural Tourism in a Changing World* (pp. 89–103). Cleveland: Channel View Publications.

Cole, S. (2007) Implementing and evaluating a code of conduct for visitors. *Tourism Management* 28 (2), 443–451.

Connell, D. (1997) Participatory Development: An approach sensitive to class and gender. *Development in Practice* 7 (3), 249–259.

Cooper, C., Fletcher, J., Gilbert, D. and Wanhill, S. (1993) *Tourism Principles and Practice*. Harlow: Longman.

Corner, L. (1989) East and West Nusa Tenggara: Isolation and poverty. In H. Hill (ed.) *Unity and Diversity: Regional Economic Diversity in Indonesia since 1970.* Oxford: Oxford University Press.

Crehan, K. (1997) *The Fractured Community. Landscape of Power and Gender in Rural Zambia.* Berkeley: University of California Press.

Crick, M. (1989) Representations of international tourism in the social sciences: Sun, sex, sights, savings, and servility. *Annual Review of Anthropology* 18, 307–344.

Crick, M. (1992) Life in the informal sector: Street guides in Kandy, Sri Lanka. In D. Harrison (ed.) *Tourism and the Less Developed Countries* (pp. 135–147). New York: John Wiley and Sons.

Crick, M. (1994) *Resplendent Sites, Discordant Voices*. Reading: Harwood Academic.

Crouch, H. (1979) The trend to authoritarianism: The post-1945 period. In H. Aveling (ed.) *The Development of Indonesian Society* (pp. 166–204). St Lucia: University of Queensland Press.

Crystal, E. (1978) Tourism in Toraja (Sulawesi Indonesia). In V. Smith (ed.) *Hosts and Guests. The Anthropology of Tourism* (pp. 109–126). Oxford: Basil Blackwell.

Cushman, G. (1999) Independent enrepreneurship: The case of Gili Air, Lombok, Indonesia. In K. Bras, H. Dahles, M. Gunawan and R. Greg (eds) *Entrepreneurship and Education in Tourism* (pp. 173–184). Proceeding ATLAS Asia Inauguration Conference.

Daeng, H. (1988) Ritual feasting and resource competition in Flores. In M. Dove (ed.) *The Real and Imagined Role of Culture in Development* (pp. 254–267). Honolulu: University of Hawaii Press.

Dahles, H. (1999) Tourism and small entrepreneurs in developing countries: A theoretical perspective. In H. Dahles and K. Bras *Tourism and Small Entrepreneurs: Development, National Policy, and Entrepreneurial Culture: Indonesian Cases.* (pp. 1–19). New York: Cognizant Communication Corporation.

Dahles, H. (2002) The politics of tour guiding, image management in Indonesia. *Annals of Tourism Research* 29, (3), 783–800.

Dahles, H. and Bras, K. (1999) Entrepreneurs in romance, tourism in Indonesia. *Annals of Tourism Research* 26 (2), 267–293.

Dahles, H. and van Meijl, T. (2000) Local perspectives on global tourism in Southeast Asia and the Pacific region: Introduction. *Pacific Tourism Review* 4, 53–62.

Dalton, B. (1995) *Indonesia Handbook* (6th edn). Chico, CA: Moon Publications.

D'amore, L. (1983) Guidelines to planning in harmony with the host community. In P. Murphy (ed.) *Tourism in Canada: Selected Issues and Options* (pp. 135–159). Victoria, BC: University of Victoria.

Daniel, Y. (1996) Tourism dance performances: Authenticity and creativity. *Annals of Tourism Research* 23 (4), 780–797.

Dann, G. (1981) Tourist motivation: An appraisal. *Annals of Tourism Research* 9 (2), 187–219.

Dann, G. (1996a) *The Language of Tourism: A Sociological Perspective*. Oxford: CABI Publishing.

Dann, G. (1996b) The people of tourist brochures. In T. Selwyn (ed.) *The Tourist Image: Myths and Myth Making in Tourism* (pp. 61–82). Chichester: Wiley.

Dearden, P. and Harron, S. (1992) Case study: Tourism and the hill tribes of Thailand. In B. Weiler and C.M. Hall (eds) *Special Interest Tourism* (pp. 95–104). London: Belhaven Press.

De Burlo, C. (1996) Cultural resistance and ethnic tourism on South Pentacost, Vaanuatu. In R. Butler and T. Hinch (eds) *Tourism and Indigenous Peoples* (pp. 255–275). London: International Thomson Business Press.

de Kadt, E. (1979) *Tourism: Passport to Development?* Oxford: Oxford University Press.

Dinas Parawisata Prop. Dati1 NTT (1998) Buku Informasi: Pengembangan dan peluang investasi usaha kawasan parawisat unggulan Nusa Tengara Timur. Kupang: Dinas parawisata.

Dougoud, R. (2000) Souvenirs from Kambot (PNG): The sacred search for authenticity. In M. Hitchcock and K. Teague (eds) *Souvenirs: The Material Culture of Tourism* (pp. 223–237). Aldershot: Ashgate.

Dove, M. (1988) Introduction: Traditional culture and development in contemporary Indonesia. In M. Dove (ed.) *The Real and Imagined Role of Culture in Development*. Honolulu: University of Hawaii Press.

Draine, C. and Hall, B. (1991) *Culture Shock: Indonesia*. London: Kuperard.

Economic Intelligence Unit Limited (2005) Indonesia industry: Tourism takes another hit.

Echols, J. and Shadily, H. (1989) *Kamus Indonesia Inggris* (3rd edn). Jakarta: Gramedia.

Erb, M. (1998) Tourism space in Manggarai, Western Flores, Indonesia: The house as a contested Place. *Singapore Journal of Tropical Geography* 19 (2), 177–192.

Erb, M. (2000) Understanding tourists, interpretations from Indonesia. *Annals of Tourism Research* 27 (3), 709–736.

Erb, M. (2001a) Conceptualising culture in a global age: Playing Caci in Manggarai. Seminar paper South East Asian Studies programme, National University of Singapore.

Erb, M. (2001b) Uniting the bodies and cleansing the village: Conflicts over heritage in a globalising world. Conference paper, EUROSEAS, SOAS, London University.

Fallon, F. (2001) Land conflicts and tourism in Lombok. *Current Issues in Tourism* 4 (6), 481–501.

Featherstone, M. (1990) Introduction. In M. Featherstone (ed.) *Global Culture: Nationalism, Globalisation and Modernity: Theory, Culture and Society*. London: Sage.

Fennell, D. (1999) *Ecotourism: An Introduction*. London: Routledge.

Flores Paradise (2005) Mengola isu sensitif parawisata. *Flores Paradise Tourism News* November p. 5.

Forshee, J. (1998) Sumba Asli: Fashioning culture along expanding exchange circles. *Indonesia and the Malay World* 26 (75), 106–121.

Forshee, J. (2001) *Between the Folds: Stories of Cloth, Lives and Travel from Sumba*. Honolulu: University of Hawaii Press.

Forth, G. (1981) *Rindi: An Ethnographic Study of a Traditional Domain in Eastern Sumba*. The Hague: Nijhoff.

Forth G. (1996) To chat in pairs. *Canberra Anthropology* 19 (1), 31–51.

Forth, G. (1998) *Beneath the Volcano: Religion, Cosmology and Spirit Classification among the Nage of Eastern Indonesia*. Leiden: KITLV Press.

Foster, G., Scudder, T., Colson, E. and Kemper, R. (1979) Conclusion: The long-term study in perspective. In G. Foster, T. Scudder, E. Colson, and R. Kemper (eds) *Long-term Field Research in Social Anthropology*. London: Academic Press.

Fox, J. (1977) *Harvest of the Palm. Ecological Change in Eastern Indonesia*. Cambridge, MA: Harvard University Press.

Fox, J. (ed.) (1980) *The Flow of Life*. Cambridge, MA: Harvard University Press.

Fox, J. (1998) Foreword: The linguistic context of Florenese culture. *Anthropologi Indonesia* 56 (xxii), Mei–Juli, 1–12.

France, L. (1998) Local participation in tourism in the West Indian Islands. In E. Laws, B. Faulkner, and G. Moscardo (eds) *Embracing and Managing Change in Tourism: International Case Studies* (pp. 222–234). London: Routledge.

Furnham, A. (1984) Tourism and culture shock. *Annals of Tourism Research* 11, 41–57.

Gede Raka (2000) Entrepreneurship for tourism: Issues for Indonesia. In K. Bras, H. Dahles, M. Gunawan, and G. Richards (eds) *Entrepreneurship and Education in Tourism* (pp. 29–36). Proceedings ATLAS Asia Inauguration Conference. Bandung: ITB.

Geertz, C. (1960) *The Religion of Java*. Chicago: University of Chicago Press.

Gibson, T. (1995) Having your house and eating it: Houses and siblings in Ara, South Sulawesi. In J. Carsten and S. Hugh-Jones (eds) *About the House, Lévi-Strauss and Beyond* (pp. 129–148). Cambridge: Cambridge University Press.

Giddens, A. (1991) *Modernity and Self Identity*. Cambridge: Polity Press.

Go, F. (1997) Entrepreneurs and the tourism industry in developing countries. In H. Dahles (ed.) *Tourism, Small Entrepreneurs and Sustainable Development* (pp. 5–22). Tilburg: ATLAS.

Goffman, E. (1961) *Encounters: Two Studies in the Sociology of Interaction*. New York: Macmillan.

Goffman, E. (1974) *Interaction Ritual*. Harmondsworth: Penguin.

Goodwin, H. (1995) Training for local participation. *In Focus* 16, 6.

Goodwin, H. (1999) Backpackers good, package tourists bad? *In Focus* 31 (Spring), 12–13.

Goodwin, H. *et al.* (1997) *Tourism, Conservation and Sustainable Development* (Vol. III). Komodo National Park: Indonesia DFID.

Graburn, N. (1978) Tourism: The sacred journey. In V. Smith (ed.) *Host and Guests. The Anthropology of Tourism* (pp. 17–32). Oxford: Basil Blackwell.

Graburn N. (1984) The evolution of tourist arts. *Annals of Tourism Research* 11, 393–419.

Graburn, N. (1987) Tourism: The sacred journey. In V. Smith (ed.) *Host and Guests. The Anthropology of Tourism* (pp. 21–36). Philadelphia: University of Pennsylvania Press.

Graburn, N. (2000) Foreword. In M. Hitchcock and K. Teague (eds) *Souvenirs: The Material Culture of Tourism* (pp. xii–xvii). Aldershot: Ashgate.

Graburn, N. and Moore, R. (1994) Anthropological research on tourism. In B. Ritchie and C. Goeldner (eds) *Travel Tourism and Hospitality Research: A Handbook for Managers and Researchers*. New York: John Wiley and Son.

Greenwood, D. (1972) Tourism as an agent of change: A Spanish Basque case. *Ethnology* 11 (1), 80–91.

Greenwood, D. (1978) Culture by the pound: An anthropological perspective on tourism as cultural commoditization. In V. Smith (ed.) *Host and Guests. The Anthropology of Tourism* (pp. 129–138). Oxford: Basil Blackwell.

Greenwood, D. (1989) Culture by the pound: An anthropological perspective on tourism as cultural commoditization. In V. Smith (ed.) *Host and Guests. The Anthropology of Tourism* (2nd edn) (pp. 171–185). Philadelphia: University of Pennsylvania Press.

Grimes, C., Therik, T., Grimes, B. and Jacob, M. (1997) *A Guide to the People and Languages of Nusa Tenggara*. Kupang: Artha Wacana Press.

Gunawan, M. (1997) National planning for Indonesia's tourism. *Pacific Tourism Review* 1, 47–56.
Gunawan, M. (1999) Indonesian tourism: Development policies and the challenge for research and education. In K. Pookong and B. King (eds) *Asia-Pacific Tourism: Regional Co-operation, Planning and Development* (pp. 147–164). Victoria: Hospitality Press Ltd.
Gunn, C. (1994) *Tourism Planning: Basics, Concepts, Cases*. New York: Taylor and Francis.
Gurung, G., Simmons, D. and Devlin, P. (1996) The evolving role of tourist guides: The Nepali experience. In R. Butler and T. Hinch (eds) *Tourism and Indigenous Peoples* (pp. 107–128). London: International Thomson Business Press.
Hall, M. (1997) *Tourism in the Pacific Rim: Developments, Impacts and Markets* (2nd edn). Melbourne: Addison Wesley / Longman.
Hall, M. (2000) Tourism in Indonesia: The end of the New Order. In M. Hall and S. Page (eds) *Tourism in South and Southeast Asia: Issues and Cases* (pp. 157–166). Oxford: Butterworth-Heinemann.
Hall, M. and Page, S. (eds) (2006) *Tourism in South and Southeast Asia: Issues and Cases*. Oxford: Butterworth-Heinemann.
Hampton, M. (1997) Unpacking the rucksack: A new analysis of backpacker tourism in South East Asia. In W. Nuryanti (ed.) *Tourism and Heritage Management* (pp. 365–380). Yogyakarta: Gadjah Mada University Press.
Hampton, M. (1998) Backpacker tourism and economic development. *Annals of Tourism Research* 25 (3), 639–660.
Hannerz, U. (1990) Cosmopolitans and locals in world culture. In M. Featherstone (ed.) *Global Culture* (pp.237–521). Newbury Park, CA: Sage.
Hannerz, U. (1996) *Transitional Connections*. London: Routledge.
Harrison, D. (1992) International tourism and the less developed countries: The background. In D. Harrison (ed.) *Tourism and the Less Developed Countries*. New York: John Wiley and Sons.
Harrison, D. (1996) Sustainability and tourism: Reflections from a muddy pool. In L. Briguglio, B. Archer, J. Jafari and G. Wall (eds) *Sustainable Tourism in Small Island States: Issues and Policies* (pp. 69–89). London: Pinter.
Harrison, D. (2001) Introduction. In D. Harrison (ed.) *Tourism in the Less Developed World: Issues and Cases* (pp. 1–22). Oxford: CABI Publishing.
Harrison , D. and Price, H. (1996) Fragile environments, fragile communities? In H. Price (ed.) *People and Tourism in Fragile Environments*. Chichester: Wiley.
Harron, S. and Weiler, B. (1992) Review. Ethnic tourism. In B. Weiler and C.M. Hall (eds) *Special Interest Tourism* (pp. 83–95). London: Belhaven.
Hashimoto, A. (2002) Tourism and socio-cultural development issues. In R. Sharpely and D. Tefler (eds) *Tourism and Development: Concepts and Issues* (pp. 202–230). Clevedon: Channel View Publications.
Hastrup, K. and Olwig, K. (1997) Introduction. In K. Olwig and K. Hastrup (eds) *Siting Culture* (pp. 1–14). London: Routledge.
Henderson, J. (1999) Asian Tourism and the financial crisis: Indonesia and Thailand Compared. *Current Issues in Tourism* 2 (4), 294–303.
Hicks, D. (1976) *Tetum Ghosts and Kin. Fieldwork in an Indonesia Community, Tetum, East Timor*. Palo Alto, CA: Mayfield.
Hicks, D. (1990) *Kinship and Religion in Eastern Indonesia*. Gothenburg: ACTA Universitis Gothoburgensis.

Hinch, T. and Butler, R. (1996) Indigenous tourism: A common ground for discussion. In R. Butler and T. Hinch (eds) *Tourism and Indigenous Peoples* (pp. 3–21). London: International Thomson Business Press.

Hitchcock, M. (1985) *Indonesian Textile Techniques*. Aylesbury: Shire Publications.

Hitchcock, M. (1991) *Indonesian Textiles*. London: British Museum Press.

Hitchcock, M. (1993) Dragon tourism in Komodo eastern Indonesia. In M. Hitchcock, V. King and M. Parnwell (eds) *Tourism in South East Asia* (pp. 303–315). London: Routledge.

Hitchcock, M. (1996) *Islam and Identity in Eastern Indonesia*. Hull: University of Hull Press.

Hitchcock, M. (2000) Introduction. In M. Hitchcock and K. Teague (eds) *Souvenirs: The Material Culture of Tourism* (pp. 1–17). Aldershot: Ashgate.

Hitchcock, M. (2001) Tourism and total crisis in Indonesia: The case of Bali. *Asia Pacific Business Review* 8 (2), 101–120.

Hitchcock, M. and Kerlogue, F. (2000) Tourism, development and batik in Jambi. *Indonesia and the Malay World* 28 (82), 221–242.

Hitchcock, M. and King,V. (1997) Introduction: Malay–Indonesian identities. In M. Hitchcock and V. King (eds) *Images of Malay–Indonesian Identity* (pp. 197–221). Oxford: Oxford University Press.

Hitchcock, M., King, V. and Parnwell, M. (1993) Tourism in South East Asia: Introduction. In M. Hitchcock, V. King and M. Parnwell (eds) *Tourism in South East Asia* (pp. 1–31). London: Routledge.

Hitchcock, M. Stanley, N. and Sui King Chung (1997) The south-east Asian 'living museum' and its antecedents. In S, Abram, J. Waldren and D. Macleod *Tourists and Tourism – Identifying with People and Places* (pp. 1–17). Oxford: Berg.

Holden, A. (2005) *Tourism Studies and the Social Sciences*. Abingdon: Routledge.

Hoskins, J. (1986) So my name shall live: Stone dragging and grave building in Kodi, West Sumba. *Bijdragen Tot de Taal Land-en-Volkenkunde* 142 (1), 31–51.

Hoskins, J. (1987) Entering the bitter house: Spirit worship and conversion in West Sumba. In R. Kipp and S. Rodgers (eds) *Indonesian Religions in Transition* (pp. 136–160). Tucson: University of Arizona Press.

Howell, S. (1995a) Whose knowledge and whose power? A new perspective on cultural diffusion. In R. Fardon (ed.) *Counter Works: Managing the Diversity of Knowledge*. London: Routledge.

Howell, S. (1995b) The Lio house. In J. Carsten and S. Hugh-Jones (eds) *About the House. Lévi Strauss and Beyond* (pp. 149–69). Cambridge: Cambridge University Press.

Howell, S. (1996) *For the Sake of Our Future: Sacrificing in Eastern Indonesia*. Leiden: Research School Centre for Non-Western Studies.

Hudiyanto, O. (2005) The Balinese people–forgotten again, www.asiafoodworker. net/indonesia (accessed 10/11/05).

Hughes, G. (1995) The cultural constraints of sustainable tourism. *Tourism Management* 16, 49–60.

Hughes, H. (1996) Redefining cultural tourism. *Annals of Tourism Research*. 23 (3), 707–709.

Hughes-Freeland, F. (1993) Packaging dreams: Javanese perceptions of tourism and performance. In M. Hitchcock *et al.* (eds) *Tourism in South East Asia* (pp. 138–154). London: Routledge.

Human Development Report (2001) http://hdr.undp.org/reports/global/2001/en/.

Hunter, W. (2001) Trust between culture: The tourist. *Current Issues in Tourism* 4 (1), 42–67.

Hutajulu, R. (1997) Parawisata Etnik: Dampak parawisata terhadap upacara tradisional pada masyarakat batak Toba. *Jurnal Seni Pertunjukan* VIII, 13–32.

Huxley, L. (2004) Western backpackers and the global experience: An exploration of young peoples interactions with local cultures. *Tourism, Culture and Communication* 5, 37–44.

Iso-Ahola, S. (1982) Towards a psychological theory of tourism motivation. A rejoinder. *Annals of Tourism Research* 9 (2), 256–262.

Jafari, J. (1989) Soft tourism. *Tourism Management* 9 (1), 32–84.

Johnston, B. (1992) Anthropology's role in stimulating responsible tourism. *Practicing anthropology* 14 (2), 35–38.

Joop Ave (n.d.) *Indonesia Tourism Gearing Up for the Nineties*. Jakarta: Directorate General of Tourism.

Joppe, M. (1996) Sustainable community tourism development revisited. *Tourism Management* 17 (7), 475–479.

Just, P. (2001) *Dou Donggo Justice. Conflict and Morality in an Indonesian Society*. Lanham, MD: Rowman and Littlefield Publishers Inc.

Kabupaten Ngada (1998) *Ngada dalam angka 1998*. Bajawa: BPS.

Kadir Din (1997) Indigenization of tourism development: Some constraints and possibilities. In M. Oppermann (ed.) *Pacific Rim Tourism* (pp. 77–81). Oxford: CAB International.

King, V. (1993) Tourism and culture in Malaysia. In M. Hitchcock, V. King and M. Parnwell (eds) *Tourism in South East Asia* (pp. 97–106). London: Routledge.

King, V. (1999) *Anthropology and Development in South East Asia. Theory and Practice*. Oxford: Oxford University Press.

King, V. and Wilder, W. (2003) *The Modern Anthropology of South East Asia: An Introduction*. London: Routledge-Curzon.

Koentjaraningrat (1971) *Manusia dan kebudayaan di Indonesia*. Jakarta: Penerbit Djambatan.

Kottak, C.P. (1999) *Assault on Paradise: Social Change in a Brazilian Village* (3rd edn). Boston: McGraw Hill College.

Kripendorf, J. (1987) *The Holiday Makers*. Oxford: Butterworth-Heinemann.

Kuntjoro-Jakti, D. (1997) The role of the private sector in cultural tourism: An Indonesian perspective. In Weindu Nuryanti (ed.) *Tourism and Culture: Global Civilisation in Change* (pp. 175–179). Yogyakarta: Gadjah Mada University Press.

LaMoshi, G. (2003) Tourism ailing, Jakarta toughens terrorism stance. *Asian Times* 17 April.

Lathief, H. (1997) Toraja yang sedang bergeser. *Jurnal Masyrakat Seni Pertunjuk Indonesia* VIII, 59–71.

Lea, J. (1988) *Tourism and Development and the Third World*. London: Routledge.

Leiper, N. and Hing Nerilee (1998) Trends in Asia Pacific tourism in 1997–98 from optimism to uncertainty. *International Journal of Contemporary Hospitality management* 10 (7), 245–251.

Lett, J. (1983) Ludic and liminoid aspects of charter tourism in the Caribbean. *Annals of Tourism Research* 10, 35–56.

Lévi-Strauss, C. (1983) *The Way of Masks*. London: Jonathan Cape.

Lewis, E.D. (1988) *People of the Source: The Social and Ceremonial Order of Tana Wai Brama on Flores*. Dordrecht: Foris.

Li, T.M. (2000) Articulating indigenous identity in Indonesia: Resource politics and the tribal slot. *Comparative Studies in Society and History* 42, 149–179.

Li, Y. and Butler, R. (1997) Sustainable tourism and cultural attractions: A comparative experience. In M. Oppermann (ed.) *Pacific Rim Tourism* (pp. 107–116). Oxford: CAB International.

Lickorish, L. (1991) *Introduction to Tourism*. Oxford: Butterworth-Heinemann.

LOC (Library of Congress) (2005) http://memory.loc.gov/frd/cs/idtoc.html (accessed 20/10/05).

Long, V. and Kindon, S. (1997) Gender and tourism development in Balinese villages. In M. Thea Sinclair (ed.) *Gender Work and Tourism* (pp. 91–119). London: Routledge.

Lutz, N. (1998) Bilingualism and linguistic politics in Andora, East Flores. *Anthropologi Indonesia* 56 (XXII), 86–94.

MacCannell, D. (1976) *The Tourist: A New Theory of the Leisure Class*. New York: Schocken.

MacCannell, D. (1984) Reconstructed ethnicity: Tourism and cultural identity in third world communities. *Annals of Tourism Research* 11, 375–391.

MacDonald, S. (1997) A people's story: Heritage, identity and authenticity. In C. Rojek and J. Urry (eds) *Touring Cultures: Transformations of Travel and Theory* (pp. 155–175). London: Routledge.

McGregor, A. (2000) Dynamic texts and tourist gaze: Death, bones and buffalo. *Annals of Tourism Research* 27 (1), 27–50.

MacIntosh, R. and Goeldner, C. (1990) *Tourism Principles, Practices and Philosophies* (6th edn). New York: John Wiley and Sons.

McKean, P. (1978) Towards a theoretical analysis of tourism: Economic dualism and cultural involution in Bali. In V. Smith (ed.) *Hosts and Guests* (pp. 93–108). Oxford: Basil Blackwell.

MacLeod, D. (1999) Tourism and the globalisation of a Canary Island. *Journal of the Royal Anthropology Institute* 5 (3), 443–457.

MacLeod, D. (2004) *Tourism, Globalisation and Cultural Change – An Island community perspective*. Clevedon: Channel View Publications.

Madeley, J. (1999) *Big Business, Poor Peoples*. London: Zed Books.

Mancini, M. (1990) *Conducting Tours: A Practical Guide*. Cincinnati: South Western Publishing Co.

Mansperger, M. (1992) Yap: A case of benevolent tourism. *Practicing anthropology* 14 (2), 10–14.

Matheson, A. and Wall, G. (1982) *Tourism: Economic, Physical and Social Impacts*. Harlow: Longman.

Maurer, J.L. (1997) A New Order sketchpad of Indonesian history. In M. Hitchcock and V. King (eds) *Images of Malay–Indonesian Identity* (pp. 209–226). Oxford: Oxford University Press.

Meethan, K. (2001) *Place, Culture, Consumption*. Basingstoke: Palgrave.

Michaud, C. (2002) External resource flows to the health sector in Indonesia, http://www.who.int/macrohealth/documents/michaud_annexb.pdf (accessed 10/10/05).

Mochtar Naim (1985) Implications of *merantau* for social organisation in Minangkabau. In L. Thomas and F. Benda-Beckmann (eds). *Change and Continuity in Minanagkabau: Local Regional and Historical Perspectives on West Sumatra* (pp. 111–117). Athens: Ohio University Press.

Molnar, A. (1998) Considerations of consequences of rapid agricultural modernisation among two Ngadha communities. *Anthropologi Indonesia* 56 (2), 47–59.

Molnar, A. (2000) *Grandchildren of the Ga'e Ancestors. Social Organisation and Cosmology among the Hoga Sara of Flores.* Leiden: KITLV Press.

Moscardo, G. and Pearce, P. (1999) Understanding ethnic tourists. *Annals of Tourism Research* 26 (2), 416–434.

Mowforth, M. and Munt, I. (1998) *Tourism and Sustainability: New Tourism in the Third World.* London and New York: Routledge.

Muller, K. (1991) *East of Bali from Lombok to Timor.* Berkeley, CA: Periplus Editions.

Murphy, P. (1985) *Tourism: A Community Approach.* London and New York: Routledge.

Nash, D. (1978) Tourism as a form of imperialism. In V. Smith (ed.) *Hosts and Guests: The Anthropology of Tourism* (pp. 33–48). Oxford: Blackwell.

Nash, D. (1989) Tourism as a form of imperialism. In V. Smith, (ed.) *Hosts and Guests: The Anthropology of Tourism* (2nd edn) (pp. 37–52). Philadelphia: University of Pennsylvania Press.

Nash, D. (1996) *Anthropology of Tourism.* London: Pergamon.

Needham, R. (1972) *Belief, Language and Experience.* Oxford: Blackwell.

Needham, R. (1984) The transformation of prescriptive systems in Eastern Indonesia. In P.E. Josselin de Jong (ed.) *Unity in Diversity: Indonesia as a Field of Antropological Study* (pp. 221–233). Dordrecht: Foris Publications.

Ness, S. (2002) *Where Asia Smiles – An Ethnography of Philippine Tourism.* Philadelphia: University of Pennsylvania Press.

Ngada dalam angka (1996) Bajawa: Kantor Statistik.

Olsen, K. (2002) Authenticity as a concept in tourism research. *Tourism Studies* 2 (2), 159–182.

Oppermann, M. (1993) Tourism space in developing countries. *Annals of Tourism Research* 20 (4), 535–536.

Oppermann, M. and Chon, K.S. (1997) *Tourism in Developing Countries.* London: International Thomson Business Press.

O'Riordan, T. and Church, C. (2001) Synthesis and context. In T. O'Riordan (ed.) *Globalism, Localism and Identity* (pp. 3–24). London: Earthscan.

Osbourne, S. (2004) Indonesia begins charging for Visas UPI, www.kabar-irian. com/pipermail/kabar-indonesia/2004-February/000668.html (accessed November 2005).

Parnwell, M. (1993) Tourism and rural crafts in Thailand. In M. Hitchcock, V. King, and M. Parnwell (eds) *Tourism in South East Asia* (pp. 234–257). London: Routledge.

Parnwell, M. and Arghiros, D. (1996) Introduction: Uneven development in Thailand. In M. Parnwell and D. Arghiros (eds) *Uneven Development in Thailand* (pp. 1–27). Aldershot: Ashgate.

Pearce, D. (1989) *Tourism Development.* Harlow: Longman.

Pearce, P. (1994) Tourism–resident impacts: Examples, explanations and emerging solutions. In W. Theobald (ed.) *Global Tourism* (pp. 103–123). Oxford: Butterworth-Heinemann.

Pearce, P. (1995) From culture shock and cultural arrogance to cultural exchange: Ideas towards sustainable socio-cultural tourism. *Journal of Sustainable Tourism* 3 (3), 143–154.

Pearce, P., Edwards, K. and Lussa, S. (1998) Facilitating tourist–host social interaction. An overview and assessment of the cultural assimilator. In E. Laws, B. Faulkner and G. Moscardo (eds) *Embracing and Managing Change in Tourism* (pp. 347–364). London: Routledge.

Perry, W. (1918) *The Megalithic Culture of Indonesia*. London: Longman, Green and Co.

Picard, M. (1990) Cultural tourism in Bali: Cultural performances as tourist attractions. *Indonesia* 49, 37–74.

Picard, M. (1993) Cultural tourism in Bali: National integration and regional differentiation. In M. Hitchcock, V. King and M. Parnwell (eds) *Tourism in Southeast Asia* (pp. 71–98). London: Routledge.

Picard, M. (1996) *Bali: Cultural Tourism and Touristic Culture*. Singapore: Archipelago Press.

Picard, M. (1997) Cultural tourism, nation-building, and regional culture: The making of a Balinese identity. In M. Picard and R. Wood (eds) *Tourism Ethnicity and the State in Asian and Pacific Societies* (pp. 181–214). Honolulu: University of Hawaii Press.

Pond, K. (1993) *The Professional Guide: Dynamics of Tour Guiding*. New York: Van Nostrand Reinhold.

Pretty, J. (1995) The many interpretations of participation. *In Focus* 16, 4–5.

Prideaux, B., Laws, E. and Faulkner, B. (2003) Events in Indonesia: Exploring the limits of formal tourism management trends forecasting methods in complex crisis situations. *Tourism Management* 24, 475–487.

Prior, J. (1988) *Church and Marriage in an Indonesian Village*. Frankfurt am Main: Verlag Peter Lang.

Pursall, R. (2005) From backpacker to flashpacker. Conference paper ATLAS SIG Meeting – Backpackers Research Group 2005: *The global nomad – an expert meeting on backpacker tourism*. Kasetsart University, Bangkok, Thailand, 1–3 September.

Rahyu Supanggah (1994) Seni Flores yang Menggeliat. *Suara Merdeka* 10th December.

RARE Centre for Tropical Conservation (2003) *Linking Biodiversity Conservation and Sustainable Tourism in World Heritage Sites*. Site assessment report. Komodo National Park, Indonesia.

Redfield. R. (1960) *The Little Community and Peasant Society and Culture*. Chicago: University of Chicago Press.

Reisinger, Y. and Turner, L. (1997) Cross-cultural differences in tourism: Indonesian tourists in Australia. *Tourism Management* 18 (3), 139–147.

Reisinger, Y. and Turner, L. (2003) *Cross-cultural Behaviour in Tourism: Concepts and Analysis*. Oxford: Butterworth-Heinemann.

Richards, G. (1996) *Cultural Tourism in Europe*. Tilburg: Atlas.

Ricklefs, M. (1993) *A History of Modern Indonesia since c.1300* (2nd edn). London: Macmillan.

Richter, L. (1993) Tourism policy-making in South East Asia. In M. Hitchcock, V. King and M. Parnwell (eds) *Tourism in South East Asia* (pp. 179–199). London: Routledge.

Robertson, R. (1992) *Globalisation: Social Theory and Global Culture*. London: Sage.

Robinson, M. (1999a) Collaboration and cultural consent: Refocusing sustainable tourism. *Journal of Sustainable Tourism* 7 (3&4), 379–397.

Robinson, M. (1999b) Cultural conflicts in tourism: Inevitability and equality. In M. Robinson and P. Boniface (eds) *Tourism and Cultural Conflicts* (pp. 1–32). Oxford: CABI Publishing.

Rodenburg, E. (1980) The effects of scale in economic development: Tourism in Bali. *Annals of Tourism Research* 7 (2), 177–196.

Rodgers, S. (1985) *Power and Gold: Jewellery of Indonesia, Malaysia and the Philippines*. Geneva: Barbier-Muller Museum.

Rojek, C. (1997) Indexing, dragging and the social construction of tourist sights. In C. Rojek and J. Urry (eds) *Touring Cultures: Transformations of Travel and Theory* (pp. 52–74). London: Routledge.

Russell-Smith, J. (2005) New era for fire management in Indonesia, http://savanna.ntu.edu.au/publications/savanna_links32/fire_management_in_.html (accessed 12/10/05).

Saju, P. and Sawega, A. (1994) Kreativitas Kolektif dari Timur. *Kompas* 11 December.

Salazar, N. (2005) Tourism and glocalisation 'local' tour guiding. *Annals of Tourism Research* 32 (3), 628–646.

Sanger, A. (1988). Blessing or blight? The effects of touristic dance drama on village life in Singapadu. In *The Impact of Tourism on Traditional Music* (pp. 79–104). Kingston: Jamaica Memory Bank.

Saremba, J. and Gill, A. (1991) Value conflicts in mountain park settings. *Annals of Tourism Research* 18, 455–472.

Schelling, V. (1998) Globalisation ethnic identity and popular culture in Latin America. In R. Keily and P. Marfleet (eds) *Globalisation and the Third World* (pp. 141–161). London: Routledge.

Scheyvens, R. (2002) Back-packer tourism and third world development. *Annals of Tourism Research* 29 (1), 144–164.

Scheyvens, R. (2003) *Tourism for Development, Empowering Communities*. New York: Prentice Hall.

Schmidt, J., Hersh, J. and Fold, N. (1998) Changing realities and social transition in South East Asia. In J. Schmidt, J. Hersh and N. Fold (eds) *Social Change in South East Asia* (pp. 1–22). Harlow: Longman.

Scholte, J. (1997) Identifying Indonesia. In M. Hitchcock and V. King (eds) *Images of Malay–Indonesia Identity* (pp. 21–44). Oxford: Oxford University Press.

Scholte, J. (2002) What is globalisation? The definitional issue – Again. CSGR Working Paper No. 109/02, University of Warwick.

Schuerkens, U. (2003) The sociological and anthropological study of globalisation and localisation. *Current Sociology* 5 (3/4), 209–222.

Schwarz, A. (1999) *A Nation in Waiting. Indonesia's Search for Stability*. St Leonards: Allen Unwin.

Scott, J. (1976) *The Moral Economy of the Peasant: Rebellion and Subsistence in South East Asia*. New Haven: Yale University Press.

Selwyn, T. (1994) The anthropology of tourism. In A. Seaton *et al.* (eds) *Tourism: The State of the Art* (pp. 729–736). Chichester: John Wiley and Sons.

Selwyn, T. (1996) Introduction. In T. Selwyn (ed.) *The Tourist Image. Myths and Myth Making in Tourism* (pp. 1–32). Chichester: John Wiley and Sons.

Seymour, R. and Turner, S. (2002) Otonomi Dareah: Indonesia's decentralisation experiment. *New Zealand Journal of Asian Studies* 4 (2), 33–51.

Sharpely, R. (1993) *Tourism and Leisure in the Countryside*. Huntingdon: Elm.

Sharpley, R. (2000) The consumption of tourism revisited. In M. Robinson, P. Long, N. Evans, R. Sharpley and J. Swarbrooke (eds) *Motivations, Behaviour and Tourist Types. Reflections on International Tourism* (pp. 381–392). Sunderland: The Centre for Travel and Tourism in association with the British Educational Publishers.

Sharpley, R. (2002) Tourism: A vehicle for development? In R. Sharpley and D. Tefler (eds) *Tourism and Development: Concepts and Issues* (pp. 11–34). Clevedon: Channel View Publications.

Simmons, D. (1994) Community participation in tourism planning. *Tourism Management* 15 (2), 98–108.

Simpson, D. and Wall, G. (1999) Environmental impact assessment for tourism: a discussion and an Indonesian example. In D. Pearce and R. Butler (eds) *Contemporary Issues in Tourism Development*. London: Routledge.

Sinclair, T. (1997) Issues and theories of gender and work in tourism. In T. Sinclair (ed.) *Gender, Work and Tourism* (pp. 1–15). London: Routledge.

Slamet-Vilsink, I. (1995) *Emerging Hierarchies. Processes of Stratification and Early State Formation in the Indonesian Archipelago: Pre-history and Ethnographic Present*. Leiden: KITLV Press.

Smedal, O. (1993) Making place: Houses, lands, and relationships among Ngadha, Central Flores. Doctoral thesis, University of Oslo.

Smedal, O. (1998) Hierarchy, stratification, power, subversion and other possible related concepts: A view from Ngadaland, Central Flores. Unpublished PhD thesis, University of Bergen.

Smedjebacka, K. (2000) Modern influences on East Sumba textiles. In M. Hitchcock and Weindu Nuryanti (eds) *Building on Batik* (pp. 285–294). Aldershot: Ashgate.

Smith, V. (ed.) (1978) *Hosts and Guests: The Anthropology of Tourism*. Oxford: Blackwell.

Smith, V. (2001) The nature of tourism. In V. Smith and M. Bryant (eds) *Hosts and Guests Revisited: Tourism Issues of the 21st Century* (pp. 53–68). New York: Cognizant Communication Corporation.

Soejono, S. (1997) Dampak Industri parawisata pada seni pertunjukan. *Jurnal Masyarakat Seni Pertunjuk Indonesia* VIII, 101–111.

Soemardjan, S. and Breazeale, K. (1993) *Cultural Change in Rural Indonesia. Impact of Village Development*. Surakarta: Sebelas Maret University Press.

Sofield, T. (1995) Indonesia's National Tourism Development Plan. *Annals of Tourism Research*. 22 (3), 690–693.

Sofield, T. (2000) Rethinking and reconceptualizing social and cultural issues in South and South East Asian tourism development. In M. Hall and S. Page (eds) *Tourism in South and South East Asia: Issues and Cases* (pp. 45–57). Oxford: Butterworth-Heinemann.

Sofield, T. (2003) *Empowerment for Sustainable Tourism Development*. Oxford: Pergamon.

Sofield, T. and Birtles, A. (1996) Indigenous peoples' Cultural Opportunity Spectrum for Tourism (IPCOST). In R. Butler and T. Hinch (eds) *Tourism and*

Indigenous peoples (pp. 396–432). London: International Thomson Business Press.

Spreitzhofer, G. (1998) Backpacker tourism in South East Asia. *Annals of Tourism Research* 25, 979–983.

Stanley, N. (1998) *Being Ourselves for You: The Global Display of Cultures.* London: Middlesex University Press.

Steege, K., Sam, S. and Bras, K. (1999) Mountain guides in Lombok. Path finders up Gunnung Rinjani. In H. Dahles and K. Bras, (eds) *Tourism and Small Entrepreneurs* (pp. 112–127). New York: Cognizant Communication Corporation.

Sufwandi Mangkudilaga (1996) The concept of the development of tourism in Indonesia. In W. Nuryanti (ed.) *Tourism and Culture: Global Civilisation in Change* (pp. 327–335). Yogyakarta: Gadja Mada University Press.

Suzuki, P. (1959) *The Religious System and Culture of Nias, Indonesia.* The Hague: Excelsior.

Swain, M. (1989) Developing ethnic tourism in Yunan China: Shalin Sani. *Tourism Recreation Research* 14 (1), 33–40.

Swain, M. (1990) Commoditizing ethnicity in Southwest China. *Cultural Survival Quarterly* 14 (1), 26–29.

Sweeny, A. and Wanhill, S. (1996) Hosting the guest: Changing local attitudes and behaviour. In L. Briguglio, B. Archer, J. Jafari and G. Wall (eds) *Sustainable Tourism in Islands and Small States: Issues and Policies* (pp. 148–159). London: Pinter.

Taylor, C. (1997) *South East Asia on a Shoestring* (9th edn). London: Lonely Planet.

Taylor, J. (2001) Authenticity and sincerity in tourism. *Annals of Tourism Research* 28 (1), 7–26.

Telfer, D. (2002) The evolution of tourism and development theory. In R. Sharpley and D. Telfer (eds) *Tourism and Development: Concepts and Issues* (pp. 35–78). Clevedon: Channel View Publications.

Timothy, D. (1999) Participatory planning: A view of tourism in Indonesia. *Annals of Tourism Research* 26 (2), 371–391.

Tosun, C. and Timothy, D. (2003) Arguments for community participation in tourism development. *The Journal of Tourism Studies* 14 (2), 2–11.

Tourism Concern (1992) *Beyond the Green Horizon.* Godalming: World Wildlife Fund.

Traube, E. (1986) *Cosmology and Social Life. Ritual Exchange Among the Mambai of East Timor.* Chicago: University of Chicago Press.

Travel Impact Newswire (2003) Indonesia from Feast to Famine. Travel Impact Newswire No. 36 16/9/03.

Tribe, J. (1997) The indiscipline of tourism. *Annals of Tourism Research* 24 (3), 638–657.

Tribe, J. (2005) *The Economics of Recreation, Leisure and Tourism* (3rd edn) Oxford: Elsevier.

Turnbridge, J.E. and Ashworth, G.J. (1996) *Dissonant Heritage: The Management of the Past as Resource in Conflict.* Chichester: John Wiley.

Turner, P. (1998) *Indonesia's Eastern Islands.* Hawthorn: Lonely Planet.

Umbu Peku Djawang (1991) The role of tourism in NTT development. In C. Barlow, A. Bellis and K. Andrews (eds) *Nusa Tenggara Timor: The Challenge of Development, Political and Social Change.* Monograph 12, Canberra: ANU University.

UNDP Indonesia Human Development Report (2004) http://www.undp.or.id/pubs/ihdr2004/ihdr2004_full.pdf (accessed November 2005).

UNESCAP (2004) http://www.unescap.org/ttdw/Publications/TFS_pubs/pub_2017/pub_2017_ch2.pdf (accessed November 2005).

Urbanowicz, C. (1978) Tourism in Tonga: Troubled times. In V. Smith (ed.) *Hosts and Guests: The Anthropology of Tourism* (pp. 83–92). Oxford: Blackwell.

Urry, J. (1990) *The Tourist Gaze: Leisure and Travel in Contemporary Societies*. London: Sage.

Usman, S. (2001) Indonesia's decentralisation policy. Initial experiences and emerging problems. Conference paper, EUROSEAS, SOAS, London University.

van der Dium, R., Peters, K. and Akama, J. (2006) Cultural tourism in African communities: A comparison between cultural manyattas in Kenya and cultural Tourism in Tanzania. In M. Smith and M. Robinson (eds) *Cultural Tourism in a Changing World* (pp. 104–123). Clevedon: Channel View.

Van den Berghe, P. (1992) Tourism and the ethnic division of labor. *Annals of Tourism Research* 19, 234–249.

Van den Berghe, P. and Keyes, C. (1984) Introduction: Tourism and re-created ethnicity. *Annals of Tourism Research* 11, 343–352.

Van der Hoop, Th. (n.d.) *Megalithic Remains in South Sumatra*. Thiemercie, Zutphen, the Netherlands.

Van Harssell, J. (1994) *Tourism: An Exploration*. NJ: Prentice-Hall, Inc.

Van Niel, R. (1979) From Netherlands East Indies to Republic of Indonesia 1900–1945. In H. Aveling (ed.) *The Development of Indonesian Society* (pp. 106–165). St Lucia: University of Queensland Press.

Van Wouden, F.A.E. (1935) *Types of Social Structure in Eastern Indonesia*. English translation by R. Needham (1968). The Hague: Martinus Nijhoff.

Vel, J. (1994) *The Uma Economy. Indigenous Economics and Development Work in Lawonda, Sumba*. Den Haag: CIP data Koninklijke bibliotheek.

Visser, L. (1997) Ritual performance and images of good governance in Halmahera. In M. Hitchcock and V. King (eds) *Images of Malay–Indonesian Identity* (pp. 180–200). Oxford: Oxford University Press.

Volkman, T. (1985) *Feasts of Honour. Ritual and Change in the Toraja Highlands*. Chicago: University of Illinois Press.

Volkman, T. (1987) Mortuary tourism in Tana Toraja. In R. Kipp and S. Rodgers (eds) *Indonesian Religions in Transition* (pp. 161–168). Tucson: University of Arizona Press.

Volkman, T. (1990) Visions and revisions: Toraja culture and the tourist gaze. *American Ethnologist* 17 (1), 91–110.

Waldren, J. (1996) *Insiders and Outsiders: Paradise and Reality in Mallorca*. Oxford: Berghahn Books.

Wall, G. (1997) Indonesia: The impact of regionalization. In F. Go and C. Jenkins (eds) *Tourism and Economic Development in Asia and Australasia* (pp. 138–149). London: Pinter.

Walters, M. (1995) *Globalisation*. London: Routledge.

Wang, N. (1999) Rethinking authenticity in tourism experience. *Annals of Tourism Research* 26 (2), 349–370.

Warburton, D. (1998) A passive dialogue: Community and sustainable development. In D. Warburton (ed.) *Community and Sustainable Development*. London: Earthscan.

Warpole, M. and Goodwin, H. (2000) Local economic impacts of dragon tourism in Indonesia. *Annals of Tourism Research* 27 (3), 559–576.

Waterson, R. (1990) *The Living House: An Anthropology of Architecture in South-East Asia*. Oxford: Oxford University Press.

Waterson, R. (1995) Houses and hierarchies in island South East Asia. In J. Carsten and S. Hugh-Jones (eds) *About the House. Lévi Strauss and Beyond* (pp. 47–68). Cambridge: Cambridge University Press.

Webb, P. (1986) *Palms and the Cross. Socio-economic Development in Nusa Tenggara* Townsville: James Cook University.

Weiler, B. and Ham, S. (2001) Perspectives and thoughts on tour guiding. In A. Lockwood and S. Medlik (eds) *Tourism and Hospitality in the 21st Century* (pp. 255–264). Oxford: Butterworth-Heinemann.

Weiller, B. and Davis, D. (1993) An exploratory investigation into the roles of the nature based tour leader. *Tourism Management* April, 91–98.

Weindu Nuryanti (1998) Tourism and regional imbalances: The case of Java. *Indonesia and the Malay World* 26 (75), 136–144.

Wheat, S. (1999) Editorial: Guide books. *In Focus* 34, 3.

Wheeler, T. (1990) *Indonesia: A Travel Survival Kit* (2nd edn). Hawthorn: Lonely Planet.

Wickens, E. (2000) Rethinking tourists' experiences. In M. Robinson *et al.* (eds) *Motivations, Behaviour and Tourist Types. Reflections on International Tourism.* (pp. 455–472). Sunderland: Centre for Travel and Tourism in association with Business Education Press.

Williams, S. (1998) *Tourism Geography*. London: Routledge.

Wilson, D. (1993) Time and tides in the anthropology of tourism. In M. Hitchcock, V. King and M. Parnwell (eds) *Tourism in South East Asia* (pp. 32–47). London: Routledge.

Windiyaningsih, C. (2004) The rabies epidemic on Flores island, Indonesia (1998–2003). *Journal of the Medical Association Thailand* 87 (11), 1389–1395.

Wiradji, S. (2005) Hope lives on for ailing tourism industry. *Jakarta Post*, www.thejarkartapost.com/special/ttb20 (accessed 07/11/05).

Wood, R. (1984) Ethnic tourism, the state and cultural change in Southeast Asia. *Annals of Tourism Research* 11, 353–374.

Wood, R. (1993) Tourism, culture and the sociology of development. In M. Hitchcock, V. King and M. Parnwell (eds) *Tourism in South East Asia* (pp. 48–70). London: Routledge.

Wood, R. (1997) Tourism and the state: Ethnic options and the construction of otherness. In M. Picard and R. Wood (eds) *Tourism, Ethnicity and the State in Asian and Pacific Societies* (pp. 1–34). Honolulu: University of Hawaii Press.

World Bank (2002) *Vulnerability of Bali's Tourism Economy. A Preliminary Assessment.* Interim Consultative Group on Indonesia, 1/11/02.

WTO (1998) Indonesia Presentation at WTO high level meeting on the economic impacts of tourism. Kobe, Japan, 25–27 November 1998, www.mct.go.kr/conf/wto (accessed 12/10/02).

WTO (1999) *Tourism 2020 Vision Executive Summary*. Madrid: WTO.

Yamashita, S. (1994) Manipulating ethnic tradition: The funeral ceremony and television among the Toraja. *Indonesia* 58, 69–82.

Zainal Kling (1997) Adat: Collective self image. In M. Hitchcock and V. King (eds) *Images of Malay–Indonesian Identity* (pp. 45–51). Oxford: Oxford University Press.

Zeppel, H. (1993) Getting to know the Iban: The tourist experience of visiting an Iban long house in Sarawak. In V. King (ed.) *Tourism in Borneo.* Borneo Research Council proceedings. Papers from the biennial international conference. Kota Kinabalu, Malaysia, July (1992) .

Index